KU-157-990

937
JONE
A
PLUT
C

61 A

STET FORTUNA DOMUS

DONORUM DEI DISPENSATIO FIDELIS

BIBLIOTHECAE
SCHOLAE HERGENSIS
LIBER.

PLUTARCH AND ROME

Plutarch and Rome

C. P. JONES

CLARENDON PRESS · OXFORD

Oxford University Press, Ely House, London W.1

GLASGOW   NEW YORK   TORONTO   MELBOURNE   WELLINGTON
CAPE TOWN   IBADAN   NAIROBI   DAR ES SALAAM   LUSAKA   ADDIS ABABA
DELHI   BOMBAY   CALCUTTA   MADRAS   KARACHI   LAHORE   DACCA
KUALA LUMPUR   SINGAPORE   HONG KONG   TOKYO

© OXFORD UNIVERSITY PRESS 1971

FIRST PUBLISHED 1971
REPRINTED (with corrections) 1972

Reproduced and printed by photolithography and bound in
Great Britain at The Pitman Press, Bath

PREFACE

THE vicissitudes of Plutarch's reputation are themselves a chapter in the history of culture. Deposed in the last century from his high position as a historian and a moralist, he came to be regarded as little more than a lifeless receptacle, valuable mainly for what he had preserved of earlier literature. His works became a quarry in the scramble for lost sources, and his reputation dwindled by comparison with the cloudy trophies of which he was the involuntary saviour.

It was always unlikely that an author should have made himself so inert a medium for the transmission of borrowed knowledge. More recent investigation has provided correctives. Plutarch's knowledge of the classical poets is not drawn entirely from handbooks; when his dependence on prose anthologies was thought to have been proved, the proof turned out to be illusory, the result of the use of his own works by later authors.

The rediscovery of Plutarch as a literary personality is welcome. It invites a new approach, from the direction of history. If his independence as an author can be proved, so also can his position in his own time be re-examined. Not that he can be turned into a major figure of imperial history, any more than he can be restored to a position equal to that of the classical writers. But he can be shown to have been affected by currents prevailing in his day, and these currents may prove to help with the understanding of his works.

Rome is the foil, the inescapable background for Plutarch's activity and thought. His life was passed entirely under the Caesars in a province of their empire. In the course of time he came constantly into contact with Rome: as the friend of Roman officials, the priest of a shrine favoured by the emperors, and as a citizen with honorary positions in the Roman hierarchy. Among Greek authors, his interest in Rome is unequalled: the *Parallel Lives* prove it, and also the *Roman Questions* and numerous passages in his essays and dialogues.

There is another justification for a study of Plutarch in relation with Rome, besides its importance in his life. In recent years historians of the early and high empires have pursued two lines with particular profit. One is the part taken by provincials in imperial history and literature. The other, closely cognate, is the relation between the two halves of the empire, east and west. These two paths have led in turn to a reconsideration of the Greek renaissance of the second and third centuries, and for a clear reason: this movement owes much of its vitality to the encouragement, both fortuitous and deliberate, of Rome. Plutarch lived at the beginning of this period, and is at once an observer and an early representative of it. Not only, therefore, can the history of his time illustrate his works, but they themselves are a source, often neglected, for contemporary manners and thought.

What follows has two parts. The first reviews the evidence for Plutarch's life and society. In the second, those of his writings that reveal his attitude to Rome are considered, as far as possible in order of composition: the *Roman Questions*, since their interest is mainly antiquarian, have not received separate treatment. While Rome provides the organizing principle, the primary subject is Plutarch.

I wish to thank Harvard University for its generous support of my graduate work and for the hospitality of its Department of the Classics and Widener Library, and Professor John H. Finley for three happy years in Eliot House. I am equally grateful to the University of Toronto for financial assistance towards the completion of the manuscript, and to the less tangible support of a congenial and accommodating Department of Classics in University College.

The thesis out of which this book has grown was proposed and directed by Professor Herbert Bloch, whose sympathy for Plutarch has been no less an example than his patience and learning. Several friends have given me the benefit of their criticism: Professor T. D. Barnes, the late Professor F. M. Heichelheim, Mr. Russell Meiggs, Dr. Fergus Millar, Dr. R. M. Ogilvie, and Professor G. V. Sumner. Professor A. Momigliano has encouraged and deepened my interest in Plutarch from an early stage. I am indebted to Professor Syme, not only for his helpful interest in this book, but also for the lessons that his work has taught a generation: to see the ancients on their own terms and not to confuse the comfortable and the true. Above all, I thank my teacher and friend Professor Glen W. Bowersock, who has aided this book at every step, from earliest draft to final proof, and whose own work has influenced every page of mine.

University College, Toronto   C.P.J.
October 1970

CONTENTS

ABBREVIATIONS

I. Periodicals etc.

AE	*L'Année épigraphique*
AJP	*American Journal of Philology*
BCH	*Bulletin de correspondance hellénique*
BMC	*Catalogue of Coins in the British Museum*
CIG	*Corpus Inscriptionum Graecarum*
CIL	*Corpus Inscriptionum Latinarum*
CP	*Classical Philology*
CQ	*The Classical Quarterly*
FGrHist	F. Jacoby, *Die Fragmente der griechischen Historiker*
GRBS	*Greek, Roman, and Byzantine Studies*
HA	*Historia Augusta*
HSCP	*Harvard Studies in Classical Philology*
IG	*Inscriptiones Graecae*
IGR	*Inscriptiones Graecae ad res Romanas pertinentes*
ILS	H. Dessau, *Inscriptiones Latinae Selectae*
JÖAI	*Jahreshefte des österreichischen archäologischen Instituts*
JRS	*Journal of Roman Studies*
LSJ[9]	Liddell and Scott, *Greek-English Lexicon*, 9th edn., revised by H. Stuart Jones, 1925–40
McCrum and Woodhead, *Documents of the Flavian Emperors*	M. McCrum and A. G. Woodhead, *Select Documents of the Principates of the Flavian Emperors A.D. 68–96* (Cambridge, 1961)
OGIS	W. Dittenberger, *Orientis Graeci Inscriptiones Selectae*
Philostr. *VS*	Philostratus, *Vitae Sophistarum*
PIR	*Prosopographia Imperii Romani*
RE	Pauly-Wissowa-Kroll, *Real-Encyclopädie der classischen Altertumswissenschaft*
REA	*Revue des études anciennes*
REG	*Revue des études grecques*
REL	*Revue des études latines*
Rostovtzeff, *SEHRE*[2]	M. Rostovtzeff, *The Social and Economic History of the Roman Empire*, 2nd edition revised by P. M. Fraser (Oxford, 1957)

SEG	*Supplementum Epigraphicum Graecum*
Smallwood, *Documents of Gaius, Claudius and Nero*	E. M. Smallwood, *Documents illustrating the Principates of Gaius, Claudius and Nero* (Cambridge, 1967)
Smallwood, *Documents of Nerva, Trajan and Hadrian*	E. M. Smallwood, *Documents illustrating the Principates of Nerva, Trajan and Hadrian* (Cambridge, 1966)
*Syll.*³	W. Dittenberger, *Sylloge Inscriptionum Graecarum*, 3rd edition
TAM	*Tituli Asiae Minoris*
TAPA	*Transactions of the American Philological Association*

II. Works of Plutarch

The following is a list of the *Lives* and *Moralia* of Plutarch to which reference has been made in the following pages, and indicates the abbreviations used. References to the *Lives* are by the edition of Cl. Lindskog and K. Ziegler, *Plutarchi Vitae Parallelae* (Leipzig, Teubner, 1914–39; 2nd edition by K. Ziegler, 1957–), to the *Moralia* by Frankfurt pages, and to the Catalogue of Lamprias and the fragments by the editions of F. H. Sandbach, *Plutarchi Moralia* 7 (Leipzig, Teubner, 1967), *Plutarch's Moralia* 15 (Cambridge, Massachusetts, Loeb Classical Library, 1969).

Lives

Aem(ilius Paullus)	*Demetr(ius)*
Ages(ilaus)	*Demosth(enes)*
Agis-Cleom(enes)	*Dio*
Alc(ibiades)	*Eum(enes)*
Alex(ander)	*Fab(ius) Max(imus)*
Ant(onius)	*Flam(ininus)*
Arat(us)	*Galba*
Arist(ides)	*Gracchi*
Art(axerxes)	*Luc(ullus)*
Brut(us)	*Lyc(urgus)*
Caes(ar)	*Lys(ander)*
Cam(illus)	*Mar(ius)*
Cato mai(or)	*Marc(ellus)*
Cato min(or)	*Nic(ias)*
Cic(ero)	*Numa*
Cimon	*Otho*
Coriol(anus)	*Pelop(idas)*
Crass(us)	*Per(icles)*

Philop(oemen)
Phoc(ion)
Pomp(eius)
Publ(icola)
Pyrrh(us)
Rom(ulus)

Sert(orius)
Solon
Sulla
Themist(ocles)
Thes(eus)
Timol(eon)

Moralia

Ad princ(ipem) inerud(itum)
Adv(ersus) Col(otem)
Amat(orius)
An seni sit ger(enda) resp(ublica)
Anim(ine) an corp(oris) aff(ectiones sint peiores)
Consol(atio) ad ux(orem)
De animae procr(eatione) in Tim(aeo)
De cap(ienda) ex inim(icis) util(itate)
De cohib(enda) ira
De curios(itate)
De def(ectu) orac(ulorum)
De E Delph(ico)
De esu carn(ium)
De exil(io)
De fort(una) Alex(andri)
De fort(una) Rom(anorum)
De frat(erno) am(ore)
De garrul(itate)
De glor(ia) Ath(eniensium)
De Herod(oti) malign(itate)
De Is(ide) et Osir(ide)
De laude ips(ius)
De poet(is) aud(iendis)
De primo frigido

De prof(ectibus) in virt(ute)
De Pyth(iae) orac(ulis)
De sera num(inis) vind(icta)
De soll(ertia) anim(alium)
De superstit(ione)
De tranqu(illitate) animi
De tribus reip(ublicae) gen(eribus)
De tuenda san(itate)
De vit(ando) aere al(ieno)
De vit(ioso) pud(ore)
Maxime cum princ(ipibus) phil(osopho esse) diss(erendum)
Mul(ierum) virt(utes)
Non posse suav(iter) vivi (secundum Epicurum)
Praec(epta) coniug(alia)
Praec(epta) ger(endae) reip(ublicae)
Quaest(iones) conviv(ales)
Quaest(iones) Gr(aecae)
Quaest(iones) Plat(onicae)
Quaest(iones) Rom(anae)
Quom(odo) adul(ator) ab amico internosc(atur)
Reg(um) et imp(eratorum) apophth(egmata)

Part I

I

CHAERONEA

PLUTARCH and Chaeronea, the names are inseparably joined. That is not merely an accident of birth. The antiquities of his city appear constantly in his writing.[1] Even at the height of his fame, he could not bring himself to leave Chaeronea, if that would make it poorer by one citizen, and Greeks who deserted their homes to chase after governmental positions earned his scorn.[2]

In Plutarch's day, such devotion to a city of minor importance is unusual. In Greek-speaking lands, the great centres of culture exercised a powerful effect on educated men, at the expense of their ancestral cities.[3] Plutarch's attachment indicates that a study of his relations with Rome must begin with Chaeronea.

According to legend, Chaeronea was the first city that the Boeotians, as they migrated southwards from Thessaly, founded in the region to which they were to give their name.[4] The legend reflects an important fact: Chaeronea is the westernmost city of Boeotia, and overlooks the main road from Thermopylae and the north as it emerges from Phocis by way of a narrow defile into the Boeotian plain. Boeotia is in fact a series of adjoining plains, which make it one of the most fertile regions of Greece, and the plain into which the road enters as it follows the course of the river Cephisus is named after Chaeronea.[5]

The position of the city, situated on an outcrop of Mount Parnassus, links it as much with eastern Phocis as with Boeotia. Hence it is not surprising that Plutarch's closer friends come from Tithora or Hyampolis in Phocis as well as Thebes or Thespiae,

[1] e.g. *Thes.* 27. 8, *Cimon* 1. 1 ff., *Demosth.* 19. 2, *Alex.* 9. 3, *Lys.* 29. 4, *Sulla* 16–19, *quaest. Rom.* 267 D, *de fort. Rom.* 318 D, *de curios.* 515 C.

[2] *Demosth.* 2. 2, *praec. ger. reip.* 814 D.

[3] Philostr. *VS* 490 (Favorinus), 516 (Scopelian). Of course such Greeks might maintain contacts with their original cities: cf. Philostr. *VS* 532 (Polemo), Artemidorus, *Oneirocr.* 3. 66, p. 235 Pack.

[4] *Cimon* 1. 1.

[5] On the topography of Chaeronea: A. Philippson-E. Kirsten, *Die griechischen Landschaften* 1. 2 (1951), 431–2.

2

from Thessaly as well as from Athens and the Peloponnese.[6] More important, Chaeronea's situation puts it within comparatively easy reach of the foremost shrine of Greece, Delphi.[7] Delphi and Chaeronea were to be the twin poles of Plutarch's adult life.

By means of its proximity to the arterial road running between northern and southern Greece, the city was linked to another important route that crossed Boeotia from Creusis on the Corinthian gulf to the narrowest part of the Euripus facing Chalcis: a bridge here joined it to Euboea.[8] This road carried traffic between the celebrated three seas of Boeotia, the Corinthian gulf and the northern and southern Aegean: these seas connected the region to three areas of the empire: Italy and the West, Macedonia and the Hellespont, and Egypt and the Orient.[9] Chaeronea had its own link to the Corinthian gulf, for a road branching off the main route to Delphi went south-west to the port of Phocian Anticyra.[10] Chaeronea's participation in one of Boeotia's unique natural advantages adds to its importance in Plutarch's life. With the proximity of Delphi, its sea connections contributed to the cosmopolitan nature of his society by facilitating the visits of friends from every part of the Roman world. One occasion epitomizes them all, the celebration of the Pythian games that brought together a Spartan who had sailed far down the Red Sea and a Tarsian who had explored the Western Isles of Scotland.[11]

Besides its ease of communication with other cities, Chaeronea enjoyed its share of the fertility for which Boeotia was noted. Its territory included the large plain that bears its name, and the marshiness of the soil favoured the growth of flowers which were used in the manufacture of a well-known medication. This

---

[6] Cf. Thucydides, 4. 76. 3 (Phocians in Chaeronea), *Cimon* 1. 9 (a Chaeronean family now settled in Phocis), *de sera num. vind.* 558 A (a family, perhaps Plutarch's, well connected both in Boeotia and in Phocis). On Plutarch's Greek friends, see K. Ziegler, *RE* 21 (1951), 665 f. and below, pp. 39 ff.

[7] For the route from Chaeronea to Delphi, cf. *Lys.* 29. 4, F. Schober, *Phokis* (1924), map at end. Plutarch and Delphi: below, pp. 26, 31–2.

[8] On this route: J. Hatzfeld, *Les Trafiquants italiens dans l'Orient hellénique* (1919), 69–70.

[9] Cf. Strabo, 9. 400, quoting Ephorus, *FGrHist* 70 F 119, and also Pseudo-Scymnos, 488–501, quoted by Jacoby, ad loc. *FGrHist* II C (1926), 69.

[10] Illustrated by Schober, op. cit. map at end. Cf. *Ant.* 68. 7.

[11] *De def. orac.* 410 A.

industry was large enough to catch the attention of the traveller Pausanias in the late second century.[12]

It is easy to underestimate the importance of Chaeronea. Plutarch emphasizes the smallness of his city even under the prosperous conditions of the second century, and the remains bear him out, particularly those of the diminutive theatre.[13] But when he calls the city small, he does so in a passage in which the standard for comparison is Athens, one of the most populous cities in Greece. Moreover, even a small city could support a few wealthy families, and the antiquities also include remains of at least one very luxurious villa of Roman date.[14] The fact that the wealth of a prominent family could bear little relation to the importance of the city in which it lived is clearly illustrated by Acraephiae on the other side of Lake Copais from Chaeronea. Even when Acraephiae was in the depths of poverty under Gaius, its leading citizen was one of the notables of all Achaea.[15]

The history of Chaeronea before Plutarch's birth had been determined entirely by its geography. Its plain was tactically the natural place for an army defending southern Greece to resist invaders who had already passed Thermopylae. Hence it has given its name to two famous battles. In the first, Philip of Macedon decisively crushed the combined Greek army attempting to block his path. In Plutarch's day the struggle of Greece and Macedon was already ancient history: both had long since passed under the Roman yoke. The second major battle of Chaeronea, a part of Sulla's campaign in Greece in the first Mithridatic war, is of more significance in Plutarch's background. It lived more vividly in local tradition, and the war which it helped to decide confirmed Roman supremacy over Greece.

Chaeronea was involved early in the war when a three-day struggle took place there between the legate Braetius Sura and Mithridates' general Archelaus.[16] But the famous battle, in

[12] Paus. 9. 41. 7.

[13] Demosth. 2. 2. For a survey of the archaeological findings: U. Kahrstedt, Das wirtschaftliche Gesicht Griechenlands in der Kaiserzeit (1954), 108–9.

[14] G. Soteriadis, REG 25 (1912), 265–6, Kahrstedt, op. cit. 109.

[15] Viz. Epaminondas son of Epaminondas, IG 7. 2711–13, especially 2711, lines 8 ff. Cf. the inscription of Claudian date published by L. Robert, BCH 59 (1935), 438–52 = Opera Minora Selecta 1. 279–93, testifying to the generosity of other Acraephians in time of depression.

[16] Sulla 11. 6–8, App. Mithr. 114. Cf. Th. Reinach, Mithridates Eupator (1895), 148–9, R. K. Sherk, Roman Documents from the Greek East (1969), 121–3, and the decree

which Archelaus was defeated by Sulla, occurred a year later. In the course of it, Archelaus attempted to capture the city, but was foiled by the tribune Gabinius after the citizens had warned Sulla of the plan.[17] Later in the same year Sulla again defeated the Mithridatic army in the plain of Orchomenus, Chaeronea's neighbour and traditional rival. These two battles left an imprint that was still visible in Plutarch's day and even later. He himself saw, as Pausanias did after him, the two trophies set up by Sulla after Chaeronea, and he could report that pieces of the weapons carried by Archelaus' army were still being found in the marshes of Orchomenus nearly two hundred years after the battle.[18]

It was inevitable that the presence of war should cause hardship to the cities of Boeotia. Because of its strategic importance, Chaeronea was firmly held by the Romans throughout the war, and a document of this period of its history happens to have been preserved at Delphi. It is a decree of the city passed in honour of a Thracian chieftain billeted on it by Sulla, probably in the winter of 87/6.[19] The Thracian is praised for keeping his troops from harming the city, and in return for his protection is enrolled with all his descendants among its benefactors. The apparent disproportion between the service and the reward indicates what an occupied city, even one on the winning side, could normally expect.

Chaeronea had in fact not always been so lucky. An incident that had probably occurred when the Romans were occupying the city in the winter of 88/7 is of interest for the importance accorded to it by Plutarch.[20] The commander of a cohort quartered on the city fell in love with a local youth of aristocratic descent called Damon, and unable to win him by persuasion decided to use force; 'my city', says Plutarch, 'was then in a wretched state and insignificant because of its smallness and poverty'. From this a series of disasters followed. The youth

of Thespiae in Braetius' honour, A. Plassart, *Mélanges Charles Picard* 2 = *Revue archéologique* 31–2 (1949), 830–2, no. 11. On the correct form of the name, less probably 'Bruttius', G. W. Bowersock, *AJP* 91 (1970), 225.

[17] *Sulla* 16. 14.

[18] Trophies: *Sulla* 19. 10, Paus. 9. 40. 7. Fragments: *Sulla* 21. 8.

[19] Published by M. Holleaux, *Études d'épigraphie et d'histoire grecques* 1 (1938), 143–63.

[20] *Cimon* 1–2. 1. On the date: Reinach, op. cit. 149, n. 1. Münzer's argument for a later date, that Chaeronea was not occupied by the Roman side until 86 (*RE* 13 [1926], 380–1) was refuted by the new inscription from Delphi (preceding n.).

formed a band that assassinated the commander and other Romans, and in order to make amends the city council was obliged to condemn the whole group to death. In revenge the boy and his followers broke in upon the magistrates at dinner and murdered them. It happened that the Roman Licinius Lucullus was in the area serving under Sulla, and after an investigation decided that Chaeronea was itself the victim of an injustice, and withdrew the garrison. The city continued to be harassed by Damon and his followers, who had now taken to banditry, until the citizens lured him back with an offer of pardon and then killed him. Even so, all was not over. Orchomenus hired a 'Roman informer' to accuse the citizens of Chaeronea collectively for the murder of Roman citizens. The case was heard by the governor of Macedonia, and only a second intervention by Lucullus saved the city from destruction.

The story vividly depicts the poverty and desperation of a small city in the last decades of the Roman republic. Except that it was lucky enough to be saved by a Roman who was also a noted philhellene, its experiences were probably not exceptional. The interest of the story is that it took place in a city that was later to produce a philosopher interested in history. The episode of Damon, like Sulla's campaigns, left traces that were still visible in Plutarch's day.[21] This incident of Chaeronea's past is directly connected with Plutarch's works, since it was as his own monument to Lucullus' benefaction that he included him in the *Parallel Lives*.[22]

It is probable that Chaeronea suffered further in the civil wars. As in the first Mithridatic war, the presence even of a friendly army could be ruinous. Now there was the added danger that if a city chose the losing side loyalty to Rome was no excuse.[23] Chaeronea's fate in this period is unknown except for an incident in the campaign of Actium. The need to man and supply Antonius' forces fell all the more heavily since Greece had already suffered so much. His captains pressed into service travellers, muleteers, harvesters, and even youths below military age; the cities were deprived of money, slaves, and baggage-animals.[24]

[21] *Cimon* 1. 8, 2. 2.
[22] *Cimon* 2. 3.
[23] Megara was sacked in 48 as a punishment for resisting Caesar's legate, Q. Fufius Calenus, Cass. Dio, 42. 14. 3–4, cf. Ser. Sulpicius *apud* Cic. *ad fam.* 4. 5. 4.
[24] *Ant.* 62. 1, 68. 6.

In Chaeronea all the citizens, among them Plutarch's great-grandfather, were compelled to carry grain down to Anticyra on the Corinthian gulf, while Antonius' agents hurried them along with whips. They were about to take up a second load when the news of Actium came. This saved the city: immediately the agents and soldiers fled, and the citizens divided the grain among themselves.[25] Shortly afterwards Octavian sailed into Athens and distributed surplus grain among all the cities.[26]

There will have been many communities in Greece like Chaeronea which remembered for generations the depression of the late republic and the revival that began with the establishment of monarchy at Rome. One of the recurrent justifications of the empire was economic: the prosperity that only peace could guarantee. Even so, improvement came slowly and with difficulty. Writing under Augustus, Strabo describes Tanagra and Thespiae as the only cities of Boeotia still flourishing: the others were ruins and names. Even when outdated sources and the viewpoint of an Asian Greek are allowed for, his account will not be far from the truth.[27] As the decades passed Chaeronea like other cities of Greece began to recover more rapidly. By the time of Plutarch's birth about the middle of the first century, the marks of war and depression had probably been largely effaced.[28]

The family into which Plutarch was born claimed descent from ancient heroes of Boeotia and Phocis, or was closely linked with one that did,[29] and had lived in Chaeronea for at least three generations before his.[30] That in itself suggests wealth, and the suggestion is borne out by other indications. Because affluence was so familiar a feature of his society, it did not usually draw comment, and hence Plutarch does not refer directly to his own.

[25] *Ant.* 68. 6–8.

[26] *Ant.* 68. 6, cf. G. W. Bowersock, *Augustus and the Greek World* (1965), 85.

[27] Strabo, 9. 410, cf. 403; for his account of Chaeronea, see 414. On Strabo's exaggeration see J. A. O. Larsen, *An Economic Survey of Ancient Rome* 4 (1938), 466 ff.

[28] Note that the Ptoian games at Acraephiae were revived about A.D. 40 after a lapse of 30 years, *IG* 7. 2712, lines 55 ff. Cf. Rostovtzeff, *SEHRE*² 91–3. Plutarch's comment on the state of Chaeronea in the first Mithridatic war is instructive for the reign of Trajan, τῆς πατρίδος ἡμῶν τότε λυπρὰ πραττούσης, *Cimon* 1. 3, and on nearby Tithora in the same period, οὔπω τοσαύτην πόλιν ὅση νῦν ἐστι, *Sulla* 15. 5.

[29] *De sera num. vind.* 558 A. Cf. B. Einarson, *CP* 47 (1952), 99 and 50 (1955), 253–5, arguing that this statement refers to Plutarch's own ancestry, disputed by Ziegler, *Hermes* 82 (1954), 499–501.

[30] *Ant.* 68. 7.

By analogy, and because Boeotia was primarily agricultural, it can be assumed that the family's capital was in land.[31] How much the family had been affected by the depression of previous decades cannot be estimated, but by Plutarch's generation it must have been worth at least the 400,000 sesterces necessary to qualify him as a knight.[32] It has already been seen that Chaeronea could well have supported a family of such means, and in fact Plutarch's was probably not the only one. A compatriot of his became a professional sophist, and that was a calling which usually only the wealthy could afford.[33]

The high degree of culture attained by Plutarch and his forebears is another sign of their affluence: Lucian observed that three things were indispensable for higher education, time, wealth, and a conspicuous social position.[34] The picture that Plutarch gives of his affable and learned grandfather shows that at least by his generation the family could already afford the cost in money and leisure to acquire a good education and pursue knowledge in later life.[35] Plutarch's father had less interest in culture but his tastes were equally expensive, hunting and horse-breeding.[36] He gave his sons an education on which no expense was spared. Plutarch's early travels in Greece and Asia, his rhetorical training, his association with Ammonius, a leading philosopher of Athens, will all have required the usual prerequisites of a higher education noted by Lucian.[37] The same impression of comfortable leisure is conveyed by Plutarch's dialogues.[38] Clearly he was less rich than some of the Greeks of

[31] Cf. A. H. M. Jones, *The Greek City from Alexander to Justinian* (1940) 265–6, Rostovtzeff, *SEHRE*² 254.

[32] Plutarch as a knight: below, p. 29. It is theoretically possible that the sum was made up by one or more of his Roman friends: cf. Pliny, *Epp.* 1. 19. 2.

[33] Viz. the sophist Nigros, *de tuenda san.* 131 A, *quaest. conviv.* 692 B. The Chaeronean who is supposed to have become an Asiarch *c.* A.D. 100 (*Syll.*³ 824 B, with Pomtow's n.) would be a further indication of local prosperity, but 'Aσιάρχης is evidently a name, cf. *IG* 14. 1422, line 6. Wilamowitz held that Plutarch's family was the only one in Chaeronea with a claim to wealth and education, *Reden und Vorträge* 2⁴ (1926), 249, disputed by K. Ziegler, *RE* 21 (1951), 641–2.

[34] Lucian, *Somn.* 1.

[35] Cf. Ziegler, art. cit. 642.

[36] Hunting: *de soll. anim.* 959 B (on the identification of the speaker with Plutarch's father, see Ziegler, art. cit. 644). Horses: *quaest. conviv.* 642 A.

[37] Plutarch's travels: below, p. 15. Training: below, pp. 14 ff. Ammonius: C. P. Jones, *HSCP* 71 (1966), 205–13, and below, pp. 16 ff.

[38] Cf. *quaest. conviv. passim*, and especially 667 C (ἐν ἀφθόνοις πᾶσι), 692 B (χορηγίαν ... πολυτελῆ).

his day, and even some of his own friends, but he had no qualms about classing himself among 'the cultivated'.[39]

Plutarch belonged by birth to a class with an inherited claim to local supremacy. Chaeronea had the usual constitution of a Boeotian city at this period: the assembly still met, but real power lay with the council, and within that with an annually changing board of magistrates headed by the archon eponymous.[40] Plutarch soon received instruction from his father on how to behave in politics: for instance, he should avoid claiming even his due of gratitude if doing so would make him unpopular.[41] Years later Plutarch passed the advice on to a beginner who wanted his political guidance, and no doubt many of his injunctions reflect the accumulated experience of a family used to influence.

It will also have been from his family that Plutarch inherited some of his many connections with other local aristocracies. His friend Philinus, for instance, belonged to a leading house of Thespiae, and the connection between the two families appears to go back to a previous generation.[42] In particular, Plutarch's attachment to Delphi, where he was later to be priest, will certainly have been inherited from his ancestors. His grandfather Lamprias had been a friend of the voluble old doctor from Amphissa, Philotas, who eventually settled and practised in Delphi, and it was probably there that Lamprias had known him.[43] Friendships between citizens of Chaeronea and Delphi were in any case facilitated by the proximity of the two cities and their traditional ties.[44]

[39] Cf. the accounts of Claudius Hipparchus, the grandfather of the sophist Herodes Atticus (Philostr. VS 547–8, PIR² C 801). Among Plutarch's friends, note the sophist Callistratus, quaest. conviv. 667 D, and the Spartan Cleombrotus, de def. orac. 410 A. οἱ χαρίεντες, quaest. conviv. 667 D.

[40] H. Swoboda, Klio 10 (1910), 331–3. This constitution is attested as late as the reign of Aurelian, BCH 29 (1905), 101.

[41] Praec. ger. reip. 816 D.

[42] On this family, see now C. P. Jones, HSCP 74 (1970), 223–55. One of its members, Aristo, may have been a cousin of Plutarch's father, art. cit. 232.

[43] Philotas and Lamprias: Ant. 28. 3–12. Philotas and Delphi: SEG 1. 181, on which see W. A. Oldfather, CP 19 (1924), 177.

[44] Note the inscription of Amatocus set up by the Chaeroneans at Delphi in the 80s B.C. (above, p. 6, n. 19); the statue of the first century A.D. commemorating ὁμόνοια between the two cities (Syll.³ 816); the herm set up by them both to Plutarch c. 120 (Syll.³ 843); the Chaeroneans made citizens of Delphi, probably in the late second century (Syll.³ 824, and above, p. 9, n. 33).

Nevertheless, the influence on Plutarch of his city and background must not be exaggerated. Ultimately it was his natural endowments and not his circumstances that made him what he became. Plutarch's distinction brought him into contact with a society wider than his family's, and in particular with eminent Romans. One of these friends was to obtain the Roman citizenship for him:[45] while the wealth of his family put him in a class to which Rome was traditionally well disposed, the citizenship, with its prospects of further distinction, was the reward of his own merits.

Similarly, Plutarch's family had the means to give him the best education, but none of its members had been distinguished in culture before him: by contrast, many of them were so thereafter, and prided themselves on their descent from him. The most notable is his nephew Sextus, the teacher of Marcus Aurelius (with whom he stood in high esteem) and Lucius Verus.[46] The Platonist Apuleius of Madauros made the hero of his *Metamorphoses* a descendant of 'the renowned Plutarch' and Sextus: that is less likely to be borrowed from life than to be a literary tribute which commemorates the great fame enjoyed by Plutarch in the generations immediately after his own.[47] Plutarch's son Autobulus, to whom he dedicated his essay on the *Timaeus* of Plato, also became a minor Platonist.[48]

In the third century the sophist Nicagoras, the holder of the rhetorical chair at Athens, proclaimed his descent from Plutarch and Sextus; his son Minucianus was also a distinguished sophist, and his grandson, again named Nicagoras, an eccentric Neoplatonist.[49] A lesser philosopher of the same period as the elder Nicagoras rejoiced to be called 'sixth in descent from Plutarch'.[50]

In the next century also, the sophist Himerius prided himself

[45] Viz. L. Mestrius Florus, see below, pp. 22, 48–9.

[46] *PIR*[1] S 488. Marcus' opinion: Εἰς ἑ. 1. 9, *Suda*, Σ 235 Adler.

[47] Apul. *Metam.* 1. 2, cf. 2. 3. Cf. G. W. Bowersock, *Rheinisches Museum* 108 (1965), 288–9, P. Veyne, *Revue de philologie* 39 (1965), 250–1.

[48] *De animae procr. in Tim.* 1012 A; *IG* 7. 3423 = *Syll.*[3] 844 A. Evidently Plutarch's son, and not a descendant of the same name, as Pomtow argues, *Syll.*[3] 843–5, n. 4.

[49] Nicagoras: W. Stegemann, *RE* 17 (1936), 216–18. Descent from Plutarch and Sextus: *Syll.*[3] 845 = *IG* 2/3². 3814, cf. 4831. Minucianus: Stegemann, *RE* 15 (1932), 1986–8. The younger Nicagoras: *OGIS* 720–1, Stegemann, *RE* 17 (1936), 218, no. 9. On the Athenian descendants of Plutarch, see now F. Millar, *JRS* 59 (1969), 16–17.

[50] *IG* 7. 3425 = *Syll.*[3] 844 B.

that his wife and son could count Plutarch, Sextus, Nicagoras, and Minucianus among their ancestors.[51] Himerius' claim, like Apuleius', is demonstrably a reflection of contemporary esteem for Plutarch, through whom, so he told the Athenians, 'you educate all people'. For the slightly younger Eunapius, Plutarch is 'the delight and lyre of all philosophy'.[52] The proliferation of notables called 'Plutarch', among them a great Neoplatonist, is another mark of the Chaeronean's fame, since it was customary for men of culture to borrow the names of earlier luminaries.[53]

So great is the distinction that Plutarch brought to Chaeronea and his family that their contribution to him can easily be neglected. To do so would be an error: his background determined much of his later development. But his own distinction is due in large part to his involvement with other places and persons than those he knew from birth, and above all with a world governed by Rome.

[51] Himer. 7. 4, 8. 21.

[52] Himer. 7. 4. Eunap. *Vit. Philosoph.* 454.

[53] Cf. p. 30, n. 16 below. On the relatives and connections of Plutarch of Athens: É. Évrard, *L'Antiquité classique* 29 (1960), 108 ff., 391 ff. A. Cameron, *Athenaeum* 45 (1967), 150, n. 3.

II

PLUTARCH'S CAREER: YOUTH

IT is characteristic that the author of over fifty biographies
has left no autobiography. The story of his life, as was already
observed in antiquity, can only be pieced together from hints
scattered throughout his works.[1] Nor is there enough information
to provide a full and even record. What there is divides con-
veniently into three main periods, roughly corresponding to three
epochs of imperial history. The formative period, that of his
youth and education, falls approximately under Nero, that of his
maturity (the least known) under the Flavians, and his old age,
in which he wrote the majority of his extant works, under Nerva
and his successors. This division is more, however, than a con-
venience. Living under the imperial system, and being a man
interested and involved in the present, Plutarch felt the effect of
changes brought about by contemporary affairs. His life is part
of the history of his time.

His birth cannot be more precisely dated than to the forties,
probably the early forties, of the first century A.D.[2] It is not even
certain that he was born in Chaeronea, since a man's πατρίς is
not necessarily the city of his birth.[3] Chaeronea, however, was
the place in which his family had lived for generations, and
there he probably received his earliest training.

By the age of seventeen or so Plutarch was able to begin his
higher education, and make the choice between the various
branches of study that offered to a young man of means. The
chronology of his development in these years is very uncertain,
though if it could be established it would be of great interest in
relation to his later career. The one assured fact is that in 66 or 67
he was already a disciple of the Egyptian Ammonius and was
soon to join the Academy after passing through a stage of extreme

---

[1] Eunap. *Vit. Philosoph.* 454: ὁ θεσπέσιος Πλούταρχος τὸν ἑαυτοῦ βίον ἀναγράφει
τοῖς βιβλίοις ἐνδιεσπαρμένως.
[2] He was νέος in 66 or 67 (*de E Delph.* 391 E, cf. 385 B): this may easily signify
an age as great as 30, cf. Xen. *Mem.* 1. 2. 35, Philostr. *Vita Apoll.* 3. 39.
[3] R. Syme, *Tacitus* (1958), 614. Cf. Artemidorus on Daldis, 235. 12 ff. Pack.

interest in mathematics.[4] Of this stage nothing more is known: there is, by contrast, evidence for yet another early interest of his to which he never directly confesses.

After 67, when he had become a philosopher of the Platonic persuasion, Plutarch had the traditional mistrust of the Academy for rhetoric, and often expressed his impatience with the schools of the sophists.[5] Yet several works survive in the Plutarchean corpus, some of them undoubtedly genuine, which bear all the marks of a highly trained rhetor.[6] These works have rightly been taken as evidence for a rhetorical period in his early development to which he did not care to allude later, even though it left its mark on his mature works; and Plutarch retained the belief that the art of persuasion, properly used, was of great value. Since it appears that by 67 he was deeply interested in mathematics and was soon to join the Academy, this rhetorical period and the works assigned to it probably belong late in the reign of Nero when the author would have been about twenty-five. There was only one city of old Greece where such a training could have been acquired, and what Plutarch later mentions as his 'move to Athens' is probably to be connected with this early period.[7]

One of his rhetorical works, the declamation on the fortune of Rome, will be considered later for what it shows or fails to show about Plutarch's early attitude to Rome.[8] More important in a study of his career is the fragment, if it is genuine, of a diatribe comparing the effects of disturbances in the body and in the soul.[9] Near the end of this piece the speaker deplores the spectacle in front of him: the throng he sees has not assembled 'bringing the first-fruits of Lydian harvests to Ascraean Zeus' or to honour Dionysus with nocturnal ceremonies, but for a bout of litigation 'that inflames Asia at yearly intervals'.[10] The reference is clearly to the assizes (*conventus*) held in various cities of the province by

---

[4] *De E Delph.* 387 F, τηνικαῦτα προσεκείμην τοῖς μαθήμασιν ἐμπαθῶς, τάχα δὴ μέλλων εἰς πάντα τιμήσειν τὸ 'μηδὲν ἄγαν' ἐν 'Ακαδημείᾳ γενόμενος.

[5] E.g. *praec. ger. reip.* 802 E, 815 B, *Luc.* 7. 4, *Cic.* 51. 1, *Lyc.* 9. 5, *Pomp.* 77. 3. On Philostr. *Epp.* 73 see below, Appendix I.

[6] Fr. Krauss, *Die rhetorischen Schriften Plutarchs und ihre Stellung im plutarchischen Schriftenkorpus* (diss. Munich, 1912). It should be noticed, however, that criticism of the sophists is to be found in these works also: *de glor. Ath.* 351 A.

[7] *Demosth.* 31. 1, παραβαλεῖν ἡμᾶς 'Αθήναζε.   [8] Below, pp. 67 ff.

[9] *Moralia* 500 B-502 A. Krauss, op. cit., does not discuss the work.

[10] *Anim. an corp. aff.* 501 E-F.

the proconsul or his legate, and though the indications are oblique they combine to suggest strongly that the scene is the Asian city of Smyrna.[11]

Plutarch in the Smyrna of Nero's reign is a prospect highly relevant to his early rhetorical phase.[12] Smyrna is well known as the centre of the movement later to be called the Second Sophistic, which was just beginning in Plutarch's youth. It was Nero who gave this movement its impetus by the favour he showed to its first great representative, Nicetes Sacerdos. Nicetes taught in Smyrna, and it may be that Plutarch's visit was connected with the great teacher's presence there. Nor should it be forgotten that one of Plutarch's Roman friends, the orator Julius Secundus, also appears to have been a follower of Nicetes.[13]

Another journey of Plutarch's youth took him to Alexandria, possibly part of one grand tour that also included his visit to Smyrna. Nothing is known of his stay in Egypt, though he is likely to have visited the famous Museum. From Alexandria Plutarch returned home to Chaeronea.[14]

An incident of his youth is known only from one passing reference, and yet is important in his relations with Rome. Still a young man, he was chosen to go on a deputation with another to the proconsul of Achaea: it is not indicated whose interests he represented, though Chaeronea is likely. When the other ambassador had to be left behind, Plutarch successfully carried out his mission alone. Even so his father advised him to claim only half the credit when reporting back.[15]

The anecdote is not precisely dated, since Plutarch only says that he was 'still young', [16] but it would fit well in his rhetorical

---

[11] This emerges from the fact that part of ancient Lydia apparently fell into the city's *conventus*-district, narrowing the possibilities down to Ephesus, Pergamum, Sardis, and Smyrna: J. Keil, *RE* 13 (1927), 2194–5. Of these the cult of Dionysus at Smyrna was outstanding, and attracted proconsuls and emperors in the time of Aelius Aristides, *Or.* 17. 6, 21. 4, 50. 85 Keil.

[12] For a summary of opinions about the setting of the work see W. C. Helmbold, *Plutarch's Moralia* 6 (Loeb, 1939), 378 (Wilamowitz's discussion is now reprinted in his *Kleine Schriften* 4 [1962], 210–11). The possibility remains that the work is spurious or, as Wilamowitz assumed (art. cit. 210), a dialogue.

[13] Smyrna and the Second Sophistic: G. W. Bowersock, *Greek Sophists in the Roman Empire* (1969), 17 ff. Nicetes: Bowersock, op. cit. 9, 24. Julius Secundus: below, pp. 50–1.

[14] *Quaest. conviv.* 678 C ff. That he was young at the time is shown by the presence of his grandfather at the feast marking his return, cf. K. Ziegler, *RE* 21 (1951), 654.

[15] *Praec. ger. reip.* 816 C f.   [16] Ibid. νέον ἔτι.

period, when his training had already made him a valuable asset to his city. It is a small instance of an old practice in Greek diplomacy, the use of men of culture as ambassadors to governors, generals, or emperors: the Second Sophistic provides several parallels to Plutarch's mission.[17] If it is correctly dated to Nero's reign rather than Vespasian's,[18] it perhaps marks Plutarch's first direct contact with the ruling power. A time was to come when he would be an intimate of proconsuls and honoured by emperors.

If Plutarch's rhetorical period and the travels connected with it are rightly placed before his conversion to the philosophy of the Academy, this phase will have ended late in the reign of Nero. The person most responsible for the change was evidently the Egyptian Ammonius, the only person whom Plutarch names as a teacher. Ammonius taught in Athens and also held the high office of hoplite general three times there: the combination of philosophy and administration recalls the later career of his pupil.[19] It will have been from Athens that with several of his fellow pupils Plutarch accompanied Ammonius to Delphi when Nero visited Greece.[20]

Apart from Plutarch's embassy to the proconsul, the period of Nero's visit to Greece and the subsequent years of faction and civil wars were probably the first events that made Rome and its affairs impinge sharply on him. Again, his movements and experiences in these few years are largely conjectural: but the period is so important in his literary and political development that conjecture must be attempted.

First, his visit to Delphi with Ammonius. Plutarch says simply that the party went 'some time ago, on the occasion of Nero's visit'.[21] It might seem only to follow that they travelled to the shrine in the fourteen or so months that the emperor was travelling about Greece. However, since the treatise in question was evidently written in Delphi and sent to a friend in

---

[17] G. W. Bowersock, *Augustus and the Greek World* (1965), 10–11, 86–7, *Greek Sophists in the Roman Empire* (1969), 43 ff. Cf. especially the Arabian Heliodorus before Caracalla, Philostr. *VS* 625–6.

[18] A Flavian date is preferred by E. Groag, *Die römischen Reichsbeamten von Achaia bis auf Diokletian* (1939), 41.

[19] C. P. Jones, *HSCP* 71 (1966), 205 ff.

[20] This visit is the background of the dialogue *de E Delphico*, 385 B ff.

[21] *De E Delph.* 385 B, πάλαι ποτὲ καθ' ὃν καιρὸν ἐπεδήμει Νέρων.

Athens,[22] 'Nero's visit' ought to refer to something more specific than the emperor's stay in Greece: his appearance at Delphi in the Pythian games. Nero was a demanding guest: even if later accounts are exaggerated, the notables of the province could hardly have failed to come as spectators of the imperial performances.[23] Ammonius, prominent as a philosopher and magistrate of Athens, may have judged it discreet to make the journey to Delphi, while his pupils accompanied him and continued their learned discussions throughout the tour. Plutarch does not allude to the occasion again, still less indicate that he had seen the emperor perform at Delphi: but it is a possibility that cannot be discounted.

Another event of Nero's stay may also have been witnessed by Plutarch. Towards the end of the year 67, a proclamation was issued bidding as many as possible to be present at the Isthmian games on 28 November. There the emperor, victorious in every competition and eager to thank the Greeks for their reception, declared Achaea free from direct rule and the payment of tribute.[24] Decades later Plutarch was to describe him standing on a platform to read the proclamation in his own voice, and the same event appears depicted as the author represents it on contemporary coins.[25] Again Plutarch gives no indication that he was a witness, and it does not greatly matter: what is certain is that the withdrawal of the proconsuls, the ending of tribute, and the troubles of the following years affected the world of a young member of the provincial aristocracy.

For the next two years, from the beginning of the revolt against Nero in early 68 to Vespasian's return to Italy in 70, the history of Achaea partly diverges from that of the rest of the empire. Unlike the civil wars at the end of the republic, those that followed the fall of Nero did not involve fighting on Greek soil. Plutarch's activities in these years are a blank: it is not even

[22] The Delphic setting is apparent from 384 E, 385 A–B. On the addressee, Serapion of Athens, see now G. W. Bowersock, *Greek Sophists in the Roman Empire* (1969), 67–8.

[23] Nero at the Pythia: Suet. *Nero* 25. 1, Cass. Dio, 63. 14. 2, 20. 3, 5. Spectators: Suet. *Nero* 23. 2, *Vesp.* 4. 4, Cass. Dio, 63. 15. 2–3, Philostr. *Vita Apoll.* 5. 7.

[24] The preliminary proclamation and the speech are preserved in the famous inscription of Acraephiae, *IG* 7. 2713 = *ILS* 8794 = *Syll.*³ 814 = Smallwood, *Documents of Gaius, Claudius and Nero* no. 64. On the date, 67 and not 66, A. Stein, *Gnomon* 1 (1925), 342–3.

[25] Description: *Flam.* 12. 13. Coins: *BMC* Corinth, nos. 568–70.

recorded that he was in Achaea. But it is fair to presume that he profited from the lessons they had for an observer of history and of the human character.

Though no longer a battleground for Roman armies, Achaea did not become an enclave of peace. Internally, the removal of proconsular authority meant that the inherited passion for faction could be satisfied to the full.[26] Besides the routine pursuance of ancestral feuds, a new source of disturbance appeared early in 69. A false Nero, the first of several, made his base on an island in sight of the Attic coast and began to attract malcontents and slaves, to the terror of the affluent and joy of the oppressed.[27] This will have given new fuel to the fury of domestic faction. These were grim years in the internal affairs of Greece,[28] and they may have given the young Plutarch his first practical lessons in politics. His later treatises on the subject show an abhorrence of faction and a liking for firm rule, guaranteed by the friendly presence of Roman power.[29] Vespasian brought the episode to an end by cancelling Greek liberty among the first enactments of his rule.[30]

The year 70 not only closes a period of imperial history, the rule of the Julio-Claudians and the subsequent civil wars, but may also be taken as the end of one stage of Plutarch's career. By now probably little less than thirty, the author had reached intellectual maturity and under the guidance of Ammonius had become a philosopher of the Academy, to which he was to adhere for the rest of his life. He had also begun his involvement in public affairs both as actor and spectator.

Plutarch's view of Nero could not be a simple one. Like other Greek writers he was influenced favourably by Nero's philhellen-

[26] Paus. 7. 17. 4, Philostr. *Vita Apoll.* 5. 41, Syncellus, p. 646 Dindorf. See also below, n. 30.

[27] Tac. *Hist.* 2. 8–9. Cf. R. Syme, *Tacitus* (1958), 518, P. A. Brunt, *Latomus* 18 (1959), 558, n. 3, B. M. Levick, *Roman Colonies in Southern Asia Minor* (1967), 166, n. 4.

[28] χρόνοι ἐπιπονωτάτων ἅμα καὶ σφαλερωτάτων καιρῶν, *Syll.*[3] 796 A = (with improvements due to A. Wilhelm) Smallwood, *Documents of Gaius, Claudius and Nero* no. 65, line 11. On the date of the inscription: A. D. Momigliano, *JRS* 34 (1944), 115–16.

[29] *Praec. ger. reip.* 798 A ff. on which see below, pp. 110 ff.

[30] Suet. *Vesp.* 8. 4, Paus. 7. 17. 4, Philostr. *Vita Apoll.* 5. 41, Syncellus, p. 646 Dindorf. Philostratus and Syncellus both date the event to the beginning of the reign: Jerome places it in 74 in his translation of Eusebius' *Chronicle* (ed. R. Helm, *Die gr. Chr. Schriftsteller* 47 [1956], 188). But Jerome has evidently borrowed the notice from Eutropius, 7. 19, where it appears without a date, and his evidence has no independent weight: cf. Mommsen, *Gesammelte Schriften* 7 (1909), 610.

ism. In the vision of Thespesius of Soli which is Plutarch's Myth
of Er, the soul of Nero is represented as that of 'one to whom the
gods owed some benefit because he had freed the best and the
most dear to them of all his subjects'.[31] As a moralist, Plutarch
saw Nero's nature as an essentially good one corrupted by
flattery.[32] But he was too much of a realist to let such considerations outweigh the external effects of Nero's character, the
'damnable procurators' that harassed the provinces, the
grasping freedmen, the self-indulgence that nearly overturned
the empire.[33] In the final judgement Nero was a tyrant and his
overthrow a noble act.[34]

By contrast with Nero, Plutarch's references to the next three
emperors and the years of civil war are few. The *Lives of Galba
and Otho*, the only survivors of a series that originally went from
Augustus to Vitellius,[35] are literary products that reveal little
about the author's personal impressions and experiences. There
is a striking comparison of the Roman empire to the Titans
reeling in conflict with the gods,[36] and the grisly details recounted
by friends who had been present on the battlefront must have
confirmed a philosopher's horror of bloodshed.[37] But as yet
Plutarch was not involved in the affairs of the empire. While the
course of his intellectual career had already been set, the social
and political pattern of his life had still to form.

[31] *De sera num. vind.* 567 F f. Cf. the comment of Philostr. *Vita Apoll.* 5. 41: 'Nero
freed Greece by an act of unusual wisdom.'
[32] *Quom. adul. ab amico internosc.* 56 E, 60 D. Cf. *de cohib. ira* 461 F f., *praec. ger.
reip.* 810 A.
[33] Procurators: *Galba* 4. 1. Freedmen: cf. the reference to the exactions of Acratus,
praec. ger. reip. 815 D, with Tac. *Ann.* 16. 23. 1, Dio Prus. 31. 148. The empire: *Ant.*
87. 9.
[34] Tyrant: *de frat. am.* 488 A (on the reference here, C. P. Jones, *JRS* 56 [1966],
70 and below, p. 52, n. 22), *de garrul.* 505 C. Deposition: *Galba* 1. 9.
[35] The series is known only from the Lamprias Catalogue, nos. 26, 27, 29–33, and
from one or two fragments (frs. 5 and perhaps 182 Sandbach). See further below,
pp. 72 ff.
[36] *Galba* 1. 6.
[37] *Otho* 14. 2. Plutarch's tone, however, is notably dispassionate.

III

PLUTARCH'S CAREER: THE FLAVIANS

UNDER the rule of the Flavians Plutarch passed from youth to the proximity of old age.[1] These years might be expected to have witnessed the peak of his literary activity. Instead they were occupied with travel and other duties. Only later, in his retirement, did he have the leisure and inclination to compose the works on which his reputation chiefly rests. But this central period, ill documented and little known, is the time in which the Plutarch familiar from the *Parallel Lives* and the *Table Talk* was formed.

A Greek of the upper class, Plutarch travelled as a matter of course to visit his friends in other cities, to attend festivals, or simply to relax in a resort.[2] The more important of his journeys took him elsewhere. In a passage of the *Demosthenes* written comparatively early in his retirement he claims, recalling his visits to Rome and Italy, that he had been so busy with political duties and those who sought his company as a philosopher that he had not had time to practise Latin.[3] This passage, as oblique and casual as all Plutarch's references to himself, is the starting-point for a study of his activities in these middle years.

Although Plutarch often shows his familiarity with Rome, and sometimes with other cities of Italy, this is the only occasion on which he indicates the purpose of his visits. By long tradition, cultivated Greeks had been chosen by their countrymen to represent their cities or their provinces at Rome, and often combined such duties with lectures there.[4] It is reasonably

---

[1] I.e. from about 25 in 66–7 (above, p. 14) to about 55 in 96. Old age began at about 60: cf. Sen. *de brev. vit.* 20. 4, Plut. *Lyc.* 26. 1, and on Vespasian at 60, Tac. *Hist.* 2. 81. 2, 4. 8. 4.

[2] Cf. K. Ziegler, *RE* 21 (1951), 653–4, and below, p. 42.

[3] *Demosth.* 2. 2: ἐν δὲ ʽΡώμῃ καὶ ταῖς περὶ τὴν Ἰταλίαν διατριβαῖς οὐ σχολῆς οὔσης . . . ὑπὸ χρειῶν πολιτικῶν (for this phrase cf. *Mar.* 32. 2) καὶ τῶν διὰ φιλοσοφίαν πλησιαζόντων. On the date of the *Demosth.* C. P. Jones, *JRS* 56 (1966), 66–70.

[4] Thus in the second century B. C. Crates of Mallos, Suet. *de gramm.* 2. 2, and the embassy of philosophers on behalf of Athens in 156/5, *Cato mai.* 22 (v. Arnim, *RE* 10 [1919], 1965).

certain that the political duties that Plutarch mentions were also of a diplomatic nature, the sequel to his early success before the proconsul of Achaea. His familiarity with diplomatic protocol appears from one of the *Roman Questions*, in which the discussion concerns the duty of foreign ambassadors to register with the prefects of the treasury of Saturn. Elsewhere embassies to Rome are several times cited, according to the context, as the glory or the burden of the politician's career.[5] Plutarch does not say on whose behalf he visited Italy. He may have represented Chaeronea, his adoptive city of Athens,[6] the shrine of Delphi, or most probably the provincial league.[7] Because he is reticent about this side of his activity, as about all his public duties, it does not follow that he was politically inconsequential.[8]

As Plutarch became better known, both because of his official duties and through the friendship of Romans who visited Greece, he may also have travelled to the capital simply as a philosopher. One of his Roman friends might ask him for his company on the journey back to Rome, or send him an invitation from Italy. On such visits, despite his freedom from political duties, his time would be occupied by lecturing to select audiences, giving private advice to his friends, or visiting them in their cities of origin and on their estates.[9]

The dating of these journeys is hazardous. Plutarch indicates that he had visited Rome and Italy several times, and none of his stays need have been of long duration.[10] An anecdote about a dog that performed before Vespasian in the theatre of Marcellus may derive, though not necessarily, from his own experience.[11] So also may his description of Epponina, the wife of the Gallic rebel Julius Sabinus, as she taunted the old emperor while

---

[5] *Quaest. Rom.* 275 B–C, *de exil.* 602 C, *praec. ger. reip.* 805 A, *adv. Col.* 1126 E.

[6] *Quaest. conviv.* 628 A, cf. C. P. Jones, *HSCP* 71 (1966), 207 and n. 11.

[7] On this league in Plutarch's day, U. Kahrstedt, *Symbolae Osloenses* 28 (1950), 70–5, J. Deininger, *Die Provinziallandtage der römischen Kaiserzeit*, Vestigia 6 (1965), 90–1. An embassy of the league to Caligula: *IG* 7. 2711 = (lines 21 ff.) *ILS* 8792 = Smallwood, *Documents of Gaius, Claudius and Nero* no. 361.

[8] 'A man whose public life was confined, generally speaking, to the municipal level', D. A. Russell, *Greece and Rome* 15 (1968), 130.

[9] Below, Ch. VI.

[10] Cf. K. Ziegler, *RE* 21 (1951), 653–7, R. H. Barrow, *Plutarch and his Times* (1967), 36–42.

[11] *De soll. anim.* 973 E-974 A. Cf. Suet. *Vesp.* 19. 1.

awaiting public execution.[12] Another indication of a visit during that reign is provided by Plutarch's reference to Julius Secundus, the orator from whom he obtained information about Otho, since Secundus appears to have died about 80.[13] If that shows that Plutarch already had in mind his biographies of the emperors from Augustus to Vitellius, another incident may be datable to the reign of Vespasian. On one occasion he travelled in northern Italy with the consular Mestrius Florus and visited Bedriacum, Brixellum, Ravenna, and possibly other cities.[14] It was Mestrius who obtained the Roman citizenship for him, and he may have done so from Vespasian.[15]

Plutarch's career under Titus and Domitian is equally little known. There is evidence that he was in Athens in the early 80s, and present at the Pythian games in the middle of the decade.[16] He was probably also in Greece a little later when Sosius Senecio, then a young man but soon to assume great importance in Plutarch's career, was there as quaestor.[17] Plutarch may have been in Rome again at a momentous time, the winter of 88–9. That seems to be implied by a strange story that he tells about Domitian's victory over Antonius Saturninus becoming known in the capital at the very hour it happened.[18] Plutarch's description of unchaste Vestal Virgins being buried alive might also reflect a well-known instance of this practice in 89 or 90.[19] Lastly, some experience of that uneasy time might seem reflected in his treatise on divine justice, in which he describes the soul of Nero undergoing punishment in the afterlife. About 89, a recurrent belief that Nero was still alive gained ground when the Parthians were reported to be aiding him in a bid to recover his throne.[20]

More important still for its effect on Plutarch is a visit to Rome

---

[12] *Amat.* 770 C-771 C.

[13] Cf. C. P. Jones, *HSCP* 72 (1968), 279 ff. especially 282, and below, p. 50.

[14] *Otho* 14. 2 (Bedriacum), 18. 2 (Brixellum), *Mar.* 2. 1 (Ravenna). On the date of the *Lives of the Caesars*, see below, p. 72.

[15] *Syll.*³ 829 A = Smallwood, *Documents of Nerva, Trajan and Hadrian* no. 487. Cf. also L. Mestrius Autobulus and L. Mestrius Soclarus from Chaeronea, evidently Plutarch's sons: *Syll.*³ 844 A, *IG* 9. 1. 61, lines 41–2.

[16] *Publ.* 15. 4, cf. S. B. Platner and T. Ashby, *A Topographical Dictionary of Ancient Rome* (1929), 300. Pythia: *de def. orac.* 410 A, with the discussion of R. M. Ogilvie, *Phoenix* 21 (1967), 108–19.

[17] Below, p. 55.

[18] *Aem.* 25. 5–7.

[19] *Numa* 10. 8–13, cf. A. N. Sherwin-White, *The Letters of Pliny* (1966), 283.

[20] *De sera num. vind.* 567 E–568 A. Cf. Tac. *Hist.* 1. 2. 1, Suet. *Nero* 57. 2.

that occurred some time later. In the *Table Talk* he tells of a conversation between his friend Avidius Quietus and the erudite Aufidius Modestus in which Aufidius jokingly suggested that Quietus had taken bribes in his province.[21] From Plutarch's confirmation that Quietus had been an exemplary proconsul it follows that his province had been Achaea, and this is confirmed by epigraphical evidence that appears to fix the year as 91/2.[22] Plutarch was therefore in Rome some time after the summer of 92, and his anecdote would suggest that it was not long after.[23]

A better-known incident may now be adduced. One of Plutarch's lectures in Rome was attended by the famous Arulenus Rusticus. When a soldier came through the audience bringing a letter from Caesar to Rusticus, Plutarch stopped to give him time to read it. Rusticus declined to disturb the lecture, thus winning general admiration.[24] Although there is no sure indication of date, the atmosphere that Plutarch's narrative conveys would accord with a date not long before Rusticus' execution in 93.[25]

There is also his description of the luxury of Domitian's new palace, a spectacle of gold and stone, which was not completed until 92. If Plutarch's reference to the opulent royal chambers, baths, and mistresses' quarters in the building comes from autopsy, that would be further evidence of a visit, presumably of an ambassadorial kind, in that year or later.[26]

Lastly, a vague scrap of information that may not lead anywhere. At some time about 93 the younger Pliny, acting on the

---

[21] *Quaest. conviv.* 632 A.

[22] *Fouilles de Delphes* 3. 1. 538 = *Syll.*[3] 822 = McCrum and Woodhead, *Documents of the Flavian Emperors* no. 318. Cyllus' tenure ran from 91 to 94 (Pomtow on *Syll.*[3] 822, n. 2, A. B. West, *CP* 23 [1928], 263), and Quietus' consulate can now be dated to early 93 (Syme, *Tacitus* [1958], 638). Hence 91/2 fits best for the proconsulate (McCrum and Woodhead retain the impossible date of 95).

[23] Macrobius when adapting this passage assumed that Quietus had just returned from his province, *Sat.* 7. 3. 15.

[24] *De curios.* 522 D–E.

[25] R. H. Barrow, *Plutarch and his Times* (1967), 38, reasonably conjectures that the letter was sent by Domitian to Rusticus as consul; he was consul in the last four months of 92 (Degrassi, *Fasti Consolari* [1952], 28). There is no reason to doubt that this consul is the famous Rusticus, as Sherwin-White does, *The Letters of Pliny* (1966), 95, followed by D. A. Russell, *Greece and Rome* 15 (1968), 132, n. 7: cf. *PIR*[2] I/J 730.

[26] *Publ.* 15. 5. Cf. Platner and Ashby, op. cit. 159, K. Ziegler, *RE* 21 (1951), 655–6.

request of the same Arulenus Rusticus, defended the wife of a certain Timon: part of the case turned on a decision of the exiled praetorian, Mettius Modestus.[27] It happens that Plutarch had a brother also called Timon, who like Plutarch had friends at Rome in the two brothers Avidius Nigrinus and Quietus.[28] Plutarch himself was known to Arulenus Rusticus, and both Rusticus and Quietus had been followers of Thrasea Paetus.[29] There is a remote chance, therefore, that Plutarch's relatives were brought for a hearing to Rome about the year 93.[30] If that is correct, it could be conjectured that Mettius Modestus had delivered his decision while proconsul of Achaea and that his exile had caused his proconsular acts to be questioned or revoked.

If Plutarch was in Rome in 92 or 93, an important consequence for his career may follow. In 93, or possibly in 94, Domitian's patience became exhausted with a group of senators and their womenfolk who adhered to the memory of Thrasea Paetus, the victim of Nero. Seven persons, among them Arulenus Rusticus, were executed or sent into exile. To mark his displeasure with their Greek associates, Domitian followed their trials with the expulsion of philosophers from Rome and Italy.[31]

Plutarch's connection with this group is clear. Among his Roman friends Arulenus Rusticus was executed; Avidius Quietus had also been a follower of Thrasea, though his career continued smoothly. Plutarch's admiration for Junius Mauricus, the brother of Arulenus who was now sent into exile, had been expressed in a work that may well be earlier than 93, the *Lives of the Caesars*.[32] His references to Thrasea Paetus, however, are less indicative, since they date from the reign of Trajan.[33]

[27] Pliny, *Epp.* 1. 5. 5. On the date, cf. Fluss, *RE* 15 (1932), 1500, H.-G. Pflaum, *Les Carrières procuratoriennes équestres* 1 (1960), 119 ff.

[28] *De frat. am.* 487 D–E. On the Avidii in Greece, below, p. 52.

[29] Pliny, *Epp.* 6. 29. 1, 9. 13. 15, 17.

[30] The thesis that the two Timons were to be identified was propounded by R. Volkmann, *Leben, Schriften und Philosophie des Plutarch von Chaeronea* (1869), 1. 24–5; contested by Wilamowitz, *Commentariolum Grammaticum* 3 (1889), 28, n. 2 (= *Kleine Schriften* 4 [1962], 655, n. 2), and not taken seriously since. On the career of Mettius Modestus, *PIR*¹ M 404, C. P. Jones, *Phoenix* 22 (1968), 123.

[31] Syme, *Tacitus* (1958), 76, 656–7, Sherwin-White, op. cit. 763–71.

[32] *Galba* 8. 8, ἄνδρα τῶν ἀρίστων καὶ ὄντα καὶ δοκοῦντα. On the date of the *Lives of the Caesars*: above, p. 22, below, p. 72.

[33] *Praec. ger. reip.* 810 A, *Cato min.* 25. 2, 37. 1.

There is a chance that Plutarch himself was affected by Domitian's ban,[34] even if he was not forced to leave Rome like the Stoic Epictetus,[35] or endangered in some other way. Already he had protection in Avidius Quietus and probably in Sosius Senecio, now perhaps of praetorian rank and favoured by Domitian. But Plutarch may have felt it advisable to forestall trouble by a voluntary departure, and to stay away from Rome for the foreseeable future.

The effects of this period on him may be seen in various ways. His attitude to the Flavians is notably hostile. Vespasian is characterized as cruel and unhappy.[36] Domitian is the type of arrogance, superstition, and tasteless extravagance.[37] But, at least in Plutarch's attitude to Domitian, it is difficult to separate the author's own experience from the general revulsion of the Greek and Roman upper class against the emperor. A more tangible consequence of Plutarch's alienation may be seen in the pattern of his literary activity. The number of his works that can be positively dated to the Flavian period is extremely small by comparison with those written later.[38] That could be in part the result of embassies and lectures, which took from him the time to write as it did the time to practise Latin. But another cause may be suspected, the danger of writing in a period when even the most innocuous work could be construed as an attack on the emperor.[39] A man already busy with public duties did not need much incentive to stop writing altogether.[40]

With his activities as an ambassador and counsellor, Plutarch must certainly have incurred throughout his mature life the usual responsibilities of a man of his position in the society of Greece. These might involve a year as the chief magistrate of Chaeronea or the still-surviving Boeotian league: Plutarch may

---

[34] Cf. R. Flacelière, *L'Antiquité classique* 32 (1963), 43.

[35] A. Gellius, 15. 11. 5. Note that Philostratus places the trial of Apollonius of Tyana in 93, *VA* 8. 1 ff. and especially 8. 7. 11.

[36] *Amat.* 771 C. A neutral reference to Vespasian's luck, *Publ.* 15. 2.

[37] *Numa* 19. 7, *quaest. Rom.* 276 E, *Publ.* 15. 3–6. For the effect of Domitian's reign on a contemporary philosopher, Epictetus, cf. C. G. Starr, *CP* 44 (1949), 20 ff.

[38] C. P. Jones, *JRS* 56 (1966), 61 ff.

[39] Note the sophist Maternus put to death because of a declamation against tyrants, Cass. Dio, 67. 12. 5, and the younger Helvidius Priscus because of a supposed reference to Domitian in a masque, Suet. *Dom.* 10. 4. Cf. the elder Pliny under Nero, Pliny, *Epp.* 3. 5. 5.

[40] Cf. Tac. *Agr.* 3. 1.

even have become chairman of the provincial assembly, the Helladarch, as did several of his friends.[41]

There were also the various duties connected with the shrine of Delphi. A wealthy citizen of Chaeronea, especially if he had a reputation as a public figure and a friend of Roman officials, could not easily avoid election as one of Boeotia's two represent-atives on the Amphictyonic council; or as an honorary citizen of Delphi he could represent that city also. While on the council, he could serve one or more terms as its executive, the epimelete. Membership of the Amphictyony was not necessary for another post, that of supervising the conduct of the Pythian games as agonothete.[42]

Finally, Plutarch succeeded to the highest position in the hierarchy of the shrine and became one of the two permanent priests.[43] In that office his diplomatic experience would have been highly desirable to deal with the intervention of a proconsul or emperor, or to obtain funds for some new building project.[44] Plutarch's tenure may have begun under Domitian, who took a close interest in the operation of the shrine, or rather under Nerva or Trajan.[45]

With the duties of public life, Plutarch had also those of raising a family. He had apparently married young, and had several sons and daughters.[46] A man with his views on education is likely to have devoted much of his time to his family.[47] This may further explain his silence in his middle years: by the time that he wrote

[41] Archon: *quaest. conviv.* 642 F, 693 F. Boeotarch: *an seni sit ger. resp.* 785 C, *praec. ger. reip.* 813 D. Helladarch: cf. his friends Lucanius (*quaest. conviv.* 675 D), Polycrates (*Arat.* 1. 5, cf. *PIR²* C 969), Pulcher (*de cap. ex inim. util.* 86 B ff. cf. *PIR²* C 1424). Cf. Ziegler, *RE* 21 (1951), 657–9.

[42] Amphictyons: cf. *an seni sit ger. resp.* 785 C, *Syll.³* 829 A. Epimelete: *Syll.³* 829 A. Agonothete: *an seni sit ger. resp.* 785 C.

[43] *Quaest. conviv.* 700 E, *Syll.³* 829 A. Cf. Ziegler, art. cit. 659–62.

[44] The emperors and Delphi: É. Bourguet, *De rebus Delphicis imperatoriae aetatis* (1905), 59–93 (on the letter of Claudius, Bourguet, 63–4, see now A. Plassart, *REG* 80 [1967], 372–8). Domitian: *Syll.³* 821 A = *ILS* 8905 = *Fouilles de Delphes* 3. 4. 120 = McCrum and Woodhead, *Documents of the Flavian Emperors* no. 463 (a); *Syll.³* 821 B–E = McCrum and Woodhead, no. 463 (b–e).

[45] Cf. G. Daux, *Chronologie delphique* (1943), 90, J. Jannoray, *REA* 47 (1945), 257, preferring a Domitianic date. Plutarch's reference to his 'many Pythiads' of service, *an seni sit ger. resp.* 792 F, could easily cover a period of 98–115.

[46] Marriage: *amat.* 749 B ff. cf. C. P. Jones, *JRS* 56 (1966) 71. On the number of his children, cf. Ziegler, *RE* 21 (1951), 648–9, P. H. De Lacy and B. Einarson, *Plutarch's Moralia* 7 (Loeb, 1959), 575–6.

[47] *De poet. aud.* 15 A, *Cato mai.* 20. 4–7.

the *Table Talk*, for instance, most of his children were grown up and married.[48]

In the Flavian era, Plutarch was absorbed with a variety of duties. Whether or not by his own choice, he appears not to have written much in these years: the treatise on brotherly love and (less certainly) the series of the *Lives of the Caesars* are the only works that can be dated to this period with any assurance.[49] There is no sign that he returned to Domitian's Rome, and he may have stayed away for several years.[50]

In Rome, the emperor had become an autocrat. There may also have been vexation for Plutarch in Greece, in the form of itinerant philosophers and strange portents.[51] He began to approach old age. There seemed no prospect that he would outlive the robust Domitian or that the latest ban on philosophers would weaken into nullity as past ones had. Then, in September 96, the news came that Domitian had been assassinated. That winter the Athenian Dionysia were celebrated with unusual magnificence. Plutarch was present at the festival.[52]

[48] *Quaest. conviv.* 666 D ff., 719 C ff., 725 F, 735 C ff. (sons), 620 A, 636 A, 642 C, 700 E (daughters).

[49] *Caesars*: below, p. 72. *De frat. am.*: below, p. 52.

[50] Note the long absence referred to at *quaest. conviv.* 727 B.

[51] Philostratus makes Apollonius of Tyana reside in Greece from 93 to 95, *Vita Apoll.* 8. 7. 11, 8. 24. Note Apollonius' visit to the oracle of Trophonius at Lebadea, *Vita Apoll.* 8. 19, where Plutarch's brother was priest, *de def. orac.* 431 C–D. Portent: Philostr. *Vita Apoll.* 8. 23.

[52] *Quaest. conviv.* 628 A, cf. *IG* 2/3². 3112. Date: J. A. Notopoulos, *Hesperia* 18 (1949), 12; *PIR²* I/J 151 returns to the obsolete range of 75/6–87/8.

IV

PLUTARCH'S CAREER:
FROM NERVA TO HADRIAN

THE following years, down to Plutarch's death in about 120, represent the zenith of his career as a philosopher and public figure. The accession of Trajan put an end to the anarchy that had threatened during Nerva's tenure, and literature flourished under the new regime. Now Plutarch had an incentive to write; and he was getting old. Instead of travelling to the West, he divided his time mainly between Chaeronea and Delphi: even Athens now seemed far away.[1] He thus had the leisure to gather such materials as he needed for his writing, to make his first acquaintance with Latin authors, and to give instruction to visitors.[2]

While he had renounced the duties that entailed extensive travel, he continued to be involved in local politics. At Chaeronea he held minor posts in the civic administration, and at Delphi continued as one of the priests, if he did not first assume the position in this period.[3] He is also attested in these last years as epimelete of the Amphictyons, supervising the erection of a statue for the new emperor Hadrian.[4] Old age, he assured his friend Euphanes, was no excuse to retire from public life.[5]

Although Plutarch had almost entirely stopped travelling to Rome, these same years saw him receive the high respect of the emperors and their friends. These are the years in which men prominent in the society of Trajan's Rome came to visit Plutarch, or wrote to him with a request for some edifying treatise.[6] The most influential of all was the consular to whom the *Parallel Lives* and the *Table Talk* are dedicated, Q. Sosius Senecio.

[1] *Demosth.* 2. 1–2 (Chaeronea), *de E Delph.* 384 E (Delphi).
[2] *Demosth.* 2. 1–2 (materials, Latin), *de poet. aud.* 15 A, *de E Delph.* 385 A (instruction).
[3] Chaeronea: *praec. ger. reip.* 811 B f. (on the date, C. P. Jones, *JRS* 56 [1966], 72). Priesthood and date: above, p. 26, n. 45.
[4] *Syll.*[3] 829 A.
[5] *An seni sit ger. resp.* 783 A ff.   [6] See below, Ch. VI.

Sosius was twice consul under Trajan and received the rare honour of a public statue from him.[7]

Eventually, perhaps with the mediation of Sosius and others, honours came to Plutarch from the emperor himself. The most signal of these is recorded only in a confused notice of a Byzantine lexicon, where it is stated that Trajan 'gave him a share in the dignity of consuls'. Despite the lexicographer's imprecision, it is evident that he is referring to the *ornamenta consularia*.[8] The ornaments corresponded to the grades of the senatorial *cursus honorum* and were for bestowal on those outside the senate. The consular kind were the highest of all; usually given for personal services to the emperor,[9] they were occasionally awarded to distinguished men of literature. Before Plutarch, Quintilian had received them from Domitian as the tutor of his adopted sons and the holder of the chair of rhetoric at Rome.[10] Later the eminent sophist Apsines of Gadara was awarded them by Maximinus.[11] If Plutarch had performed some particular service for Trajan equal to that of Quintilian for Domitian, it is not recorded: more likely the *ornamenta* marked general recognition of his eminence.

A consequence that follows from this award bears on Plutarch's public career. Magisterial *ornamenta* were almost always bestowed on those of equestrian rank. It is nowhere attested that Plutarch, the first Roman citizen in his family, was also enrolled among the knights; but since this honour was considerably more common than the *ornamenta*, it is unlikely that he had not already received it, either from Trajan or some earlier emperor.[12] Previously it had been usual for knights to pass through the *tres militiae*, but as the knighthood was bestowed more widely exceptions became more common, especially among those who were men of letters

[7] Below, pp. 54 ff.

[8] *Suda*, Π 1793 Adler: μεταδοὺς δὲ αὐτῷ Τραιανὸς τῆς τῶν ὑπάτων ἀξίας προσέταξε μηδένα τῶν κατὰ τὴν ᾽Ιλλυρίδα ἀρχόντων παρὲξ τῆς αὐτοῦ γνώμης τι διαπράττεσθαι. Cf. *Suda*, A 4735 on Apsines of Gadara, ὑπατικοῦ λαβὼν ἀξίωμα. Thus E. Groag, *RE* 3 A (1927), 1190 (suggesting the mediation of Sosius): A. Stein, *Der römische Ritterstand* (1927), 274.

[9] As by Nero to his guardian Asconius Labeo, Tac. *Ann.* 13. 10. 1.

[10] Auson. *grat. act.* 7. 31, p. 361 P. ascribing his elevation to Domitian's cousin Flavius Clemens. Cf. *PIR*² F 59.

[11] *Suda*, A 4735 Adler; cf. *PIR*² A 978, and now *Hesperia* 10 (1941), 260, no. 65, G. W. Bowersock, *Greek Sophists in the Roman Empire* (1969), 5–6.

[12] Thus A. Stein, op. cit. 274, E. Groag, *Die römischen Reichsbeamten von Achaia bis auf Diokletian* (1939), 146.

rather than of affairs.[13] There is no sign that Plutarch had seen service in the field. Equestrian rank would also imply a level of affluence which accords with the known facts about his background. He is unlikely, however, to have possessed the fluency in Latin which had been expected of knights in his youth.[14]

The same source that preserves the notice of Plutarch's *ornamenta* contains the more obscure information that Trajan gave orders for none of the governors of Illyria to do anything without the philosopher's agreement.[15] Although this might contain a core of truth, it appears rather to reflect the administrative system of a later age. Possibly the compiler has confused Plutarch with one of his later namesakes who held high office in Greece in the fourth and fifth centuries.[16]

Less tangible evidence for the relations of Plutarch and Trajan is provided in the corpus of Plutarch's own writings. In the works of undoubted authenticity, one passing reference to a Caesar who had recently wintered on the Danube probably alludes to Trajan.[17] One of the several extant political works might appear at first sight to have been addressed to him, the treatise sometimes called a *Discourse to an Unlearned Prince*.[18] Trajan allowed Dio of Prusa to lecture to him on kingship,[19] and he had no reason to be less patient with Plutarch. There is nothing in the work, however, to indicate that it was intended for one person in particular, but rather delivered before several hearers; and it does not concern monarchs so much as rulers in general, even the magistrates of cities.[20]

Later ages, ever ready to imagine philosophers counselling monarchs, did not scruple to invent evidence for advice given

---

[13] So, apparently, Suetonius: cf. Syme, *Tacitus* (1958), 778–81, discussing *AE* 1953. 73 (a contrary opinion in A. N. Sherwin-White, *The Letters of Pliny* [1966], 127). Also perhaps the sophist Dionysius of Miletus, *PIR*² D 105.

[14] Wealth: above, pp. 8 ff. Latin: *Demosth.* 2. 2, cf. Suet. *Claud.* 16. 2.

[15] *Suda*, Π 1793 Adler (above, p. 29, n. 8). Cf. the comments of K. Latte in Ziegler, *RE* 21 (1951), 658, n. 1.

[16] On these see E. Groag, *Die Reichsbeamten von Achaia in spätrömischer Zeit* (1946), 59–62, L. Robert, *Hellenica* 4 (1948), 94 ff., 147–8. None of these is recorded in *RE*. R. H. Barrow, *Plutarch and his Times* (1967), 46, suggests not implausibly that the *Suda*'s Ἰλλυρίδα is really a slip for Ἀχαιαν.

[17] *De primo frigido* 949 E.

[18] *Ad princ. inerud.* 779 D ff. Thus, e.g. E. R. Goodenough, *Yale Classical Studies* 1 (1928), 94 ff., K. Scott, *TAPA* 60 (1929), 126 ff.

[19] Dio: *Or.* 1–4, cf. *PIR*² D 93.

[20] Audience: 781 E. City magistrates: 780 F, 781 F.

by Plutarch to Trajan. In the letter prefixed to the spurious *Apophthegms of Kings and Generals* the philosopher is made to assure the emperor that the following work, culled from his *Parallel Lives*, will save Trajan the bother of having to peruse the whole. Several features betray it as a forgery.[21] No less spurious, but more difficult to explain, is the work supposedly written by Plutarch for the benefit of Trajan that is cited by the twelfth century writer, John of Salisbury. The *Institutio Traiani* may be John's own fabrication, or a cento assembled by someone with more knowledge of Plutarch's writings than John had.[22]

If there is no sign that Plutarch communicated with Trajan in extant works, that does not mean that the two did not maintain private contacts. Besides, Plutarch could perform more useful service than by advising Trajan how to govern his empire. Above all, an emperor so concerned with the views of posterity can only have looked with satisfaction on the works that Plutarch poured out in this period, the *Parallel Lives* in particular, which were addressed to Trajan's close friend Sosius Senecio. The *Lives*, 'linking the excellent Greeks to the warlike denizens of Rome' in the words of a Byzantine poet,[23] typify their age, in which Greeks and Romans mixed together in society, in the senate, and on the *fasti*. Time had proved wrong the dire prophecies of the elder Cato: while retaining her goodwill for Greek culture, Rome had reached the height of power.[24]

The *Parallel Lives* would not have been the only work of Plutarch to please Trajan. Like the rulers of other empires, the Caesars saw the advantage of advertising their interest in the prosperity of so famous a shrine as Delphi. Trajan, continuing where Domitian had left off, confirmed the traditional rights of the city and added buildings both there and at the other meeting place of the Amphictyons, Thermopylae. Whether or not Plutarch first became priest in Trajan's reign, several of his works were now devoted to Delphi and glorified the new

---

[21] *Reg. et imp. apophth.* 172 A ff. Cf. Wyttenbach's judicious comments, *Plutarchi Chaeronensis Moralia* 6 (1810), 1041–2.

[22] S. Desideri, *La 'Institutio Traiani'* (1958). For the controversy about John's part in the work cf. Desideri's survey, 25 ff., and now Janet M. Martin, *HSCP* 73 (1969), 320–1.

[23] Agathias, *Anth. Plan.* 331.

[24] *Cato mai.* 23. 3.

construction there.[25] From being an ambassador of the Greeks to Rome, Plutarch was now an ambassador of the empire to posterity.

Despite his more confined area of activity, his diplomatic duties were not over. There were his functions as priest, and new developments occurred in the administration of the province. Not only were there the usual worries that annual proconsuls brought for prominent citizens:[26] about 107 Trajan sent a new official, a *corrector*, to intervene in the affairs of free cities like Delphi and Athens.[27] It was a delicate commission, and to avoid injuring the sensibilities of ancient cities a *corrector* might well have called in a respected philosopher who knew the ways of Greeks and Romans. After a while, even this measure proved insufficient. There is evidence that for a period Trajan made Achaea subject to his own legates, giving the senate Sardinia in exchange. One of these turned out to be the young consular C. Avidius Nigrinus, whose father and uncle had both been friends of Plutarch. One of Nigrinus' tasks was to moderate boundary disputes between Delphi and her neighbours.[28]

When the young emissary of Trajan arrived in Delphi, Plutarch will have been about 70. Nigrinus was not the only reminder of change and mortality. His father and uncle had died long since.[29] Plutarch's friend Mestrius Florus, through whom he obtained the Roman citizenship, had finally succumbed, after a lively old age prolonged by curative waters and a passion for learning.[30] Others followed as the reign drew near its end. Philopappus, the convivial prince from Commagene who had made his home in Athens, was now buried there in a sumptuous monument on the Hill of the Muses.[31] In these years Plutarch also lost his old friend and helper, Sosius Senecio.[32] At

[25] Trajan and Delphi: *Syll.*[3] 823 A–C; *Fouilles de Delphes* 3. 4. 47. Cf. É. Bourguet, *De rebus Delphicis imperatoriae aetatis* (1905), 69–72. Plutarch on the new construction: *de Pyth. orac.* 408 F ff. on the date of which see C. P. Jones, *JRS* 56 (1966), 63 ff., 72.

[26] Note the instructive consolation to a man in exile, *de exil.* 602 C, 604 B.

[27] Pliny, *Epp.* 8. 24, cf. Arr. *Diss. Epict.* 3. 7. On the date: Sherwin-White, *The Letters of Pliny* (1966), 477 ff. Cf. also C. P. Jones, *Phoenix* 22 (1968), 135.

[28] Legates: R. Syme, *Historia* 18 (1969), 359. Avidius Nigrinus: *Syll.*[3] 827 (827 C = Smallwood, *Documents of Nerva, Trajan and Hadrian* no. 446: Delphi), *SEG* 21. 498 (Athens).

[29] Below, pp. 51 ff.

[30] Mestrius: below, pp. 48–9. Waters: *quaest. conviv.* 734 D ff. Learning: *quaest. conviv.* 702 D, 734 D, Suet. *Vesp.* 22.

[31] Below, p. 59.   [32] Below, p. 57.

last it was the turn of the emperor himself. On his way to the Parthian War Trajan had lingered in Athens exchanging embassies with the enemy.[33] Less than four years later word came from the East that he was dead and Hadrian was his successor.

If Plutarch was still observing the vicissitudes of the Caesars and the affairs of Rome, he may have been pleased to learn of the new emperor. It is possible that Hadrian was already known to him as a friend of the younger Nigrinus, and perhaps of Sosius; and a few years ago he had been archon at Athens.[34] Soon, however, there were rumours that he had not been adopted but owed his elevation to the help of Trajan's wife Plotina: cultured society in Achaea was soon to have tangible proof of the dowager's influence with the new emperor.[35] The rumours were succeeded by something more palpable. Within a year of Hadrian's accession four consulars had been executed on a charge of conspiracy. One of them was Avidius Nigrinus.[36]

Now another Nigrinus was dead, and Plutarch was starting to outlive the second generation of his friends.[37] Even his writings began to grow dated as the circumstances in which they had been written changed.[38] He continued to write, in particular adding to the *Parallel Lives*, but perhaps with less fluency and less enthusiasm.

Even now, however, he did not lay aside the public career which he had pursued since his youth. Political life was like an old, familiar friend,[39] and perhaps a consolation also. In Delphi he continued to wear the crown of priesthood and assumed the

---

[33] Cass. Dio, 68. 17. 2. Cf. P. Graindor, *Athènes de Tibère à Trajan* (1931), 25; F. A. Lepper, *Trajan's Parthian War* (1948), 6, 28–30.

[34] Nigrinus: *HA* Hadr. 7. 1, cf. Syme, *Tacitus* (1958), 245. Sosius: *HA* Hadr. 4. 2 (not very reliable: on the reading, Groag, *RE* 3 A [1927], 1187). Archon: *ILS* 308, cf. Syme, 513, n. 2.

[35] Viz. in the matter of the Epicurean succession, *ILS* 7784 = *IG* 2/3². 1099 = *Syll.*³ 834 = Smallwood, *Documents of Nerva, Trajan and Hadrian* no. 442.

[36] Cass. Dio, 69. 2. 5, *HA* Hadr. 7. 1–3. Cf. Syme, op. cit. 244.

[37] The two sons of Julius Secundus, the orator he had met under Vespasian (above, p. 22), were both dead by 106 (Pliny, *Epp.* 6. 6; C. P. Jones, *HSCP* 72 [1968], 279 ff.).

[38] *Luc.* 36. 5 implies a date before 114 (C. P. Jones, *JRS* 56 [1966], 69); *Ant.* 34. 9 (no triumph over the Parthians since Ventidius') seems clearly to antedate Trajan's posthumous triumph in 117 or 118, *HA* Hadr. 6. 3, cf. J.-C. Richard, *REL* 44 (1966), 351–62.

[39] ὥσπερ ἡλικιώτην καὶ συνήθη φίλον, an seni sit ger. resp. 783 C.

duty, probably not for the first time, of serving the Amphictyonic council as its executive officer, the epimelete. In that post he was the supervisor when the council voted to honour the new emperor with a statue.[40]

Whatever his actions elsewhere, in Greece Hadrian was anxious to continue and augment his predecessor's policies. Benefactions were showered on the shrine of Delphi: ever more new buildings went up under the eye of one of the emperor's ubiquitous agents.[41] The beneficiaries knew what was expected of them. They hailed the emperor as the salvation of the city and raised statues to him everywhere.[42]

Hadrian did not overlook the opportunity to honour the doyen of Greek literature. Not that he needed Plutarch to tell him which temples needed completion or which antiquities were particularly worthy of commemoration.[43] Trajan had already granted Plutarch the *ornamenta*; now Hadrian made him procurator of Greece. Normally the procurator supervised the imperial properties in the province as the emperor's private agent, but Plutarch probably held the position only in a nominal capacity.[44] Nor does he appear to have done so for long. Soon after the beginning of the reign, when he was approaching his eightieth year, he succumbed to a painful illness.[45] The citizens of Delphi and Chaeronea united to set up his monument in the meeting-place of the Amphictyons.[46]

Plutarch's career invites comparison with his Greek contemporaries. The most similar is the philosophic rhetor, Dio of Prusa.[47] Born about the same time as Plutarch into a leading family of Prusa, Dio likewise received an ample and expensive education. There followed a long period of indecision between

---

[40] Priesthood: *an seni sit ger. resp.* 792 F. Epimelete: *Syll.*³ 829 A.

[41] *Fouilles de Delphes* 3. 4. 98 = *Syll.*³ 830, cf. *HA* Hadr. 11. 4–6.

[42] *Syll.*³ 829 A–B, 835 A–B. Note also the famous statue of Antinous at Delphi, on which see now Ch. W. Clairmont, *Die Bildnisse des Antinous* (1966), *passim*.

[43] C. P. Jones, *JRS* 56 (1966), 65–6.

[44] Syncellus, p. 659 Dindorf = *Eusebius: Die Chronik des Hieronymus*, ed. R. Helm, *Die gr. Chr. Schriftsteller* 47 (1956), 415: Πλούταρχος Χαιρωνεὺς φιλόσοφος ἐπιτροπεύειν Ἑλλάδος ὑπὸ τοῦ αὐτοκράτορος κατεστάθη γηραιός. Cf. E. Groag, *Die römischen Reichsbeamten von Achaia bis auf Diokletian* (1939), 145–7, G. W. Bowersock, *Greek Sophists in the Roman Empire* (1969), 57, n. 6, 112.

[45] Illness and death: Artemidorus, 4. 72. Date: C. P. Jones, *JRS* 56 (1966), 66.

[46] *Syll.*³ 843.

[47] *PIR*² D 93. Cf. now Bowersock, op. cit. 110 ff.

sophistry and philosophy that ended with his becoming, in the judgement of the expert Philostratus, a philosopher who was reputed to be a sophist.[48] Plutarch was also converted from rhetoric to philosophy, and continued to use his training as a speaker even when he had turned entirely from the profession. Under the Flavians Dio made friends among Roman consulars; one of them was executed by Domitian, and Dio banished from Rome and his native province.[49] The reigns of Nerva, an old friend, and Trajan saw him recalled and restored to influence. Dio expressed his gratitude by preaching to cities of the Greek East on the need for internal concord; in the same period, Plutarch composed strikingly similar *Political Precepts* for the benefit of an aspiring politician of Sardis. Always quarrelsome, Dio now found his last years clouded by local feuds and petty litigation.[50]

Though the two do not mention one another in their extant works, there were certainly contacts between them. Plutarch's young friend Favorinus, who managed to associate with most of the prominent philosophers of the day, was a pupil of Dio.[51] At least two of Plutarch's works had Dio's name in their title, a Discussion and a Speech delivered at Olympia, both πρὸς Δίωνα: the phrase may mean simply that Dio was addressed or discussed, but it may also indicate that he was attacked.[52] The Olympian speech is unlikely to be connected with Dio's own extant speech delivered there after his return from exile. Plutarch's work may rather date from an earlier period, and have something to do with Dio's attacks on philosophers.[53]

There is also the Stoic Epictetus.[54] After a long stay in Rome as a slave and a freedman, Epictetus was banished under Domitian's edict against philosophers.[55] He retired to Nicopolis in southern Epirus, and received visitors as eminent as the friends of Plutarch or Dio: a knight soon to be *praefectus annonae*

[48] Philostr. *VS* 492. Cf. A. D. Momigliano, *JRS* 41 (1951), 149–53.
[49] Dio Prus. *Or.* 13. 1. Perhaps T. Flavius Sabinus, *PIR*[2] F 355.
[50] Pliny, *Epp.* 10. 81–2.
[51] Philostr. *VS* 492. On Favorinus see also below, p. 61.
[52] Lamprias Catalogue nos. 204, 227: cf. Ziegler, *RE* 21 (1951), 706.
[53] Olympian Oration: *Or.* 11 v. Arnim. Attacks on philosophers: Synesius, *Dio* 37 A–B, Momigliano, art. cit. 152–3.
[54] *PIR*[2] E 74, F. Millar, *JRS* 55 (1965), 141 ff.
[55] A. Gellius, 15. 11. 5.

4

at Rome, a *corrector* of free cities, and a young man later to be
consul and to commit his teacher's discourses to writing, Flavius
Arrianus.[56] Like his two coevals, Epictetus could count emperors
among his friends, since he is said to have been on intimate terms
with Hadrian.[57]

In Plutarch's extant works there is no more mention of
Epictetus than of Dio, nor do the discourses recorded by Arrian
mention Plutarch. But the two philosophers cannot have been
unaware of one another. Nicopolis was one of the many cities in
which Plutarch had friends, and he sat with its delegates on the
Amphictyonic council.[58] Persons he knew in Achaea may have
visited Epirus and had interviews, not necessarily congenial,
with the resident philosopher.[59] The ubiquitous Favorinus at
some time studied with Epictetus and wrote an attack on him,
a dialogue in which a slave of Plutarch conversed with the low-
born philosopher.[60]

Another phenomenon of the age can hardly be left out of
account among the contemporaries of Plutarch, Apollonius of
Tyana.[61] For evidence there is the ample biography by Philostratus of Lemnos, though the abundance of material may be
largely due to the author's invention. The Apollonius depicted
by Philostratus has his own Roman followers, from highly
placed knights to emperors: he too is involved with the opposition to Domitian, and in fact is brought to trial before the
emperor in the very year of the expulsion of philosophers from
Rome. He in his turn departs for Greece and the East, only to be
restored to honour when his old friend Nerva succeeds Domitian.
Apollonius' relations with cities of the Greek world also recall
Plutarch, and even more the great sophists of the age: he urges

---

[56] Knights: Arr. *Diss. Epict.* 1. 10. 2–6. *Corrector: Diss. Epict.* 3. 7. Arrian:
*PIR*² F 219. On Arrian's manipulation of his material, there is now the valuable
study of Th. Wirth, *Museum Helveticum* 24 (1967), 149–89, 197–216.

[57] *HA* Hadr. 16. 10.

[58] Friends: *quaest. conviv.* 667 E ff., 698 A. Nicopolis on Amphictyonic council:
Paus. 10. 8. 4.

[59] Stein conjectured that the procurator of Epirus rebuked by Epictetus, Arr.
Diss. Epict. 3. 4, was Plutarch's friend Cornelius Pulcher, *PIR*² C 1424: cf. Millar,
art. cit. 147.

[60] A. Gellius, 17. 19. 1, Galen, *de opt. doct.* 1 = *Scripta minora* 1. 82 = fr. 30
Barigazzi.

[61] *PIR*² A 927. On the historical worth of Philostratus' *Vita Apollonii*, see now G. W.
Bowersock, introduction to the Penguin translation (1971), 14–17.

unity and concord among them, and represents their interests before emperors.[62]

There is a suspicious similarity, however, between Philostratus' picture of Apollonius and the showmen whom he describes in his later *Lives of the Sophists*. The features which Apollonius has in common with Plutarch are largely those that Plutarch shares with the Second Sophistic. That does not mean that the views and the activities of Philostratus' hero cannot usefully be compared with those of Plutarch. Philostratus was himself familiar with the emperors and with life in the Greek East; even if his picture of Apollonius is generously supplemented by his imagination, it shows the way in which a knowledgeable Greek of the third century envisaged the condition of a philosopher in the first.[63]

Plutarch and his three contemporaries are different in many ways: in their places of origin, their class, their persuasions. Even so they possess notable similarities. All have friends and followers among the Roman aristocracy, all to a greater or lesser degree incur Domitian's displeasure, all end their lives honoured by his successors. In short, the similarities between them are linked to their relations with Rome.

That is not coincidence. These four stood on the threshold of a major historical movement, the Second Sophistic.[64] To a degree not known before, the security and affluence of the Roman empire permitted a great revival in Greek culture, above all in rhetoric but also in philosophy. The course of this movement as it is chronicled by Philostratus presents many parallels to the career of Plutarch. Philostratus' subjects also go on embassies to Rome, enter the Roman administration, and attract powerful visitors and generous benefactors to the cities in which they live.[65]

[62] Knights: *VA* 5. 10 (a procurator of Baetica), 7. 16 ff. (a *praefectus praetorio*). Emperors: 5. 27 ff. (Vespasian), 6. 29 ff. (Titus), 7. 8 ff. (Nerva). Enemies of Domitian: 7. 8 ff. Trial: 8. 1 ff. Date: 8. 7, section 11. In Greece: 8. 15 ff. Nerva's accession: 8. 27. Concord: 1. 15 (Aspendus), 4. 8–9 (Smyrna), 6. 38 (Syrian Antioch). Interests: 6. 34 (Tarsus).

[63] On Philostratus, see *PIR²* F 332, Bowersock, *Greek Sophists in the Roman Empire* (1969), 1 ff.

[64] Bowersock, op. cit. *passim*.

[65] Embassies: e.g. *VS* 520 f. (Scopelian), 531 (Polemo). Administration: e.g. *VS* 524 (a procurator). Visitors and benefactors: e.g. *VS* 531 (Polemo), 582 (Aristides).

There are also obvious differences. Most of Philostratus' sophists do not have the close attachment to one shrine or deity that Plutarch does. Their flamboyant calling did not easily allow them to spend time in a place that was not a centre of rhetoric; and Delphi was not, even though a statue or some other honour there still brought prestige to a sophist or a philosopher.[66] The notable exception is Aelius Aristides, who devoted much of his life to the Asclepieum in Pergamum: but Pergamum was in any case a sophistic centre of considerable importance, and the devotees in the sanctuary gave Aristides ample encouragement to display his art.[67]

Other differences between Plutarch and the great sophists can be ascribed to the nature of his calling. Plutarch did not have the armies of young disciples that were expected of a great sophist: while his circle of acquaintances was very wide, his only known successors, with the exception of Favorinus, are members of his own family.[68] A sophist needed disciples to defend him against his rivals, and his reputation depended largely on his performances and his imitators: a philosopher owed his distinction as much to his influence with laymen as to the training of new professionals.

In many respects the career of Plutarch is a reflection of a larger historical fact, the absorption of Greek men of culture into the social and administrative conditions of the empire. But among the sophists and philosophers of the age, he has a unique place precisely because of his surviving works. They preserve as do the writings of none of his contemporaries the picture of an eminent Greek's society and his view of the world in which he lived.

[66] Note, e.g. the sophist Soterus honoured at Delphi by Ephesus, *Fouilles de Delphes* 3. 4. 265 = *SEG* 13. 362.

[67] On Aristides and Pergamum see now C. A. Behr, *Aelius Aristides and the Sacred Tales* (1968), 41 ff. Bowersock, op. cit. 70–2.

[68] Viz. his son Autobulus; *Syll.*³ 844 A, and his nephew, the celebrated Sextus, *PIR*¹ S 488.

V

PLUTARCH'S SOCIETY: *DOMI NOBILES*

WHEN Plutarch advised a politician of an eastern city always to have a friend among the most powerful men in Rome,[1] he drew a distinction of great importance for an understanding of his society. The class of which he was a member by birth was a provincial aristocracy accustomed to influence in its own territory. It was only in his adult life that he came into contact with the senators and proconsuls to whom he dedicates his works. That is why such men, when introduced as characters into Plutarch's dialogues, do not appear in those which draw on memories of his youth, for example the dialogue on love. At that time, eminent Romans were still strangers.

It is usual to divide Plutarch's friends into Greeks and Romans. For several reasons that will not do. There is only a language in common between an itinerant Cynic and a descendant of the royal house of Commagene, between a Pythagorean from Etruria and a commander of Caesar's armies. The separation of Greeks and Romans is made additionally hazardous by social circumstances that did not prevail in earlier times. Plutarch and many of his Greek friends were themselves Romans before the law, and some of his friends who held office at Rome came from Greek-speaking regions. Further, the criterion of nomenclature is no longer reliable: even when a man's names are authentically Roman, he may in fact be as Greek as Plutarch. Only epigraphical evidence, for example, shows that the Cornelius Pulcher to whom the treatise on making good use of enemies is dedicated belongs to an old house of Epidaurus.[2]

It will be better, therefore, to consider Plutarch's society in another way, and take first those of his friends that belong to his own social kind. These men, who share a high level of wealth and local influence, are the core of Plutarch's acquaintance, and

---

[1] *Praec. ger. reip.* 814 C. [2] *PIR²* C 1424.

their discourses provide the material out of which he constructed most of his dialogues. All are Greeks by birth, and most are from old Greece, but there is also a large admixture of visitors and correspondents from cities of the East.

One of the marks of this society was the ability to claim descent from figures of myth or ancient history. Plutarch's family, or one with which it was closely connected, numbered among its ancestors Opheltas, a prehistoric king of Boeotia, and Daiphantus, a hero of the Phocians in their ancient wars with Thessaly.[3] Similarly his friend Themistocles the Stoic was descended from the Athenian general and still enjoyed the honours granted to his ancestor at Magnesia on the Maeander.[4] Polycrates of Sicyon, another friend of Plutarch, was of the family of Aratus and no inferior to him in reputation or influence, so the philosopher said when dedicating to him the *Life of Aratus*.[5]

Others in Plutarch's circle came from families that had gained their distinction, or added to it, in the troubled conditions of the late republic. The well-travelled Chaeremonianus of Tralles may descend from the Chaeremon of Nysa who supported the Roman cause in the first Mithridatic war. Chaeremon's son Pythodorus moved to Tralles and there guided the family's fortunes through the vicissitudes of the civil wars: his descendants included a great sophist of the generation after Plutarch's, as well as several consuls.[6] One of Plutarch's closest friends, the Petraeus who collaborated with him and Polycrates to further the prosperity of Delphi, is also from a family that had surmounted reverses in the late republic. It was already prominent in Thessalian Hypata when one of its members, also a Petraeus, sided with Julius Caesar's legate in Achaea, L. Cassius Longinus, and through him received the Roman citizenship; subsequently Petraeus was beheaded on the orders of Brutus. Plutarch records that a Petraeus of Thessaly was burned alive in riots

[3] p. 8 above. On Opheltas, cf. *Cimon* 1. 1; on Daiphantus, *mul. virt.* 244 B, *non posse suav. vivi* 1099 E, P. A. Stadter, *Plutarch's Historical Methods* (1965), 34–41.

[4] *Themist.* 32. 6, *quaest. conviv.* 626 E. For another possible descendant of Themistocles in imperial Athens, see *IG* 2/3². 3610; otherwise restored by E. Kapetanopoulos, *BCH* 92 (1968), 494, n. 1.

[5] *Arat.* 1. 5. Evidently therefore identical with the Helladarch Ti. Claudius Polycrates, *Syll.*³ 846, cf. *PIR*² C 969.

[6] Chaeremonianus: *quaest. conviv.* 641 B. Chaeremon: *Syll.*³ 741. Pythodorus: Strabo, 555–6, 649. Polemo the sophist: Philostr. *VS* 530 ff. (*PIR*² A 862, cf. 883). On this family, G. W. Bowersock, *Augustus and the Greek World* (1965), 8, 143–4.

under Augustus. He is probably the other man's son, and owes his commemoration to Plutarch's interest in the history of his friends' ancestors.[7]

The most notable example of a house raised to power in the late republic, and observed in its vicissitudes by Plutarch, may be that of the Herculanus to whom he addresses his treatise on self-praise.[8] The man is evidently active in politics, and ought to be identical with a younger contemporary of Plutarch, C. Julius Eurycles Herculanus of Sparta.[9] He too was prominent in public affairs, both in his native city and as a Roman senator; moreover, he had some tie of propinquity with Plutarch's friend Sosius Senecio. The fortunes of the house had been founded under Augustus by the adventurer Eurycles, who obtained the citizenship and maintained his supremacy in Sparta until his downfall in the middle of the reign. Plutarch preserves a detailed account of Eurycles' part at Actium, and his lost *Life of Augustus* recorded the dynast's trial before the emperor.[10] It is also likely that a passage in the treatise on brotherly love alludes to further tribulations in the family under Nero.[11] Even though the Euryclids were one of the great dynasties of imperial Achaea, Plutarch's interest in them again reflects his own time. As he studied the past, his attention was caught by the forebears of those he knew, and his friends themselves may have supplied him with details not recorded in his sources.[12]

Plutarch's interest in the ancestors of his friends may explain his precise knowledge about Caphis of Tithora who performed services for Sulla in the first Mithridatic war. One of the author's

---

[7] Petraeus: see especially *de Pyth. orac.* 409 B, *Syll.*³ 825 A–C. Ancestors: Caes. *bell. civ.* 3. 35. 2, *praec. ger. reip.* 815 D. Bowersock, op. cit. 161, *Rheinisches Museum* 108 (1965), 279–82. Chr. Habicht, *Ancient Macedonia* (1970), 278, n. 17 (on p. 279), considers the Petraeus who supported Caesar "gewiss Larisäer", like his rival Hegesaretus: but Caesar clearly implies that they were from different cities, *varia voluntate civitatium*, ibid.

[8] *De laude ips.* 539 A. The treatise on philosophers and men in power may be addressed to the same man: *maxime cum princ. phil. diss.* 776 A, with the conjecture of Pohlenz, *Plutarchus: Moralia* 5. 1 (Teubner, 1957), 1, n.

[9] *PIR*² I/J 302. So Stein, *RE* 8 (1912), 549, no. 1 ('vielleicht'): against, E. Groag, *RE* 10 (1917), 585, no. 221, *PIR*² H 93. The question is not mentioned in *PIR*² I/J 302.

[10] *Ant.* 67. 2–4, *reg. et imp. apophth.* 207 F (from the lost *Life of Augustus*). Bowersock, *JRS* 51 (1961), 112–18; *PIR*² I/J 301.

[11] *De frat. am.* 487 F–488 A. So Groag, *Die römischen Reichsbeamten von Achaia bis auf Diokletian* (1939), 37–8; against, *PIR*² I/J 587.   [12] Cf. *Nic.* 1. 5.

closest friends, Soclarus, was from the same little Phocian city, and there is a chance that he was descended from Sulla's agent.[13]

Descent was a mark of aristocracy, but not a prerequisite: it was too easily manufactured.[14] Wealth was more important, and indeed is the one feature common to all members of Plutarch's society.

Like Plutarch, his friends had the means to travel extensively. As he had visited Egypt, so had at least two of his fellow Boeotians, and the wealthy Spartan Cleombrotus had travelled not only in Egypt and Cyrene but far down the Red Sea also, using his ample means to conduct private research.[15] Nor were Plutarch's visits to the West exceptional. Several of his friends appear with him in Rome, and one of his townsmen died during a rhetorical competition in Gaul.[16] Such visits were facilitated by an elaborate web of friendships, which guaranteed a wealthy man hospitality in cities other than his own. In return, Plutarch entertained visitors from all over Greece and Asia Minor.[17]

When they were not travelling to other lands, Plutarch and his friends had abundant leisure to spend nearer home. They could visit one another's cities at times of festival, to celebrate a friend's presidency at the local games or his success as a competitor.[18] Or they might congregate at a fashionable resort where the wealthiest competed in the appointments of their houses and the elegance of their dinner-parties.[19] These were the occasions that Plutarch used to give verisimilitude to the nine books of his *Table Talk*.

While Plutarch's dialogues mainly show his society at times of relaxation, they do not obscure its concern with public

---

[13] Caphis: *Sulla* 12. 6–8, 15. 5; for the reading Τιθορεὺς ὤν in 15. 5, L. Robert, *Hellenica* 11–12 (1960), 82–4. Note the Caphis son of Aristio from Tithora, *IG* 9. 1. 192, line 1, contemporary with Plutarch's friend, also son of an Aristio, *amat.* 749 B, *PIR*² F 369, G. W. Bowersock, *CQ* 15 (1965), 267–8. On Tithora, see Robert, *Hellenica* 2 (1946), 105–6.

[14] Cf. Suet. *Vesp.* 12, Tac. *Ann.* 12. 53. 2.

[15] Egypt: Pemptides of Thebes (*amat.* 755 E), Philinus of Thespiae (*de soll. anim.* 976 B). Cleombrotus: *de def. orac.* 410 A–B.

[16] e.g. *quaest. conviv.* 727 B–730 F. Nigros in Gaul: *de tuenda san.* 131 A, cf. *quaest. conviv.* 692 B. On rhetoric in the Gauls, cf. Syme, *Tacitus* (1958), 459, 799–800.

[17] Greece: e.g. *quaest. conviv.* 639 B (Thessaly), 698 A (Nicopolis). Asia Minor: 641 A (Tralles), 656 A (Nicaea), 698 D (Tarsus, cf. *amat.* 749 B), 710 B (Pergamum, Prusias).

[18] *Quaest. conviv.* 628 A (Athens), 638 B, 674 F (Delphi), 723 A (Corinth).

[19] *Quaest. conviv.* 667 C–D, cf. *de frat. am.* 487 F.

office. Traditionally and necessarily, such office was the province of the upper classes, and politicians who were not rich could easily go bankrupt.[20] A wide variety of duties offered. They might involve only a man's home town, or a larger unit such as the local or provincial league; they might be merely institutionalized displays of munificence, like the presidency of a festival, or such positions of importance as an embassy to a proconsul or emperor. The more generous the politician, the larger the number of offices he held. Plutarch's career included the archonship of Chaeronea, with its routine of sacrifices and dinners at which he was the host, and also his priesthood and other duties at Delphi; in addition, he went on embassies to the proconsul and to Italy, and like many ambassadors may have paid his own expenses. Again his friends' careers closely resemble his. They hold office at home and in other cities;[21] they finance the great festivals of Greece;[22] and they represent the province as its high priests and chief officials.[23] Plutarch's friends in Asia Minor are of the same kind, for example Menemachus of Sardis for whom he wrote the *Political Precepts*. Menemachus' high birth naturally made him aspire to influence in his native city.[24]

Ever since their first intervention in Greek affairs, the Romans had sided with this wealthy class, in which they found Greeks most like themselves.[25] While retaining governmental power for herself, Rome supported the rich in the control of the places they knew best, their own cities. It was an arrangement designed to benefit both parties. The local aristocracies were allowed to thrive, so long as they did not exploit their privilege to an extent

[20] *Praec. ger. reip.* 822 C-823 A, *de vit. aere al.* 830 E. Cf. Pliny, *Epp.* 10. 110, A. N. Sherwin-White, *The Letters of Pliny* (1966), 720.

[21] Thus L. Cassius Petraeus in Hypata and Delphi, *Syll.*³ 825 A–C, and note the several cities endowed by C. Julius Eurycles Herculanus, *PIR*² I/J 302.

[22] *Quaest. conviv.* 674 F (Petraeus and Pythia, cf. *Syll.*³ 825 C), 723 A (Sospis and Isthmia, cf. *Corinth: Results of Excavations conducted by the American School of Classical Studies at Athens* 8. 3, no. 226).

[23] Thus Cn. Cornelius Pulcher (*de cap. ex inim. util.* 86 B, cf. *PIR*² C 1424), Lucanius (*quaest. conviv.* 675 D), Tib. Claudius Polycrates (*Arat.* 1. 5, *de Pyth. orac.* 409 B, *quaest. conviv.* 667 E ff.; cf. *PIR*² C 969).

[24] *Praec. ger. reip.* 798 B, ἀξίως τῆς εὐγενείας ἐν τῇ πατρίδι 'μύθων τε ῥητῆρ' ἔμεναι πρηκτῆρά τε ἔργων'.

[25] On this well-known tendency, A. H. M. Jones, *The Greek City* (1940), 170–1, *Dumbarton Oaks Papers* 17 (1963), 6–7; G. W. Bowersock, *Augustus and the Greek World* (1965), 7, 100 ff.; J. Briscoe, *Past and Present* 36 (1967), 3–20.

that provoked jealousy and caused faction, while Rome retained ultimate control.[26]

It is no surprise, therefore, to find close ties between Plutarch's Greek friends and Rome. Some of them came from families that had been on friendly terms with Rome since the late republic.[27] Others had adapted quickly to the establishment of monarchy at Rome and the permanence of Roman power in Greece. Such were the forebears of Plutarch's close friend Philinus of Thespiae, who cultivated the Romans resident in their city and made dedications to the imperial house.[28] Others in Plutarch's circle were priests of the Caesars in their cities,[29] or presided over the provincial cult of Rome as Helladarchs.[30]

The ties between Plutarch's class and Rome are shown not only by his friends but also, since the audience for whom he writes naturally resembles those he knew, by the presumptions he makes about his readers. Thus his precepts on health are addressed to people who could expect to be invited to dinner by great men; his treatise on self-praise cautions against boasting about interviews with the emperor.[31] Similarly the political treatises are written for politicians familiar with the routine of entertaining the proconsul or going on embassies to Rome.[32] In the society mirrored by the *Table Talk*, a man might preen himself on the last conversation he had had with the emperor or on the salaried post that had recently been conferred on him; entertaining the proconsul and receiving his invitations were matters of course.[33] Among such people Roman consulars like Mestrius Florus could feel at ease.

By befriending eminent Greeks, Romans indulged their

[26] Eurycles of Sparta is an excellent case of a man supported by Rome until he abused his position too far: Bowersock, *JRS* 51 (1961), 112 ff. For *quies* and local responsibility for it, cf. Livy, 34. 51. 6; Acts 16: 19–20; Jos. *Ant. Iud.* 19. 311; Pliny, *Epp.* 10. 117; Apul. *Met.* 10. 6. 4; Philostr. *Vita Apoll.* 1. 15.

[27] Above, pp. 40 ff.

[28] C. P. Jones, *HSCP* 74 (1970), 223 ff.

[29] (T. Flavius) Pemptides, *amat.* 761 B, clearly identical with the ἀρχιερεύς under Galba, B. V. Head, *Numismatic Chronicle*, 3rd ser. 1 (1881), 271–2; see now S. N. Koumanoudes, Χαριστήριον εἰς ᾽Αναστάσιον Κ. ᾽Ορλάνδον 2 (1966), 1–11. Also C. Julius Eurycles Herculanus, *PIR*² I/J 302.

[30] Helladarchs: above, pp. 26, 43, n. 23.

[31] *De tuenda san.* 124 A–C, *de laude ips.* 547 D–F.

[32] *De exil.* 602 C, cf. 604 B. *Praec. ger. reip.* 805 A.

[33] *Quaest. conviv.* 630 F (conversation), 632 F (salaried post, cf. *praec. ger. reip.* 814 D), 679 C (entertaining the proconsul), 710 A (his invitations).

cultural interests and procured useful agents and advisers. The relationship could not work only for the advantage of one party. In return for their special expertise, Greeks had long since begun to expect what only Rome could give them, a share in power. In the late republic, favoured Greeks received the citizenship and Roman support in their cities of origin. Under the first Caesars, they climbed ever higher, to honourable status as knights and up the grades of the senatorial *cursus*. Plutarch's era witnessed a new stage in the process, men from the Greek East holding consulates and commanding armies.[34]

The social effects of these changes, many of which had taken place in Plutarch's lifetime, can be seen in his circle. The possession of Roman citizenship was now no longer a distinguishing mark. It can be assumed that like Plutarch almost all of his friends were citizens: among the two dozen or so known from documentary evidence, there is one doubtful exception.[35] Several of them had received the citizenship under the Flavians, whose generosity with it is well known.[36] Plutarch's failure to mention his citizenship is no attempt to maintain the appearance of a Hellene.[37] In his circle, the citizenship was like affluence, too familiar to deserve comment.

Now that the citizenship was commonplace in a society like Plutarch's, a truer mark of distinction was provided by equestrian status. Plutarch himself was a knight, and owed to his own eminence other honours usually reserved for equestrians, the consular *ornamenta* and a procuratorship. At least one of his friends had a comparable career, the Cornelius Pulcher whom he advised how to make good use of his enemies. Descended from an old family of Epidaurus which had received the citizenship under Augustus, Pulcher served as Trajan's procurator in Epirus and *iuridicus* of Hadrian in Egypt. Like his friend from Chaeronea,

---

[34] See now especially Chr. Habicht, *Istanbuler Mitteilungen* 9–10 (1959/60), 120–5; Syme, *Proceedings of the Massachusetts Historical Society* 72 (1963), 12–19; Bowersock, *Augustus and the Greek World* (1965), 140 ff. Note Plutarch's comment on the senatorial ambitions of men from Chios, Galatia, and Bithynia, *de tranqu. animi* 470 C.

[35] Viz. the poet Serapion, but the interpretation of the relevant text is not clear: cf. J. H. Oliver, *Hesperia*, Suppl. 8 (1949), 244.

[36] A. N. Sherwin-White, *The Roman Citizenship* (1939), 194 ff. Rostovtzeff, *SEHRE*² 111–12.

[37] Wilamowitz, *Reden und Vorträge* 2⁴ (1926), 251: 'er blieb Hellene, und hielt darauf, es auch zu scheinen.'

he also served his native province, and among other offices became high priest of the Achaean council.[38] It is likely that other friends of Plutarch who are not so well attested as Pulcher were also of equestrian rank, for example those that also became Helladarchs.[39] Some of them may have held office as provincial procurators.[40] There is no sign, however, that any of Plutarch's friends resembled him in receiving senatorial *ornamenta*. Nor can any of them be found in the higher grades of the equestrian career, the great secretariats and prefectures. The Greeks that had attained these positions by Plutarch's time were from wealthier regions than Greece: Egypt and the Orient.[41]

As old Greece lagged behind the Orient in the number and eminence of its equestrians, so also it was comparatively slow to produce senators. Appropriately, however, one of the first Achaean senators can also be identified as a friend of Plutarch, the Euryclid Herculanus.[42] The wealth of the Euryclids had given them a start over most families of Greece, and they had already produced eminent knights under Claudius and Nero.[43] In the later second century, when Achaean senators become more numerous, it is no surprise that they include descendants of Plutarch's friends.[44]

Herculanus is a token of things that were still to come in old Greece. Asia Minor, by contrast, had already advanced in the course of Plutarch's life to produce its first consuls and commanders of Roman armies.[45] It is doubtful whether such men

[38] *PIR*[2] C 1424; add now *SEG* 22. 289.

[39] For these cf. pp. 26, 43, n. 23 above. There is no mention of equestrian office, however, in the inscription of Polycrates, *Syll.*[3] 846.

[40] Note Plutarch's comments on salaries from the emperor, *quaest. conviv.* 632 F, and 'procuratorships worth many talents', *praec. ger. reip.* 814 D.

[41] Cf. H.-G. Pflaum, *Les Carrières procuratoriennes équestres* 1 (1960), nos. B (2), 13 *bis*, 15–17, 46, 106.

[42] Cf. p. 41, n. 9 above.

[43] *PIR*[2] I/J 302, cf. 372, 587. The senatorial career constructed for Plutarch's friend Sospis in *Corinth* 8. 3. 170 is variously implausible.

[44] Thus T. Flavius Philinus of Thespiae, *cos. suff.* in the third century and descended from Plutarch's friend of the same name, *PIR*[2] F 331, *SEG* 12. 265, C. P. Jones, *HSCP* 74 (1970), 240. Note also the consular relatives of Q. Statius Themistocles, the descendant of Plutarch's Athenian friend Serapion, *IG* 2/3[2]. 3704; cf. J. H. Oliver, *Hesperia*, Suppl. 8 (1949), stemma facing p. 248.

[45] Thus C. Antius A. Julius Quadratus from Pergamum, *cos. suff.* 94, *cos. II ord.* 105, legate of Syria *c.* 101–4 (*PIR*[2] I/J 507), C. Julius Quadratus Bassus from Pergamum, *cos. suff.* 105, *comes* of Trajan in the second Dacian war, legate of Syria during the Parthian war (*PIR*[2] I/J 508). On Sosius Senecio, see below, pp. 54 ff.

considered themselves Greeks rather than Romans, or vice versa. More probably they did not think of the appellation 'Roman' as complementary to 'Greek' but rather as something that transcended local origin. The Roman citizenship, and even more ascent into the Roman hierarchy, were now open to the aspirations of those who were qualified by wealth and culture.[46] Greeks were only the heirs to that same extension of Rome's privileges that had long ago spread over Italy and then the provinces of the West.

It was to be expected that some of these oriental senators would come into contact with Plutarch. His society was one that philhellene Italians enjoyed: still more the eastern dynasts that pursued their ancestral culture in the intervals of holding office at Rome. But such men are best not considered among Plutarch's Greek friends, but among their counterparts at Rome.

[46] The standard formulation is Aristides, *Or.* 26. 59 K. τὸ μὲν χαριέστερόν τε καὶ γενναιότερον καὶ δυνατώτερον πανταχοῦ πολιτικὸν ἢ καὶ ὁμόφυλον πᾶν ἀπεδείξατε, τὸ δὲ λοιπὸν ὑπήκοόν τε καὶ ἀρχόμενον.

VI

PLUTARCH'S SOCIETY:
ROME AND THE WEST

IN the study of a group so multifarious as the circle of Plutarch, it is impossible to operate with rigid distinctions. Its nucleus is formed by the local aristocracy to which he belonged by birth, and its diversions, its dinners, tours, and festivals, are the background for his dialogues. But more important for the historian are the friends that appear only exceptionally in his dialogues. These are the knights and senators whom he alludes to in passing as his friends, or to whom he dedicates his works.

Just as the provincial aristocrats of Plutarch's acquaintance correspond approximately to what are sometimes called his Greek friends, so these less frequently seen persons correspond to his Roman friends. They are Romans in the sense that they hold, or may be supposed to have held, positions in the imperial administration. But not all will be natives of Italy, or even have Latin as their first tongue: none can be shown to have his *patria* nearer Rome than the cities of northern Italy.

Within this diverse company, the most important group is that of Plutarch's consular friends. The first in seniority if not in influence is L. Mestrius Florus.[1] No ancestors are recorded, and little is known of his career; like other senators known to Plutarch, he may derive from northern Italy.[2] Somewhat older than his Greek friend, he will have begun his public career under Nero, and may be the Florus who preferred to appear on the stage rather than risk the emperor's displeasure.[3] Political flexibility is also indicated by his later career. Mestrius next

---

[1] *PIR*[1] M 380.

[2] Syme, *Tacitus* (1958), 596, n. 2. Note especially Plutarch's tour with Mestrius in the region of the Po (above, p. 22). The name of his son-in-law, Caesernius (*PIR*[2] C 178), is frequent in Aquileia: cf. A. Calderini, *Aquileia romana* (1930), 472–3, *PIR*[2] C 182.

[3] Arr. *Diss. Epict.* 1. 2. 12–18, cf. F. Millar, *JRS* 55 (1965), 141.

appears as one of the senators on Otho's side at Bedriacum: he had been present under duress, so he later told Plutarch.[4] He was not the only friend of the author to be with the Othonian forces in 69, and he may be presumed to have furnished some of the details in the *Lives of Galba and Otho*: before the work was written, he took Plutarch on a tour of the battlefield of Bedriacum.[5] His subsequent career was evidently successful. Vespasian, who found his pedantry amusing, gave him the suffect consulate: like all of Plutarch's consular friends, Mestrius was a *novus homo*.[6] After the lapse of about fifteen years, he attained one of the twin pinnacles of a civilian career, the proconsulate of Asia.[7]

The meagreness of the public record is amply supplied by Plutarch's portrait in the *Table Talk*. The author shows Mestrius enjoying a sprightly old age in Greece; he debates philosophical niceties, celebrates the birthdays of Socrates and Plato, and exhibits the same antiquarian tastes that had amused Vespasian long ago.[8] He is a notable example of the philhellenism which in an earlier day made Roman senators resort to cities like Naples and Tarentum.[9]

Mestrius is often called Plutarch's patron. It is true that he obtained the Roman citizenship for his friend, and his travels with Plutarch recall the republican senators who liked to journey in the company of learned Greeks, whether poets, philosophers, or historians.[10] But by Plutarch's time the relations between Greeks and Romans had undergone many changes. Though Plutarch was indebted to Mestrius for the citizenship, nothing indicates that he was closer to him than to others of his Roman friends. It is noticeable that none of the extant works is dedicated to him. Rather than being the client of one Roman, Plutarch was the friend and counsellor of many.

---

[4] *Otho* 14. 2.

[5] Ibid. See below, pp. 75, 78.

[6] Consulate: see next n. Vespasian: Suet. *Vesp.* 22.

[7] *Syll.*³ 820; *Forsch. in Ephesos* 2. 166, no. 48; *AE* 1966. 426. The usual date of 82/3 may be too early: perhaps 89/90, with the consulate *c.* 75.

[8] Age: note especially the presence of Favorinus, *quaest. conviv.* 734 D, cf. C. P. Jones, *JRS* 56 (1966), 73. In Greece: *quaest. conviv.* 626 E ff., 680 C ff., 698 E ff. Socrates and Plato: 717 D ff. Antiquarianism: 702 D.

[9] Cf. 684 F, 719 A. Naples, etc.: G. W. Bowersock, *Augustus and the Greek World* (1965), 80–4; J. H. D'Arms, *Romans on the Bay of Naples* (1970).

[10] Citizenship and travels: above, pp. 21 ff.

A second friend of Plutarch in the generation of Mestrius Florus is more elusive, though of much greater significance in the literary history of the period. Julius Secundus is only mentioned by Plutarch once, as an orator from whom he had heard about Otho's behaviour before the fatal battle of Bedriacum. Secundus should have known: he had been in charge of Otho's correspondence.[11] There is no indication that the friendship between him and Plutarch was close, and large conclusions cannot safely be drawn from it. But its implications cannot be neglected.

Born about 35, and so roughly contemporary with Mestrius, Secundus appears to be of Gallic origin; his *patria* may be Burdigala, the chief city of Aquitania. He emerges into history in 69 as Otho's secretary. If he was not already a senator then, he seems to have become one later, perhaps adlected by Vespasian and Titus in their censorship. In Vespasian's reign he became one of the chief speakers of the Roman forum, and was still comparatively young when he died, perhaps in the reign of Titus.[12]

Plutarch's acquaintance with Secundus adds another participant in the events of 69 to the number of his friends, and so has consequences for his account of that year in the *Lives of Galba and Otho*. No less important is Secundus' relation to figures of contemporary Latin literature: M. Aper, forthright and resplendent as an orator, Vipstanus Messalla, also an orator, and half-brother of the dreaded Regulus, the tragedian Curiatius Maternus, the poet Saleius Bassus, and above all Quintilian.[13] Though Secundus died young, his memory was kept alive by a new generation. Tacitus, who had been his disciple in early youth, commemorated him in the *Dialogus* and, it can be argued, helped his son Naso when the time came for the youth to aspire to senatorial honours.[14] Another of Naso's sponsors

---

[11] *Otho* 9. 3. Syme, *Tacitus* (1958), 799–800; *PIR*² I/J 559.

[12] Birthdate and origin: C. P. Jones, *HSCP* 72 (1968), 282–5. In 69: *Otho* 9. 3. Senate: Pliny, *Epp.* 6. 6. 4. As a speaker: Tac. *Dial.* 2. 1. Death: Quint. 10. 1. 120, cf. Jones, art. cit. 282–3.

[13] Aper: Tac. *Dial.* 2. 1, cf. *PIR*² A 910 and now Syme, *JRS* 58 (1968), 139–40. Messalla: Tac. *Dial.* 14. 1, cf. *PIR*¹ V 468. Curiatius: Tac. *Dial.* 14. 1, cf. *PIR*² C 1604, Syme, *Tacitus* (1958), 798–9. Saleius: Tac. *Dial.* 5. 2, cf. *PIR*¹ S 50. Quintilian: *Inst. Orat.* 10. 3. 12.

[14] Tacitus: *Dial.* 2. 1. Naso: Pliny, *Epp.* 6. 9, cf. C. P. Jones, *HSCP* 72 (1968), 283.

also claimed to have been an admirer of his father, the younger Pliny.[15]

A second group of Plutarch's friends reaches prominence under Domitian. One of these is Arulenus Rusticus, who attended the philosopher's lectures in Rome. Rusticus is also from northern Italy, more precisely from the Transpadane zone.[16] He first appears in history as a tribune in 66, eager to interpose his veto on behalf of Thrasea Paetus. Praetor in 69, he was wounded as an ambassador of Vitellius and the senate to the Flavian armies near Rome. Under the Flavians Rusticus cultivated the memory of Thrasea and the friendship of the close-knit group of senators that saw themselves as his successors. Perhaps as a gesture of reconciliation to these, Domitian admitted Rusticus to the consulate in the last months of 92, and it may have been in this period that he attended Plutarch's lecture. Another year, and he had been executed for treason.[17]

There is no sign that Plutarch knew Rusticus well, unless by chance the Timon whose wife the senator was once concerned to protect was the philosopher's brother.[18] Rusticus' effect on him will rather have been that of an example: a man who put philosophy above a communication from Caesar, and the memory of a philosophic Roman above his personal safety.

Two of Plutarch's friends also active under Domitian and well disposed to the successors of Thrasea Paetus may be considered together. These are the Avidii brothers, Nigrinus and Quietus. Both together are the recipients of the treatise on brotherly love, and Quietus alone receives the dialogue on divine vengeance.[19]

The Avidii are again from northern Italy, Faventia in the Ager Gallicus, and apparently coeval with Plutarch. Nigrinus is a shadowy figure, his only attested post being a praetorian proconsulate: there is reason to think that it was in Achaea, where Quietus also was proconsul. Unlike his brother, Nigrinus

---

[15] Pliny, *Epp.* 6. 6. 3.

[16] *PIR*[2] I/J 730. With Plutarch: *de curios.* 522 D f. His *origo:* G. E. F. Chilver, *Cisalpine Gaul* (1941), 104, Syme, op. cit. 559.

[17] Tribune: Tac. *Ann.* 16. 26. 4. Ambassador: Tac. *Hist.* 3. 80. 2. Praise of Thrasea: Tac. *Agr.* 2. 1, cf. Suet. *Dom.* 10. 3. Consulate: above, p. 23. Execution: Pliny, *Epp.* 3. 11. 3, Syme, op. cit. 656–7, A. N. Sherwin-White, *The Letters of Pliny* (1966), 765–6.

[18] Pliny, *Epp.* 1. 5. 5. See above, p. 24.

[19] *PIR*[2] A 1407, 1410. *De frat. am.* 478 A–B, *de sera num. vind.* 548 A.

seems not to have proceeded to the consulate, and nothing
further is heard of him: he may have died in the early 90s.[20]

One further detail about Nigrinus' career might be extracted
from the way Plutarch addresses the two brothers in his treatise:
the pleasure they take in upright deeds, he affirms, will make
them all the more ready to abide by their judgements, since they
are acting before noble and virtuous spectators. That phrase
recalls another in the work on divine vengeance, where 'the race
that is noblest and dearest to the gods' is a circumlocution for
the Greeks.[21] It may be suspected that Plutarch is alluding to
the joint activity of the two brothers in Achaea, and that one of
them was acting as legate in the proconsulate of the other. The
treatise would then be one of Plutarch's earliest datable works.[22]

Quietus is much the more vivid of the two. Already of mature
age under Nero, he became a friend of Thrasea Paetus,[23] in this
one respect resembling Arulenus Rusticus. Quietus' first attested
post is a legionary legateship under Vespasian or perhaps early
under Domitian.[24] His proconsulate of Achaea can probably
be dated to 91/2. In that office he received honours from Delphi
for his piety to Apollo;[25] that is relevant to the career of his
distinguished nephew, the younger Nigrinus, as well as to his
friendship with Plutarch. It was after Quietus' return from
Achaea to Rome that an incident already discussed took place.
Plutarch was present when Quietus was jokingly accused of
having taken bribes in his province.[26] Early in 93 Quietus
succeeded to the consulate, the senior *suffectus* in a year that may

---

[20] Province: Pliny, *Epp.* 10. 65. 3, 66. 2; E. Groag, *Die römischen Reichsbeamten von Achaia bis auf Diokletian* (1939), 42. Other deaths at this time: Syme, *Tacitus* (1958), 69.

[21] *De frat. am.* 478 B, τὸ χαῖρον ὑμῶν ἐφ' οἷς κατορθοῦτε ποιήσει τῇ κρίσει τὴν ἐπιμονὴν βεβαιοτέραν, ὥσπερ ἐν χρηστοῖς καὶ φιλοκάλοις θεαταῖς εὐημερούντων. Cf. de sera num. vind. 568 A, τῶν ὑπηκόων τὸ βέλτιστον καὶ θεοφιλέστατον γένος, and also Flam. 7. 6, ὡς ἐν καλλίστῳ θεάτρῳ τῇ Ἑλλάδι μέλλοντας ἀγωνίζεσθαι.

[22] Thus Groag, *PIR²* A 1410 and *Reichsbeamten* 42. For this practice, cf. Suet. *Vitell.* 5, *ILS* 990. This possibility is another argument for supposing that the 'tyrant' referred to at *de frat. am.* 488 A is Nero, cf. C. P. Jones, *JRS* 56 (1966), 70: the reference would not have been ambiguous if the work was written before 96.

[23] Pliny, *Epp.* 6. 29. 1.

[24] *ILS* 6105; dated 82–?84 by G. Alföldy, *Die Legionslegaten der römischen Rheinarmeen = Epigraphische Studien* 3 (1967), 15, not later than 79 by A. R. Birley, *Epigraphische Studien* 4 (1967), 68.

[25] *Syll.*³ 822 = *Fouilles de Delphes* 3. 1. 538 = McCrum and Woodhead, *Documents of the Flavian Emperors*, no. 318. On the date cf. p. 23, n. 22 above.

[26] *Quaest. conviv.* 632 A, cf. p. 23 above.

have seen many rewarded for service in the recently completed war against the Sarmatae. Although not particularly young, since he will by now have been close to 50, he had done well. There is no sign that his friendship with Thrasea had hindered his progress hitherto, or now imperilled him in the purge of Thrasea's kinsfolk and adherents.[27]

After Domitian's assassination, Quietus is soon found defending the interests of Thrasea's widow and daughter in the senate.[28] Like Pliny, in whose support he was then speaking, he may have acted from opportunism as well as piety. He advanced promptly to a consular command in a province of Caesar's portion, Britain:[29] the combination of an interest in philosophy with the command of Trajan's armies recurs among Plutarch's consular friends. If Quietus survived until the end of his tenure, he may have died soon thereafter, since in a letter of about 107 Pliny speaks of him as deceased, with no hint that his death was recent.[30]

The Avidii brothers are important as an illustration of the rank attained by Plutarch's Roman friends, and also for the possible implications of his acquaintance with them. He not only outlived Nigrinus and Quietus, but lived to see their respective sons rise to high eminence. The younger Quietus is the less significant, consul suffect in 111 and proconsul of Asia in 125/6.[31] His cousin Nigrinus first appears, if he has been correctly identified, as a pertinacious tribune in the year 105, and in the next year as a protector of oppressed provincials.[32] Having risen with unusual speed to be suffect consul in 110, Nigrinus was sent as the emperor's special legate to Greece, a province with which his father and uncle had been familiar.[33] Late in Trajan's reign, he is discovered in the consular command of Dacia, where he may have stayed until after the accession of Hadrian.[34] Nigrinus had

---

[27] On the consuls of 93: Syme, *Tacitus* (1958), 638–9; on the chronology of the treason trials, ibid. 656–7, Sherwin-White, *The Letters of Pliny* (1966), 763–71.

[28] Pliny, *Epp.* 9. 13. 15.   [29] *CIL* 16. 43. See now Birley, art. cit. 68.

[30] Pliny, *Epp.* 6. 29. 1.

[31] *PIR²* A 1409; L. Robert, *Hellenica* 6 (1948), 82–3; A. Degrassi, *Fasti consolari* (1952), 33.   [32] Pliny, *Epp.* 5. 13. 6, 20. 6, 7. 6. 2.

[33] *Syll.³* 827. The date is not quite assured: Groag, *Die römischen Reichsbeamten von Achaia bis auf Diokletian* (1939), 56, Syme, *Historia* 18 (1969), 359.

[34] *ILS* 2417. On the date of his departure see now Chr. Habicht, *Altertümer von Pergamon VIII*, 3; *Die Inschriften des Asklepieions* (1969), 50, arguing that it was before the death of Trajan.

progressed perhaps too fast, and his wealth and influence might make him aspire even higher. Soon after the beginning of the reign, when he had been succeeded in his province and had returned home, he was executed with three other consulars on a charge of conspiracy.[35]

Though there is no direct evidence that Plutarch knew or met the younger Nigrinus, it is an almost certain assumption.[36] Delphi was one of the cities with which Nigrinus, as the emperor's legate, was most directly concerned, and an extensive series of documents shows him settling boundary disputes between the city and its neighbours.[37] Such an undertaking could not but have involved the two priests of Apollo, of whom one was Plutarch. Even apart from business Nigrinus would have made the acquaintance of the distinguished philosopher who had dedicated works to his father and uncle. If Plutarch's circle included the younger Nigrinus, it came close to touching power and empire. Not only was Nigrinus himself of imperial calibre, but he appears to have been familiar with Trajan's kinsman and successor, Hadrian: later Hadrian claimed that he had thought of him as his heir.[38] In the course of time the imperial promise of the Avidii was fulfilled. When Hadrian eventually made his choice, it fell on Nigrinus' stepson and son-in-law, Ceionius Commodus, but Ceionius fell sick and died.[39] The emperor then picked a new successor, later to be known as Antoninus Pius, and told him to adopt Ceionius' son, the grandson of Nigrinus. The boy grew up to be the co-regent of Marcus, Lucius Verus.[40] One of his teachers, so chance ordained, was Sextus the nephew of Plutarch.[41]

The third and largest group of Plutarch's senatorial friends all come to prominence under one emperor, Trajan. Chief among them in prestige, and in proximity both to Plutarch and to the emperor, is Q. Sosius Senecio. Sosius received from Plutarch the dedications of his two most ambitious works, the *Parallel Lives*

[35] Cass. Dio, 69. 2. 5, *HA* Hadr. 7. 1, 23. 10.

[36] Ziegler, *RE* 21 (1951), 691, states it as a fact, confusing the younger Nigrinus with the elder.

[37] *Syll.*³ 827.   [38] *HA* Hadr. 7. 1, cf. Syme, *Tacitus* (1958), 245.

[39] *PIR*² C 605; Syme, *Athenaeum* 35 (1957), 306 ff.

[40] *PIR*² C 606.

[41] *HA* Verus 2. 5: the only evidence, but comparatively reliable, cf. T. D. Barnes, *JRS* 57 (1967), 65–74, especially 67.

and the *Table Talk*, as well as the treatise on progress in virtue. From the *Table Talk* it is clear that their relationship was not the distant one of a man of letters cultivating an indifferent patron: Sosius was a familiar friend of Plutarch and his sons.[42] He is a cardinal link between the philosopher and Rome.

Sosius' origin is nowhere directly attested. It is almost axiomatic that in dedicating the *Parallel Lives* to him Plutarch intended to make a symbolic gesture, the gift of a Greek man of letters to a Roman general. The symbolism may be of a different kind. There are reasons to think that Sosius was from the Greek East.[43] That is, he combines in his own person the peculiar excellences of Greece and Rome, war and the gentler arts.[44]

Sosius' career, it can be argued, is known almost in full from an acephalous inscription found at Rome.[45] He appears to have been some years, perhaps as many as twenty, junior to Plutarch. Probably they met for the first time in Greece, where Sosius was quaestor in the late 80s. In the *Table Talk* written under Trajan Plutarch recalls several conversations that the two had held both in Rome and in Greece, at Athens, Patras, and at the wedding of Plutarch's son in Chaeronea. Some of these may date to Sosius' term of duty. If the portrait given by Plutarch in his work is any guide, Sosius was a man with broad interests and an especial taste for poetry and philosophy. The sympathy between the middle-aged philosopher and the young official was to find public expression a decade later, when Plutarch dedicated his major works to Sosius, and Sosius helped to obtain public honours for Plutarch.

In the years after his quaestorship, Sosius' career prospered with the favour of Domitian. Even if he had private sympathies with the emperor's victims, in particular with the philosophers expelled from Rome in 93, he chose to follow the path of uncomplaining industry.[46] When the emperor was assassinated, Sosius

[42] On Sosius in Plutarch, Groag, *RE* 3 A (1927), 1188–92, Ziegler, art. cit. 688–9. Note especially *quaest. conviv.* 612 E (many dinners together in Greece and Rome), 666 D (Sosius present at wedding of Plutarch's son), 734 E (Sosius a ἑταῖρος of Plutarch's sons).

[43] Provincial origin suggested by Syme, *Tacitus* (1958), 599, n. 8; perhaps Cilicia, id. *Historia* 17 (1968), 101, n. 127. See now C. P. Jones, *JRS* 60 (1970), 103.

[44] Cf. the familiar formulation of Vergil, *Aen.* 6. 847 ff.

[45] *CIL* 6. 1444 = *ILS* 1022. For what follows see now C. P. Jones, art. cit. 98 ff.

[46] Tac. *Agr.* 42. 5, with the comments of Syme, *Tacitus* (1958), 24–5.

may have been commanding a legion in Lower Germany: he was swiftly promoted to govern the crucial province of Gallia Belgica. The period of his tenure was that which saw Trajan elevated from the legateship of Upper Germany to share the power with Nerva, and soon after left sole emperor. Sosius received a high reward, the ordinary consulate of 99: for a man who had never held the *fasces* before, that was an exceptional honour. In the following years, his military talents, joined to a nature that Trajan found congenial, brought him high command in the Dacian wars, and after the conquest of Dacia had been completed his career was crowned with a second ordinary consulate in 107 and other honours.

Plutarch, in the meanwhile, will not have seen his friend for many years. He may, however, have supplied Sosius with some writings to beguile the time left over from campaigning: a cultured man commanding an army might easily make such a request of his literary friends far from the battlefront.[47] Plutarch's *Table Talk*, with its reminiscences of leisurely and elegant speculation, could have been begun, perhaps completed, in the period of the Dacian wars.[48]

It may be suspected that Sosius reciprocated. At some time under Trajan Plutarch received the consular ornaments, a distinction that ranked him with the advisers of emperors and above more rich and powerful men of contemporary Achaea.[49] This, and other honours of which there is now no record, may be due to the intervention of Sosius.[50] Nor would it be surprising if Sosius had introduced to the old philosopher a young friend who shared his own philhellenic tastes and also had served in both Dacian wars, P. Aelius Hadrianus.[51] Plutarch knew another friend of the future emperor in Avidius Nigrinus.

In the year of his second consulate, Sosius was still in his prime,

[47] Pliny, *Epp.* 9. 25. 1, cf. 4. 26. 2.

[48] On the chronology of the *Table Talk*, see C. P. Jones, *JRS* 56 (1966), 72–3, and above, p. 27, n. 52. Sosius appears only in the first four books: when the introduction to the fifth was written, he and Plutarch were separated by 'shadowy mountains and roaring sea' (672 D).

[49] See above, p. 29. Ti. Claudius Atticus Herodes, father of the sophist, received praetorian ornaments, though he later entered the senate: *Corinth* 8. 2. 58 = *AE* 1919. 8 = Smallwood, *Documents of Nerva, Trajan and Hadrian* no. 198 (*PIR*² C 801).

[50] Thus Groag, *RE* 3 A (1927), 1190.

[51] Hadrian and Sosius: *HA* Hadr. 4. 2 (if that can be trusted). On the reading, Groag, art. cit. 1187.

but no civil or military employment is recorded thereafter. Perhaps his energies were spent, perhaps he no longer found public life congenial. A soldier whose fighting days ended prematurely might not have much to look forward to except a quiet death. In the end, his old friend from Chaeronea outlived him.[52]

Though Sosius had no son, the family name was perpetuated through his daughter Sosia Polla and her husband, the energetic Pompeius Falco.[53] Like the Avidii, Sosius founded a house that might not disgrace the throne of the Caesars. His great-great-grandson, Q. Sosius Falco, was *consul ordinarius* in the momentous year of 193. After the accession of Pertinax the disgruntled praetorians briefly plotted to replace the emperor with Falco.[54]

Perhaps not unlike Sosius, if he has been correctly identified, is the Saturninus to whom Plutarch dedicates his attack on Colotes, the pupil of Epicurus. Saturninus is described as a lover of culture and antiquity, and one who considers it a royal pastime to study the writings of the ancients; and he also seems to know a Platonist of Plutarch's acquaintance.[55] It happens that L. Herennius Saturninus is found as proconsul of Achaea in 98/9 intervening in the affairs of Delphi: this man is therefore probably the potentate in Plutarch.[56] If that is correct, he is another who combined an interest in philosophy with military skills. After his suffect consulate in 100, he is attested in the course of the second Dacian war as legate of Upper Moesia: his predecessor may have been Sosius.[57] Thereafter no more is heard of him, and his origin and previous career are also a blank. Nor is there any sign that he and Plutarch were close friends.

By contrast with Sosius and Herennius, both military men, another of Plutarch's consular friends may have risen by his

---

[52] Sosius appears to have died before Trajan: Groag, art. cit. 1187, cf. Syme, *Tacitus* (1958), 476. Cf. Julius Agricola, dying some nine years after his departure from Britain, in his fifty-fourth year (Tac. *Agr.* 44. 1).

[53] Pompeius Falco: *PIR*¹ R 68. On the family's stemma, Groag, *JÖAI* 18 (1915), Beibl. 265–74.

[54] Cass. Dio, 74. 8, cf. *HA* Pert. 10. 1–7 (*PIR*¹ S 557, Barbieri, *Albo* no. 481).

[55] *Adv. Col.* 1107 E, φιλόκαλον καὶ φιλάρχαιον ὄντα καὶ τὸ μεμνῆσθαι καὶ διὰ χειρῶν ἔχειν. . .τοὺς λόγους τῶν παλαιῶν βασιλικωτάτην διατριβὴν ἡγούμενον.

[56] É. Bourguet, *De rebus Delphicis imperatoriae aetatis* (1905), 71; Groag, *Die römischen Reichsbeamten von Achaia bis auf Diokletian* (1939), 49–51; *PIR*² H 126.

[57] *CIL* 16. 54; Syme, *JRS* 49 (1959), 27–9.

civilian abilities. This is the 'excellent Fundanus' who takes the
leading part in the dialogue on anger, and is also mentioned in
the treatise on tranquillity of mind. There can be no doubt that
he is C. Minicius Fundanus, known from a variety of sources
but above all as a correspondent of the younger Pliny.[58]

Fundanus appears to come from Ticinum, which like Pliny's
patria, Comum, lay in the orbit of Milan: it may also be the
origin of one of Plutarch's Latin sources, Cornelius Nepos.[59]
Fundanus is therefore another northerner among Plutarch's
friends. His career, though it included at least one legionary
legateship, was probably for the most part civilian: in the several
letters of Pliny that concern him, there is no hint of warfare, and
much that suggests an orator and man of the forum.[60] In due
course, perhaps not so soon as Pliny expected, Fundanus
succeeded to the suffect consulate in 107, a new man like all of
Plutarch's consular friends.[61] Eventually, in 122/3, he was
allotted the province of Asia, and there received a rescript from
Hadrian on the proper way to treat Christians.[62]

Fundanus may have met Plutarch during a spell of duty in
Greece as proconsul or legate,[63] or when the philosopher visited
Rome and Italy. It is clear that Plutarch knew him well. That
emerges from Fundanus' monologue in the treatise on anger.
Many of the details about the consular's circumstances and
personality, his memories of Musonius Rufus, his impulsive
nature, his treatment of his slaves, could hardly have been
invented by Plutarch. One detail is corroborated by Pliny,
Fundanus' reference to his 'little daughters'.[64]

---

[58] *PIR*[1] M 433; Groag, *RE* 15 (1932), 1820–6. *De cohib. ira* 452 F ff., *de tranqu. animi* 464 E.

[59] Syme, *Tacitus* (1958), 801. On the origin of Nepos, Wissowa, *RE* 4 (1900), 1408–9, cf. Sherwin-White, *The Letters of Pliny* (1966), 307.

[60] Pliny, *Epp.* 1. 9, 4. 15, 5. 16, 6. 6, 7. 12. For the early career, see the inscription republished by Syme, op. cit. 801, n. 3. The fact that it was found in Bosnia suggests that it was set up to Minicius as governor of Dalmatia, a consular imperial province without a legion: thus Syme, *Gnomon* 31 (1959), 515–16, followed by J. J. Wilkes, *Dalmatia* (1969), 445–6, App. II no. 18. If so, the absence of 'cos.' is surprising. Cf. the inscription set up to Avidius Quietus in Thrace by veterans that had served under him in Upper Germany, *ILS* 6105, cf. *PIR*[2] A 1410.

[61] Pliny, *Epp.* 4. 15. 5, cf. Syme, *Tacitus* (1958), 662, n. 2.

[62] Euseb. *Hist. Eccles.* 4. 9. For the date, C. P. Jones, *Phoenix* 22 (1968), 123.

[63] Thus Groag, *RE* 15 (1932), 1820–1.

[64] *De cohib. ira* 453 D (Musonius), 463 C (impulsiveness), 459 C (slaves), 455 F (daughters), cf. Pliny, *Epp.* 5. 16, C. P. Jones, *JRS* 56 (1966), 61.

The last of Plutarch's friends who is known to have attained the consulate is the King Philopappus whom he instructed on distinguishing friends from flatterers. Philopappus' generosity as agonothete of the great Dionysia is also the occasion of one of the scenes in the *Table Talk*.[65] The grandson of the last king of Commagene, whom Vespasian deposed in 72, Philopappus took up residence in Athens and participated in the city's cultural life. There Plutarch, himself an honorary citizen, will have met him and may have turned casual items of his conversation to use as history, as he did with others of his friends. Philopappus could have supplied details about his ancestor whom M. Antonius besieged unsuccessfully in Samosata, or about the first battle of Bedriacum where his father, like friends of Plutarch, had been on Otho's staff.[66]

With other descendants of Oriental kings, Philopappus was promoted in his career by Trajan, who adlected him into the senate and gave him a suffect consulate in 109.[67] He died only a few years later, and his tomb on the Hill of the Muses at Athens, still partly standing, symbolizes an age. On either side of his monumental statue his name was inscribed, on the left in Latin with his names, tribe, and honours as a Roman, on the right in Greek, with his royal titles and ancestors.[68]

Plutarch's society included at least one more senator, the mysterious Paccius for whom he wrote the treatise on the control of anger: his rank is evident from the author's reference to his senatorial shoes.[69] As with Fundanus, Plutarch alludes freely to Paccius' circumstances, his powerful friends, his high reputation as an orator, and, in a long and direct exhortation, the distress which it causes him to observe misconduct in public affairs.[70] Since the work is almost certainly of Trajanic date, it appears that Paccius was active as a speaker and a senator in the era of Pliny and Tacitus, and it is appropriate that he seems to have

[65] *Quom. adul. ab amico internosc.* 48 E, *quaest. conviv.* 628 A–B, *PIR²* I/J 151. The date of the agonothesia is probably 96/7, see above, p. 27, n. 52.

[66] *Ant.* 34. 4–7, Tac. *Hist.* 2. 25. 2. Cf. p. 41 above.

[67] *ILS* 845. Syme, *Tacitus* (1958), 510.

[68] *ILS* 845 = *OGIS* 409, 410, 412 = *IG* 2/3². 3451. For a detailed study, see M. Santangelo, *Annuario della Scuola archeologica di Atene*, 3–5 (1941–3, publ. 1948), 153 ff., especially 194–9 (= *SEG* 21. 735).

[69] *De tranqu. animi* 465 A, μνημονεύεις ὡς οὔτε ποδάγρας ἀπαλλάττει κάλτιος, κτλ. Cf. C. P. Jones, *JRS* 56 (1966), 63.

[70] *De tranqu. animi* 465 A (friendships, reputation), 468 B–F (distress).

been a friend of Minicius Fundanus.[71] He might be a kinsman, perhaps a son, of C. Paccius Africanus, the *delator* of the Neronian age who regained respectability under Vespasian,[72] and like other of Plutarch's senatorial friends he could have visited Greece in an official capacity.[73]

There remains a small group of persons mentioned by Plutarch and apparently from the West, whose status is not clearly indicated. Terentius Priscus, to whom he dedicates the treatise on the decline of oracles, is evidently the man of the same name who was a compatriot and patron of the poet Martial. The poet's allusions might suggest a knight, but better a minor senator.[74]

A person who appears more frequently in Plutarch, and was evidently well known to him, is the erudite Sextius Sulla from Carthage. He appears to have been familiar with several of Plutarch's consular friends, Mestrius Florus, Sosius Senecio, and particularly Minicius Fundanus, with whom he is the interlocutor in the dialogue on anger.[75] There is no mention of his rank, but Plutarch's description would fit a minor senator or a knight.

There is also Aufidius Modestus, a learned friend of Plutarch and his family, and the wit who joked at Avidius Quietus in Rome. He is evidently identical with the man of the same name known as a commentator on Vergil's *Georgics*. Clearly not a freedman, as the early *grammatici* had been, he may have been a knight like Suetonius; and like Suetonius he might be Umbrian by origin.[76]

Last, and difficult to fit into any category, is the hellenized

---

[71] *De tranqu. animi* 464 E.

[72] Tac. *Hist.* 4. 41. 3; Syme, *Tacitus* (1958), 668; B. E. Thomasson, *Die Statthalter der römischen Provinzen Nordafrikas* (1960), 2. 47–8. M. Hofmann, *RE* 18 (1942), 2064, no. 7, thought that Plutarch's friend might be the Neronian consul.

[73] E. Groag, *Die römischen Reichsbeamten von Achaia bis auf Diokletian* (1939), 45.

[74] *PIR*[1] T 62–3. There seems no reason to divide the man in Martial into a father and a son, as Stein does, *RE* 5 A (1934), 667–8, followed by C. P. Jones, *JRS* 56 (1966), 70. Cf. Martial, 7. 46, 12 *praefatio*, 3 (4), 62 (patronage), 8. 45 (an absence in Sicily: conceivably as proconsul or legate).

[75] *PIR*[1] S 476. *Rom.* 15. 3–4, *de cohib. ira* 452 F ff. (Fundanus), *quaest. conviv.* 650 A ff. (Florus), 636 A, cf. 635 E (Sosius).

[76] *PIR*[2] A 1390. *Quaest. conviv.* 618 F, 632 A. Commentator: Servius on *Georg.* 2, 497, 3. 53, cf. Martial, 10. 21. 1. His origin: cf. the contemporary consular Aufidius Umber (*PIR*[2] A 1395), and the Umbrian C. Aufidius Victorinus, son-in-law of Fronto (*PIR*[2] A 1393). Suetonius: Syme, *Tacitus* (1958), 780–1.

Gaul, Favorinus of Arelate, who was almost certainly of equestrian rank. He will have been known to Plutarch only at the beginning of his career, and may have been his pupil. Plutarch did not live to see Favorinus' later vicissitudes: his rivalry with the sophist Polemo, his quarrel with Hadrian, and his respectable old age.[77]

Despite the variety of Plutarch's Roman friends, he happens not to mention any of his contemporaries in Latin literature, or to be mentioned by them. The person whom he might have been likeliest to meet is the younger Pliny. They had several friends in common, particularly Sosius Senecio, and there is a remote chance that Pliny came into contact with relatives of Plutarch through Arulenus Rusticus.[78] Pliny was not indifferent to the society of learned Greeks, but it is noticeable that those he mentions are all of high social distinction and, as it happens, from a more affluent province than Achaea and one he knew well, Syria.[79] The philosopher from Chaeronea might not have been quite so presentable as these well-connected Syrians, or so considerate of Pliny's sensibilities.[80]

Plutarch also had friends in common with Cornelius Tacitus. If Tacitus knew Minicius Fundanus only distantly, he would have found Sosius Senecio congenial, and long ago he had been a follower of Julius Secundus.[81] Whatever Tacitus' opinion of contemporary Greeks and of senators who studied philosophy, it is not impossible that he noticed the writings of a Greek who concerned himself with recent Roman history and had known eyewitnesses of the events he described. There is no need to suppose that when Tacitus himself turned to writing imperial history he kept before him Plutarch's *Lives of the Caesars*. But he

---

[77] *PIR*² F 123; A. Barigazzi, *Favorino di Arelate: Opere* (1966). Rank: [Dio Prus.] 37. 25 = Barigazzi, no. 95. 25. In Plutarch: *quaest. Rom.* 271 C, *quaest. conviv.* 734 D–F, *de primo frigido* 945 F ff. Lamprias Catalogue no. 132 (= Barigazzi, Test. 20, 21, 18, 19). Polemo: Philostr. *VS* 490–1 = Barigazzi, Test. 6. 5, cf. 3; Bowersock, *Greek Sophists in the Roman Empire* (1969), 90–1. Hadrian: Philostr. *VS* 490 = Barigazzi, Test. 6. 1–3; Bowersock, op. cit. 35–6. Old age: A. Gellius, 2. 26 = Barigazzi, Test. 28, e.g.

[78] Above, p. 24.

[79] Thus Euphrates, *Epp.* 1. 10 (*PIR*² E 121); Isaeus, *Epp.* 2. 3 (*PIR*² I/J 52); Artemidorus, *Epp.* 3. 11 (*PIR*² A 1169).

[80] Note Plutarch's stern rebuke to an unnamed Roman, *de frat. am.* 479 E.

[81] Fundanus: Pliny, *Epp.* 4. 15, 1, cf. Syme, *Tacitus* (1958), 801. Senecio: cf. Syme, op. cit. 476. Secundus: Tac. *Dial.* 2. 1.

might have recalled a striking phrase here and there, or some deplorable omission. He would not have approved, for instance, if Plutarch's *Life of Tiberius* had said much about the emperor's youthful stay on Rhodes and his Greek courtiers while omitting mention of Arminius.[82]

Plutarch's *Lives of the Caesars* might also have caught the notice of the younger Pliny's protégé Suetonius Tranquillus. Suetonius' appetite for recondite information could well have drawn his attention to Plutarch's work, which appears to have been completed under the Flavians; all the more since he himself stood in the tradition of Greek enquiry and wrote some of his own works in the language.[83] Indeed, the idea of a series of imperial biographies may have been due to Plutarch, whose own attempt is the first known example of the type, and may have preceded Suetonius' by only a few years.[84] That does not mean that Suetonius, any more than Tacitus, made Plutarch a basic source. The Greek had had a different interest, morals rather than history, and his knowledge of Roman matters was often slight. But there was no book from which a conscientious researcher could not extract some profit.[85]

Plutarch's senatorial friends are a heterogeneous group. They vary widely in age, from members of Nero's senate to a proconsul of Asia under Hadrian. Their origins include northern Italy, provinces of the West, and Asia Minor. Within the group, there are also discernible similarities. All the consulars are new men. Alert and ambitious, they passed without check from Otho to Vespasian, from Domitian to Nerva: the one exception is Arulenus Rusticus, whom Plutarch may not have known very well. A majority of the consulars owe their distinction to Trajan, above all Sosius Senecio. That has a bearing on Plutarch's fortunes in the same reign, and on the circumstances under which his major works were written, notably the *Parallel Lives*.

[82] Thus the famous outburst, *Ann.* 2. 88. 3, might refer to Plutarch's *Lives of the Caesars*, if not the *Parallel Lives*: cf. Bowersock, *Augustus and the Greek World* (1965), 109, n. 2. Stay on Rhodes: Damascius, *Vita Isid.* 64 = fr. 182 Sandbach. Courtiers: *de def. orac.* 419 D.

[83] Cf. Funaioli, *RE* 4 A (1931), 625 (Περὶ τῶν παρ' Ἕλλησι παιδιῶν), 629 (περὶ βλασφημιῶν).

[84] For the relative dates of Plutarch's and Suetonius' *Lives*, see now Bowersock, *Hommages à Marcel Renard I*, Collection Latomus 101 (1969), 119 ff., especially 122.

[85] The observation of the elder Pliny, *Epp.* 3. 5. 10.

Several of them had had official duties in Greece, as quaestors, legates, or proconsuls, and these may first have met Plutarch there. Back in Rome, they would have renewed their acquaintance on his visits. Others, like Arulenus Rusticus, probably met him for the first time in the capital.

Inevitably, Plutarch was not on the same terms with them all. Some, like Terentius Priscus, he may never have met face to face, but communicated with them through intermediaries. Others, like Rusticus and Herennius Saturninus, he may have met only briefly. But those he knew best, Mestrius Florus and Sosius Senecio, appear from his dialogues to have been completely at home in his society. Mestrius and his sons-in-law are close friends of Plutarch's family.[86] Sosius is host to Plutarch's friends, and attends the wedding of his elder son.[87] Not only these two, but all Plutarch's western friends, will have known Greek: that is clear from his confession that he had had no chance to practise Latin when staying in Italy.[88] The works that he dedicates to men like Terentius Priscus and the Avidii assume more than a knowledge of the language, a thorough grounding in Greek culture.

The tradition whereby learned Greeks dispensed advice and consolation to Roman officials still flourished in Plutarch's day. This was what the younger Pliny required from the Syrian Euphrates and what knights and senators expected from Epictetus in Nicopolis.[89] In the same way Plutarch might try to reconcile quarrelling brothers, or to reassure an orator when public duties became a burden to him.[90] In his role of confessor, he would learn the personal circumstances of his friends, their foibles and domestic worries, and convention allowed him to allude to such things freely when giving his guidance.

Already in his day, however, educated Greeks were drawing level in social standing with the Romans who came to them for advice and distraction. This process was hastened on the one side by the fact that sophists and philosophers were themselves drawn from the upper classes of their cities; on the other, by the

[86] *Quaest. conviv.* 680 C ff., 734 D ff.

[87] *Quaest. conviv.* 666 D; cf. Plutarch's comment on suitable wedding-guests, 679 C.

[88] *Demosth.* 2. 2.

[89] Pliny, *Epp.* 1. 10. 10, Arr. *Diss. Epict.* 3. 7. 21, e.g.

[90] *De frat. am.* 479 E, *de tranqu. animi* 468 B ff.

penetration of Greeks into the Roman administration, which is the reason why many of the Roman friends of sophists were in fact Greek by origin.[91] Local dignitaries were not merely showing respect for culture when they married their daughters off to philosophers: they were advancing their own positions.[92]

Plutarch stands at the entrance of a new period in the history of the Roman East, the renaissance of the second and early third centuries. In that era an Athenian sophist was to be *consul ordinarius*, and a man who claimed descent from him to assume the imperial purple.[93] The process that brought this about had begun long ago, when Rome was still a republic. It had made available to Plutarch the Roman citizenship, the friendship of great Romans, and the esteem of the emperors themselves. It remains to be seen whether Plutarch ignores the new era, or welcomes it.

[91] Bowersock, *Greek Sophists in the Roman Empire* (1969), 88 and *passim*.

[92] Pliny, *Epp.* 1. 10. 8, cf. 3. 11. 7.

[93] Viz. Ti. Claudius Herodes Atticus (*PIR²* C 802) and the Gordian addressed by Philostratus, *VS praefatio*, either Gordian I or Gordian II: see now T. D. Barnes, *Latomus* 27 (1968), 581–97, Bowersock, op. cit. 6–8.

Part II

VII

THE HISTORICAL DECLAMATIONS

Probably among the earliest of Plutarch's extant works are the declamations on historical themes, on Alexander, the glory of Athens, and the fortune of the Romans. It is unwise to expect much substance from works so ephemeral in purpose. What can be done is to define that purpose and dispel misconceptions about the political thought of the young Plutarch.

The speech on the fortune of the Romans is the most relevant of the group to Plutarch's own time. The traditional title belies the work, since at the outset Plutarch makes clear that he plans not merely to praise the fortune of Rome but to show that Fortune and Virtue had both contributed to the city's greatness.[1] Because that programme is not fulfilled, and the speech ends with unusual abruptness, the last part is generally agreed to be missing. The complementary section on Roman virtue either remained unwritten or more probably was lost in transmission.[2]

It has already been argued that this group of declamations belongs to an early stage of Plutarch's development, before his apprenticeship with Ammonius and so probably in the reign of Nero.[3] That appears to raise a difficulty. The laudatory tone of the work, and its evident affinities with the conventional declamations in praise of cities, might suggest that it was delivered by Plutarch as a formal encomium of Rome on an early visit there:[4] the earliest of his visits, however, appears to have been made under Vespasian. But if Plutarch had delivered the

---

[1] De fort. Rom. 317 C, cf. 320 B, 321 B.
[2] Thus Ziegler, *RE* 21 (1951), 720. Nevertheless, the view that the speech survives virtually intact is still expressed: A. E. Wardman, *CQ* 5 (1955), 99, n. 6.
[3] Above, p. 14.
[4] So J. Palm, *Rom, Römertum und Imperium in der griechischen Literatur der Kaiserzeit* (1959), 36; R. Flacelière, *Mélanges Carcopino* (1966), 373. Palm points in particular to 321 A, τὰ καλὰ ταῦτα βασίλεια, κτλ.: but these words occur in a speech of the personified Tyche, who would naturally be represented as being in sight of Rome.

speech in Rome, he would surely have indicated that unequivo-
cally, as the rhetor Aristides does throughout the laudation of
Rome that he delivered there.[5] The plan of Plutarch's speech
marks it as a conventional controversy in which Fortune and
Virtue are made to strive for the title of having founded Rome.
The natural audience for it was a gathering of trained rhetori-
cians, perhaps in Athens where the declamation on that city's
glory was delivered.[6] Plutarch has drawn on the same stock of
themes as Aristides,[7] but his purpose is entirely different.

While the work is not a formal laudation of Rome, equally
it is not an attack, either open or covert. Certainly, hostile
Greeks had once made much of the Romans' faith in their
fortune, claiming that they owed all they possessed to the whim
of chance.[8] The emphasis that Plutarch's speech gives to Fortune
appears at first sight to show that at this early stage he sympathized with that view. On closer inspection, the speech has nothing in common with this literature of protest, if indeed it was
still being written in Plutarch's day. While the theme of Fortune
might be used in disparagement, it could also be put to use as an
item of praise, and in fact was one of the recommended ingre-
dients of formal laudations.[9] When Plutarch calls Rome's
Fortune 'the sister of Lawfulness and Persuasion and the
daughter of Forethought', he is not treating it as mere chance,
but comes close to assimilating it to a virtue.[10]

For similar reasons there is no cause to see ill will towards
Rome in a passage at the end of the extant speech. Here Plutarch
attributes to Rome's fortune the fact that Alexander of Macedon
had died before the inevitable war between them.[11] In making
that claim he must have in mind an old controversy among
historians, whether Alexander would have defeated Rome if
he had not died in Babylon. From Livy's outburst on the subject,

---

[5] Aristides, Or. 26. 1, 3, 7, etc. K.

[6] De glor. Ath. 345 F.

[7] Thus cf. 317 C with Aristides, Or. 26. 103–4 K.; 324 B with Aristides, Or. 26.
15–17 K.; 318 A–B, 325 E with Aristides, Or. 26. 12–13 K.

[8] Polyb. 1. 63. 9; Dion. Hal. Ant. Rom. 1. 4. 2. Cf. G. W. Bowersock, Augustus and
the Greek World (1965), 108–10.

[9] Cf. Menander Rhetor, Rhet. Graec. 3. 376. 25, 420. 27; W. Gernentz, Laudes
Romae (diss. Rostock, 1918), 96.

[10] De fort. Rom. 318 A. Thus, rightly, Palm, op. cit. 34. In the same sense, H. Fuchs,
Der geistige Widerstand gegen Rom (1938), 93; Ziegler, RE 21 (1951), 720.

[11] De fort. Rom. 326 A–C.

it is clear that the notion of Alexander's victory was a comfort to Greek writers still unreconciled to the inevitability of Roman rule.[12] But just as the theme of Fortune itself could be used for contrary purposes, so also could the commemoration of Alexander. Livy bridled at the notion that the heroes of the Samnite wars would have yielded to demoralized Macedonians: but there is nothing unfriendly in Plutarch's picture of the conquerors of Persia and the lords of Italy, locked in close combat for the mastery of the world. The Romans of his speech, 'athletes trained in myriad wars, warlike and manly all', are a different breed from those whom hostile Greeks saw cowering in terror at the mere name of Alexander.[13]

One small item in fact shows the closeness of Plutarch's views to those of Livy and other Roman historians. A tradition seized upon by the same Greeks made out that the Romans had sent ambassadors to Alexander on his triumphant return to Babylon. Roman writers maintained total silence on the matter, and Livy, impugning it obliquely, avowed that the Romans had never even heard of him.[14] Both in the declamations on Alexander and the *Life*, Plutarch follows the Roman tradition and ignores the story completely. Elsewhere he represents it as a claim made by Rome before all the world that Alexander would have met defeat if he had invaded Italy.[15]

The declamation on the fortune of Rome is therefore no statement of political faith. But certain ideas may be observed in it which recur in Plutarch's more mature works and are not mere flourishes of the moment. Already the notion appears that Rome's fortune had intervened in its history to let the city deal separately with its enemies instead of being overwhelmed by them: later it returns in the *Life of Caesar*.[16] Allied to this idea is that of the collaboration between fortune and divine power. Just as Plutarch speaks in the declamation of 'divine fortune', so later he represents the guardian spirit of Rome collaborating with fortune to spread Roman power over Greece.[17]

---

[12] Livy, 9. 17–19, especially 18. 6. On this see now Bowersock, op. cit. 109; H. R. Breitenbach, *Museum Helveticum* 26 (1969), 146–57.
[13] 326 C; Livy, 9. 18. 6–7.
[14] Arrian, *Anab. Alex.* 7. 15. 5–6; Livy, 9. 18. 6.
[15] *Pyrrh.* 19. 2.
[16] *De fort. Rom.* 321 F; *Caes.* 26. 2–3.
[17] *De fort. Rom.* 316 F, 322 A, 323 E, *Philop.* 17. 2.

These ideas are not Plutarch's invention. They derive from the traditions of Greek historiography about Rome, notably from Polybius.[18] But though they are not original, and appear in a rhetorical work, they may still represent the author's personal belief. One idea in particular seems to reflect the circumstances of an imperial writer and Plutarch's own convictions. This is the notion that Rome was a stable element in the chaos of history, 'an anchor in storm and change'.[19] Augustan propaganda had encouraged the Greeks to see the new dispensation as the guarantor of order and peace, and it is not surprising that the Greek literature of the principate, reflecting the views of the cultured few, should endorse such a comfortable notion.[20] It is as a member of the same class himself that Plutarch compares the instability of earlier ages to the primeval chaos, while with Rome 'power entered an order of peace and one unchanging cycle.'[21]

Another feature that anticipates the mature Plutarch is the broad acquaintance with Roman history, from the myths of Romulus and Remus to anecdotes about Julius Caesar. Just as the range of Plutarch's interest is the same as that of the *Parallel Lives*, so there is a close correspondence in details.[22] Even at this early stage he appears to possess that interest in the Roman past that distinguishes him from many Greeks, even one so well disposed as Aristides. Already he can cite Roman historians, Valerius Antias and Livy, though since he acquired the ability to read Latin only late in life these quotations cannot (and need not) derive from perusal of the original texts.[23]

The other historical declamations, those on Alexander and Athens, resemble that on the fortune of Rome in form and treatment. They too are concerned with adjudging the claims of abstractions for their influence on history: to show that Alexander was made great by Virtue and not Fortune, and Athens

---

[18] Thus, on the collaboration of τύχη and θεός in Polybius, F. W. Walbank, *A Historical Commentary on Polybius* I (1957), 17. Cf. Dion. Hal. *Ant. Rom.* 1. 5. 2–3.

[19] *De fort. Rom.* 317 A, στοιχεῖον ἀΐδιον . . . 'ἀγκυρηβόλιον σάλου καὶ πλάνης'.

[20] Ehrenberg and Jones, *Documents Illustrating the Reigns of Augustus and Tiberius*[2], no. 98a; *OGIS* 458 = Ehrenberg and Jones, no. 98 = R. K. Sherk, *Roman Documents from the Greek East* (1969), no. 65. Cf. R. Syme, *The Roman Revolution* (1939), 473–4; U. Laffi, *Studi classici e orientali* 16 (1967), 49–52, 56–9.

[21] *De fort. Rom.* 317 C; cf. Aristides, *Or.* 26. 103–4 K.

[22] e.g. cf. *de fort. Rom.* 318 C with *Sulla* 2. 7.

[23] *De fort. Rom.* 323 C (Antias), 326 A (Livy), cf. *Demosth.* 2. 2, and below, pp. 83–6.

by her men of action and not her artists. Though the treatment is rhetorical,[24] all these declamations forecast the mature Plutarch's interest in the characters of great men and in weighing ethical issues. The cocoon of cultured moralizing from which the *Parallel Lives* were to emerge is already formed. But before they were written Plutarch was to undertake a preliminary experiment in biography.

[24] For an analysis of the *de fort. Alex.* see now J. R. Hamilton, *Plutarch, Alexander: A Commentary* (1969), xxiii–xxxiii.

VIII

THE *LIVES OF THE CAESARS*

IN the history of Greek literature, biography appears comparatively late. Though the genre may have had its beginnings in the fifth century, it received form and life in the fourth, from Isocrates' *Evagoras* and Xenophon's *Agesilaus*.[1] These works started the fashion of combining laudation with ethical disquisition, and became classics as familiar to Plutarch as to every aspiring biographer.[2] Later centuries saw new developments in the art, of which an important one was serial biography, for instance kings of a country or the heads of a philosophical school. While such catalogues might sometimes pretend to scientific accuracy, they might equally be written like their first exemplars for delectation and moral improvement rather than for sober fact.

Plutarch's *Lives of the Caesars* were originally a series running from Augustus to Vitellius, of which only the *Galba and Otho* now survive.[3] While the loss makes speculation about the whole work hazardous, it is clearly important for an understanding of Plutarch's attitude to Rome. Moreover, the surviving *Lives* raise problems about Plutarch's personal circumstances and historical methods.

The date of the series cannot be established with any certainty. The best indication, such as it is, is the exclusion of the Flavian house, which suggests a date of composition before Domitian's death in 96. Various indications make it appear that some time had elapsed since the events described in the surviving part, while the spontaneously inserted praise of the senator Junius Mauricus favours a date earlier than his exile in 93.[4] Plutarch

---

[1] See now A. D. Momigliano, *The Development of Greek Biography* (forthcoming).

[2] *Evagoras*: cf. *Evag.* 77 with *Arat.* 1. 5. *Agesilaus*: *Ages. passim, quom. adul. ab amico internosc.* 55 D, *praec. ger. reip.* 784 E–F, 809 B.

[3] Lamprias Catalogue, nos. 26, 27, 29–33.

[4] *Galba* 8. 8, ἄνδρα τῶν ἀρίστων καὶ ὄντα καὶ δοκοῦντα. On Mauricus, *PIR²* I/J 771.

may well have written the *Lives of the Caesars* under Domitian, at a time when he was used to visiting Rome and knew Mauricus' brother, Arulenus Rusticus.[5]

Although the scheme of Plutarch's work recalls that of his younger contemporary, Suetonius, the two authors are far removed in purpose. While both eschew narrative history, Suetonius does so to marshal his minute facts more clearly: Plutarch professes to be concerned only with the notable actions and experiences of the Caesars.[6] In that claim he recalls a traditional distinction between the historian, whose first duty was to truth, and the biographer, who had licence to omit or adorn material as his purpose required.[7] Plutarch's statement in the *Caesars* closely resembles his assertions in the *Parallel Lives*, where again biography is distinguished from history by its selectivity and its use of personal details only as a guide to inner character.[8] Plutarch's *Caesars* are naturally much closer to his other biographies than to those of Suetonius.

Plutarch's ethical interest is clear from his practice as well as his principles. In the surviving *Lives*, the pictures of Galba and Otho are as favourable as the tradition allowed. Galba is upright and severe, his only faults parsimony and the congenital inclination of old age to follow bad advice.[9] Similarly, Otho is a study in contrasts, a man corrupt in life but not in spirit: the early days of his reign are a spring-time of hope and expectation, and his edifying death occupies about a fifth of the whole biography.[10] Certain subsidiary characters, on the other hand, are blackened irredeemably, for example Nymphidius Sabinus, T. Vinius, and Tigellinus.

Plutarch's liking for moral simplification becomes all the clearer when his account is compared to the parallel one of Cornelius Tacitus. Thus, among the several versions of Galba's last words that appear to have been current, Plutarch reports only the creditable one.[11] He inclines to believe that the armies

---

[5] So e.g. Th. Mommsen, *Gesammelte Schriften* 7 (1909), 226. On Plutarch's visits to Rome, above, pp. 20–5.

[6] *Galba* 2. 5.

[7] Polybius, 10. 21. 8, cf. Cicero, *ad fam.* 5. 12. 2–7, Nepos, *Pelop.* 16. 1. 1.

[8] *Alex.* 1; cf. pp. 103–6 below.

[9] *Galba* 29; contrast the famous obituary by Tacitus, *Hist.* 1. 49. 2–4.

[10] *Otho* 18. 3 (corruption), 1–3 (reign), 15–17 (death).

[11] *Galba* 27. 1, cf. Tac. *Hist.* 1. 41. 2, Suet. *Galba* 20. 1.

of Otho and Vitellius pondered leaving the choice of an emperor to the senate, a view that Tacitus decisively rejects.[12] Conversely, instances of extreme depravity that Tacitus ignores are included by Plutarch, for instance the grisly mutilation of Galba's head.[13]

This tendency to ennoble the principal figures and to disparage those who brought them bad advice or misfortune again anticipates the *Parallel Lives*. Even Antony, whom Plutarch professes to include in the series exceptionally as an example of bad character, is destroyed less by his innate qualities than by his evil genius, Cleopatra.[14] In both Plutarch's series of *Lives*, the laudatory traditions of the genre are reinforced by the philosopher's desire to instruct.

The *Lives of Galba and Otho* are therefore typical of their author, and presumably the lost *Lives* were no different. That conclusion is relevant to a much-discussed problem, that of the sources used by Plutarch for his account of the year 69. The prevailing view of his procedure can be summarized as follows. Between his account and the parallel parts of Tacitus' *Histories* there are many correspondences, some of which extend to whole paragraphs. These are too numerous to be explained by coincidence: and since Tacitus cannot be imagined to have consulted Plutarch, it must follow that both draw on a common source. Tacitus at least cannot have adapted his narrative of Roman history from a Greek: the unknown writer will therefore be one of the major Latin historians of these events. The two authors have not, however, followed the lost source equally closely, since they differ greatly in presentation and arrangement of their common facts. Tacitus, far superior as a historian and an artist, must have transformed the basic material to suit his needs, while Plutarch, though he may have abridged his source, reproduces faithfully the part of it that he has used. All that remains is to identify the lost historian among the rival candidates.[15]

In this view of the relationship between the two authors, Plutarch is little more than a lay figure: indeed, it owes its

---

[12] *Otho* 9. 5, cf. Tac. *Hist.* 2. 37–8.

[13] *Galba* 27. 4.

[14] *Demetr.* 1. 6; cf. especially *Ant.* 25. 1, 62. 1.

[15] R. Syme, *Tacitus* (1958), 180–90, 674–6, with previous bibliography. Subsequent discussions have not questioned the basic premises: H. Drexler, *Klio* 37 (1959), 153–78, M. Fuhrmann, *Philologus* 104 (1960), 264–9, R. Hanslik, *Wiener Studien* 74 (1961), 113–25, G. B. Townend, *AJP* 85 (1964), 337–77.

origin to a pardonable desire to look behind Tacitus' narrative at his methods of composition. It is time that the question was approached from a different direction, that of Plutarch. When the present view was formulated, Plutarch was widely considered a mere transcriber of lost sources, to which he contrived to give a gloss of novelty.[16] Only recently has a truer estimate of his achievement been reached, though it has had little effect on discussions of the present question.[17]

Plutarch's use of unwritten sources is of primary importance. It is evident from the *Table Talk* and other works that his society was devoted to long discussions on innumerable topics. The results are sometimes explicitly reported in his narrative and antiquarian works, for example the information about Antony's revels at Alexandria that came to him through a friend of his grandfather.[18] Nor is there any reason to believe that he invariably indicates to his readers which items of his knowledge derive from oral and which from written sources: such precision is not Plutarch's way.

In writing the *Lives of Galba and Otho* the biographer was concerned with events that had happened within recent memory, perhaps only twenty years before. It is in itself unlikely that these events had never been discussed in his society in such a way as to leave a mark on his writings. In fact, at least one item is stated by the author himself to derive from such a source, a strange phenomenon that his friend Mestrius Florus had observed after the first battle of Bedriacum.[19] Plutarch's description of Otho's tomb is also explicitly derived from autopsy.[20]

Another detail in these *Lives* can be referred to Plutarch himself. One of the explanations that he gives of Otho's eagerness to commit his troops to battle was 'recounted by the rhetor Secundus', and is contrasted with one that 'others were heard to give'.[21] There is no reason to think that this is transcribed from Plutarch's

---

[16] Thus F. Leo, *Die griechisch-römische Biographie* (1901), 155: 'seine Leistung ist eben die, dass ein Werk mit dem Schimmer des Neuen unter seinen Händen entsteht.'

[17] See especially C. Theander, *Plutarch und die Geschichte* (1951), P. A. Stadter, *Plutarch's Historical Methods* (1965).

[18] *Ant.* 28. 3–12. On Plutarch's oral sources see also Theander, *Eranos* 57 (1959), 99–131; Stadter, op. cit. 137–8.

[19] *Otho* 14. 2.

[20] *Otho* 18. 2.

[21] *Otho* 9. 3 ff. τοῦτο μὲν διηγεῖτο Σεκοῦνδος ὁ ῥήτωρ . . . ἑτέρων δ' ἦν ἀκούειν . . .

source. In the same *Life* he uses the expression again to refer to the experience described to him by Mestrius Florus, and it recurs with the same implication in the *Parallel Lives*.[22] Enough is known of Secundus to show that he is likely to have frequented the philhellenic circles that welcomed Plutarch to Rome, since he was a prominent orator and had attended the lectures of Nicetes, the rhetorician from Smyrna.[23]

There is furthermore no compulsion to regard the statements that Plutarch explicitly refers to Mestrius and Secundus as the only information that he had obtained from them or other of his friends. It has long been observed that his account of Nymphidius Sabinus and Galba's last days seems to derive from an eyewitness.[24] Now Mestrius is known to have been one of those senators mentioned by both Tacitus and Plutarch as Otho's unwilling followers, obliged to leave Rome with the emperor in March 69.[25] Some of Plutarch's knowledge of events both in Rome and in the north must derive from Mestrius, with whom he was later on terms of daily intercourse. The engagements of Otho's and Vitellius' troops involved, besides Mestrius, the father of another friend of Plutarch, the opulent king Philopappus.[26] When therefore Plutarch refers to unwritten accounts of those events,[27] he may be reporting what he had heard for himself and not merely transcribing the discoveries of a lost historian.

A further consideration militates against the view that Plutarch abridged the *Lives of Galba and Otho* from a lost Latin source. Fairly early in the composition of the *Parallel Lives*, he confesses that at the time of his travels to Rome and Italy he had not had time to practise Latin: it was only late in life that he had begun to read works in the language.[28] If the *Lives of the Caesars*

---

[22] *Otho* 14. 3–4, *Ant.* 28. 12, 68. 7. Cf. C. Theander, *Plutarch und die Geschichte* (1951), 7–11.

[23] C. P. Jones, *HSCP* 72 (1968), 285–6. For a possible connection of Plutarch with Smyrna and Nicetes, see above, pp. 14–15.

[24] Thus R. Syme, *Tacitus* (1958), 180–1: 'Something can be discovered about the author thus presumed. . . . He was present in Rome at the beginning of January 69.'

[25] *Otho* 14. 2; *Otho* 5. 2 with Tac. *Hist.* 1. 88. 1.

[26] Tac. *Hist.* 2. 25. 2, cf. p. 59 above.

[27] *Otho* 9. 4, ἑτέρων δ' ἦν ἀκούειν; *Otho* 14. 1, οὕτω μὲν οἱ πλεῖστοι τῶν παραγενομένων ἀπαγγέλλουσι . . .

[28] *Demosth.* 2. 2. The *Demosthenes-Cicero* was the fifth in the series of *Parallel Lives*, *Demosth.* 3. 1.

are in fact a work of an earlier period it is unlikely that they are based on a lost Latin source. Even in the *Parallel Lives* Plutarch has an evident preference for Greek sources rather than Latin: thus his account of Coriolanus is based on Dionysius of Halicarnassus, not on Livy.[29] It happens to be recorded by Josephus, if evidence were necessary, that the transactions of the year 69 had been narrated by many, both in Greek and in Latin.[30] Though Plutarch had some access to Roman sources,[31] any account that he used extensively is more likely to have been one of these lost Greek ones.

What then of the correspondences between Plutarch and Tacitus that have encouraged a general belief in the common source? Several considerations weaken their effect. One is a matter of perspective. Tabulated side by side in columns, these parallels look impressive. When the two accounts are read independently, however, the correspondences are more sparsely distributed, and the order in which they occur in the two authors is very different. Second, allowance must be made for identity of subject. Plutarch, for example, reports as his impression of Otho's tomb that 'neither by the size of the monument nor the loftiness of the inscription could it excite envy', while Tacitus states that it was 'modest and destined to endure'.[32] It requires faith to believe that Plutarch has merely transcribed what Tacitus has compressed into an epigram. It is no less difficult to accept that among the several Latin historians of these events, Plutarch and Tacitus should have lighted upon precisely the same one: all the more when the similarities of Suetonius' account are adduced to show that he too adopted the same historian for his main authority.[33]

These items may be thought sufficient to place in doubt the theory of a common source. There is something else, a hypothesis which, if false, does not weaken the general case. It is a cornerstone of the usual theory that Tacitus could not have inspected Plutarch's *Lives of the Caesars*.[34] Yet if he could write to the younger

---

[29] D. A. Russell, *JRS* 53 (1963), 21–8.   [30] *Bell. Iud.* 4. 496.
[31] Note the reference to Cluvius Rufus, *Otho* 3. 2. Usually assumed to be another borrowing from the lost source, but Plutarch cites Cluvius elsewhere, in a very different context, *quaest. Rom.* 289 C–D.
[32] *Otho* 18. 1; Tac. *Hist.* 2. 49. 4.
[33] e.g. by Mommsen, *Gesammelte Schriften* 7 (1909), 250–1.
[34] Thus Mommsen, art. cit. 227.

Pliny for details of the elder's death,[35] he may equally well have read over the account of a prominent Greek who had had friends among the witnesses of Galba's reign and Bedriacum. Just as Tacitus might have deplored shortcomings in lost *Lives* of the series,[36] so he may perhaps be seen correcting errors in the extant ones. Thus whereas Plutarch depicts one of the officers in the army of Upper Germany exhorting the troops to desert Galba for Vitellius, Tacitus turns aside to observe that, though some of them were conspicuous in raising sedition, none did so in a set speech: there was as yet no rival to make the risk worth while.[37] The same confrontation between optimism and realism can be seen when Plutarch reports from hearsay that the armies of Otho and Vitellius had meditated leaving the choice of an emperor to the senate. Tacitus notes that he had found this story in certain authors, and rebuts it in a long digression.[38] But if Tacitus had no sympathy for the Greek's outlook, he may yet have picked up a turn of phrase without making Plutarch a main source. If so, that further weakens the significance of correspondences between the two.

The *Galba and Otho* are typical of their author. Plutarch's primary interest is in moral rather than factual instruction. For this purpose educated Romans were as appropriate an audience as Greeks. If he glosses Latin terms in order to make them comprehensible to Greeks, that does not show that he did not expect to be read by Romans: the same is true of the *Parallel Lives*.[39] The attainment of perfect accuracy was alien to his purpose. The two extant *Lives*, like the *Parallel Lives*, are a mixture of information and opinions drawn from many quarters. If the author could use the results of autopsy or discussion with learned friends to supplement his narrative, so much the better: but there is no sign, for example, that he visited the Transpadane zone with the express purpose of gathering material for the *Otho*.[40]

[35] Pliny, *Epp.* 6. 16. 1.
[36] Above, p. 62.
[37] *Galba* 22. 5–8; Tac. *Hist.* 1. 55. 4.
[38] *Otho* 9. 5; Tac. *Hist.* 2. 37–8.
[39] *Galba* 12. 2, 24. 1, 24. 3. Similarly, later authors who explain Christian practices or terminology are not necessarily pagan themselves or writing for pagan audiences: Averil and Alan Cameron, *CQ* 14 (1964), 316–28, Averil Cameron, *Historia* 15 (1966), 470–1.
[40] As C. Theander has suggested, *Plutarch und die Geschichte* (1951), 8.

Of the other *Lives* of the series, there is only one of which it is now possible to form any idea, that of Augustus. To this there are two avenues of approach. The more reliable is the collection of the emperor's remarks preserved in the *Sayings of Kings and Generals*, since this work appears to consist in the main of excerpts from Plutarch's *Lives*, both extant and lost, and to have been fathered on the author at an early stage.[41] The sayings of Augustus which it preserves, though sometimes valuable for details of history,[42] do not suggest that Plutarch's biography was more than an admiring sketch: he may have conveyed the inscrutability of his subject without being able to penetrate it.[43]

The picture of the young Augustus in the *Parallel Lives* is a less helpful guide to the lost biography. His early political career, which is of course all that the *Lives* concern, is represented as cynical and bloodthirsty; there is a strong imputation of cowardice at Philippi; and his opponents are consistently represented as the champions of freedom.[44] This might at first sight appear inconsistent both with the fragments of the lost *Life of Augustus* and with Plutarch's evident acquiescence in the imperial system. There is in fact no difficulty. The notion that Augustus' rule changed with time, growing 'more kingly and public spirited', was a commonplace. It had grown naturally out of an implied claim of Augustan propaganda, that the emperor, after the necessary measures to defeat the hordes of the East, had transferred power from himself to the senate and turned a new leaf in his own history and the state's.[45] Nor is the term 'freedom' applied to the republican constitution in itself a sign of republican sympathies.[46] A close parallel to Plutarch is provided half a century later by the Greek Appian. Appian presents no less unfavourable a picture of the young Augustus than Plutarch, and similarly calls the system he helped to overthrow 'freedom', yet his own views are conventionally establish-

---

[41] *Reg. et imp. apophth.* 206 F-208 A. The view followed here is that of Wyttenbach, *Plutarchi Chaeronensis Moralia* 6 (1810), 1039–42: for a different one, Ziegler, *RE* 21 (1951), 863–5.

[42] Cf. G. W. Bowersock, *JRS* 51 (1961), 116, *CQ* 14 (1964), 120–1.

[43] Cf. the anecdotes in *Cic.* 49. 5, *Brut.* 58.

[44] *Cic.* 46. 6, *Brut.* 27. 1, 27. 4–5, 46. 2, *Ant.* 19. 4, 53. 1 (career); *Ant.* 22. 1–2 (Philippi); *Cic.* 46. 1, *Brut.* 39. 8, *Ant.* 19. 1, 89. 2 (freedom).

[45] Augustus' rule: *an seni sit ger. resp.* 784 D, cf. Cass. Dio, 66. 18. 5. Propaganda: R. Syme, *The Roman Revolution* (1939), 317, 459.

[46] Ch. Wirszubski, *Libertas* (1950), 127–9, 160.

mentarian.[47] It is also likely that in his *Life of Augustus* Plutarch presented his subject more favourably than in *Lives* of which others were the heroes, by a process of biographical distortion which is evident in the *Parallel Lives*.[48]

The other lost *Lives of the Caesars* have left even fewer traces than the *Augustus*, though from the *Galba and Otho* it is possible to surmise how Plutarch would have treated his material. Tiberius will have been a study in moral decline, all the vices breaking out as restraints vanished, though with the final verdict perhaps influenced by his philhellenic tastes.[49] Gaius will have been all depravity,[50] Claudius the prey of scheming wives and freedmen. Nero provided lessons in the deleterious effect of power on a weak and untrained mind, though allowance may have been made for flashes of virtue and, as in the *Life of Tiberius*, for devotion to the arts of Greece.[51] Vitellius, depicted as a weakling and debauchee, may have offered occasion for reflections on the uprightness and stable rule of his successors.

The *Lives of the Caesars*, to judge by the remains, were not the fruit of deep research or unorthodox views. Plutarch's interests were elsewhere, in the study of character. That is not to say that he had no interest in contemporary history, or no advice to give his readers about political behaviour. But the *Lives of the Caesars* were apolitical. In this, as in other respects, they forecast the *Parallel Lives*.

[47] On Appian's treatment of the young Augustus and 'freedom', see E. Gabba, *Appiano e la storia delle guerre civili* (1956), 177–206; for Appian's views, *praef.* 7, *bell. civ.* 1. 24, 4. 61–4.

[48] e.g. the Vettius affair of 59 B.C. is narrated by Plutarch only in the *Lucullus*, 42. 7–8, as a machination of Pompey's supporters: it is omitted from the *Pompey*.

[49] For Tiberius' philhellenic tastes in Plutarch, *de def. orac.* 419 D, fr. 182.

[50] Cf. *de superstit.* 170 E–F, fr. 211. It follows that at *Ant.* 87. 8 Plutarch cannot speak of Gaius as having ruled 'with distinction', ἐπιφανῶς: ἐπιμανῶς seems to be required, cf. duSoul quoted by Reiske in his edition of the *Parallel Lives* 5 (1776), 250.

[51] *De cohib. ira* 461 F, *praec. ger. reip.* 810 A (virtue); *de sera num. vind.* 567 F (philhellenism).

IX

THE *PARALLEL LIVES*:
SOURCES AND METHODS

AMONG Plutarch's works, the *Parallel Lives* hold a dominant place. So it was already in antiquity.[1] While the *Lives* are primarily documents for an age earlier than Plutarch's, they nevertheless contribute to the history of his own time. But no study of the *Lives*, whatever its aim, can by-pass the problem of assessing the author's own part in them: the sources that he used, his methods of composition, his purpose in writing.

These questions are particularly relevant to Plutarch's relations with Rome. If he appears to be little more than a transcriber of his sources, opinions that he expresses about Roman history and institutions may not be his own. If it emerges that at the time of writing his access to sources was limited, this will affect the verdict on his factual reliability.

One problem above all concerns Plutarch both as a student of the past and as a figure of his own day: his knowledge of Latin.[2] In the preface to the *Lives of Demosthenes and Cicero*, written early in the series but fairly late in Plutarch's life,[3] he makes his only direct statement on the subject. Virtue, and therefore happiness, were not qualities that depended on residence in a large city: but such a city, containing an abundance of books and information, was essential for one who planned a systematic history, since that required the use of rare and otherwise inaccessible

---

[1] Cf. Eunapius, *Vit. Philos.* 454, τὸ κάλλιστον αὐτοῦ τῶν συγγραμμάτων: Agathias, *Anth. Plan.* 16. 331. In the Lamprias Catalogue, the *Parallel Lives* are listed first. Of Plutarchean papyri, two are from the *Parallel Lives*, one from the spurious *de placitis philosophorum* (Roger A. Pack, *The Greek and Latin Literary Texts from Egypt*[2] [1965], nos. 1430–2: but cf. also no. 1223).

[2] On this vexed question see A. Sickinger, *De linguae Latinae apud Plutarchum et reliquiis et vestigiis* (diss. Heidelberg, 1883); W. Vornefeld, *De scriptorum Latinorum locis a Plutarcho citatis* (diss. Münster, 1901); H. J. Rose, *The Roman Questions of Plutarch* (1924), 11–19; C. Theander, *Plutarch und die Geschichte* (1951), 68–9.

[3] C. P. Jones, *JRS* 56 (1966), 66–70. Note ὀψέ ποτε καὶ πόρρω τῆς ἡλικίας, *Demosth.* 2. 2: cf. *Aem.* 10. 2, ἡλικίας . . . ἤδη πρόσω καὶ περὶ ἑξήκοντα γεγονὼς ἔτη.

books.[4] Chaeronea, however, was small, and even when Plutarch was in Italy, the pressure of duties had impeded him from acquiring a facility in Latin,[5] so that he had begun to read it only late in life. He then found that, rather than understanding what was described from the words, he was able to grasp the meaning of the words from his experience of affairs: but he did not have the time even now to acquire an appreciation of Latin style.[6]

From this preface several conclusions emerge. Without doing so directly, Plutarch appears to disclaim for his own work the status of a formal history, made as a result of systematic reading and inquiry. That accords with the distinction which he draws elsewhere between his own biographies and the more comprehensive interest of history.[7] Plutarch does not of course disavow all historical pretensions: both in the *Demosthenes and Cicero* and in other *Lives* he takes an evident pride in interjecting his own opinions and discoveries on historical topics.[8] But these additions are the result of casual and amateur inquiry: he means their presence to be counted to his credit, but not their absence to his discredit.[9]

Plutarch's statement about his Latin is part of the same disclaimer. It was not necessary for his purpose either to consult all the sources or to acquire a thorough knowledge of Latin. His unfamiliarity with it is shown by the misapprehension expressed in another work, that the Latin language had practically no prepositions.[10] It is true that in other *Lives* Plutarch does offer judgements on points of Latin style, though they may be tralatitious, and that he knows the meaning of many Latin words.[11]

---

[4] *Demosth.* 1–2. 1.   [5] γυμνάζεσθαι περὶ τὴν ῾Ρωμαϊκὴν διάλεκτον, *Demosth.* 2. 2.

[6] *Demosth.* 2. 3–4. It cannot be inferred that, because Plutarch says that he found himself (συνέβαινεν ἡμῖν) following words with difficulty, he was now past this stage: he is clearly distinguishing between his own knowledge and that required for an appreciation of style. For this imperfect cf. e.g. *Demosth.* 5. 5. ἐάσας τὰ λοιπὰ μαθήματα . . . αὐτὸς αὑτὸν ἤσκει, 'he began to train himself.'

[7] *Alex.* 1.

[8] e.g. *Demosth.* 7. 6, 9. 2, *Cic.* 49. 5. Cf. Theander, *Plutarch und die Geschichte* (1951), 2–32.

[9] Cf. *Demosth.* 1. 4, ἡμεῖς, εἴ τι τοῦ φρονεῖν ὡς δεῖ καὶ βιοῦν ἐλλείπομεν, τοῦτο . . . αὐτοῖς δικαίως ἀναθήσομεν, κτλ.

[10] *Quaest. Plat.* 1010 D.

[11] Style: *Caes.* 50. 4, cf. *Fab. Max.* 1. 8, *Cato min.* 5. 3, *Gracchi* 2. 3. Words: see especially *quaest. conviv.* 726 D-727 A, cf. L. Hahn, *Rom und Romanismus im griechisch-römischen Osten* (1906), 239–52.

His knowledge may have improved as he composed the *Lives*, but there is no sign either that he felt impeded by his lack of fluency or that he systematically tried to remedy it.

This conclusion appears at first sight to be at variance with the extensive use that Plutarch makes of Latin sources in the *Lives* and, more rarely, elsewhere.[12] In the *Lives* about twenty of these are quoted. Some are mentioned only once.[13] Others are cited more often, for example, the elder Cato and Sulla: Sulla's *Memoirs* are twice cited by book number, a practice that Plutarch seems to follow only when he has direct access to a work.[14] Plutarch sometimes comments on these sources in a way that suggests direct acquaintance with them: thus he summarizes a speech of Tiberius Gracchus to show the orator's persuasiveness and intensity, and observes that Cicero's readiness to praise others can be seen from his works.[15] Plutarch also attaches complimentary epithets to well-known works or authors, or the indefinite article to less familiar ones.[16] When his citations can be checked, they sometimes correspond so exactly with the original as to give a strong impression of first-hand knowledge.[17] To suppose that they are silently borrowed from intermediaries appears to contradict his practice, since he not infrequently admits that he knows of an author only at second hand.[18] While he clearly did not read Latin for pleasure, writing the *Parallel Lives* might seem to have impelled him to acquire a working knowledge of the indispensable sources.

To resolve this apparent contradiction it is necessary to consider the circumstances under which Plutarch wrote and the

---

[12] See now William C. Helmbold and Edward N. O'Neil, *Plutarch's Quotations* (1959), which however omits the following: L. Calpurnius Piso (*Numa* 21. 7), C. Calpurnius Piso (*Mar.* 45. 8–9), Rutilius Rufus (*Mar.* 28. 8, *Pomp.* 37. 4), and Sallust (*Luc.* 11. 6, 33. 3, *Sulla* 41. 3).

[13] e.g. C. Fannius, *Gracchi* 4. 6; Q. Dellius, *Ant.* 59. 7; P. Volumnius, *Brut.* 48. 2–5, 51. 1.

[14] Cato: H. Jordan, *M. Catonis quae extant* (1860), *incert. libr. frr.* 64–77. Sulla: Peter, *HRR* I² (1914), frs. 1, 4–8, 11–18, 20–1. Book numbers: *Sulla* 17. 2 = fr. 16, 37. 1–3 = fr. 21. Cf. the citations from Herodotus in the *de Herod. malign.* 857 A, 859 B, e.g.

[15] *Gracchi* 15. 1, *Cic.* 24. 4.

[16] Epithets: *Luc.* 42. 4, *Cic.* 2. 5. Γάϊος τις Πίσων: *Mar.* 45. 8.

[17] e.g. *Caes.* 44. 8 = Caes. *bell. civ.* 3. 92. 4; *Aem.* 10. 6–8 = Cic. *de div.* 1. 103; *Cato mai.* 23. 2–3 = Pliny, *NH* 29. 14.

[18] Instances in Rose, *The Roman Questions of Plutarch* (1924), 13, Theander, *Plutarch und die Geschichte* (1951), 54.

conventions of his age. If he himself was not fluent in Latin, that was in part a result of his western friends' fluency in Greek: on his stays in Italy he had not had time to practise the other language. The facility with which educated Romans read and spoke Greek is often noticed in the *Lives*, and when Plutarch introduces an Italian like Mestrius Florus into his dialogues talking Greek as fluently as a native, there is no reason to regard that as fantasy.[19] The bilingualism of his friends is relevant to his use of Latin sources. Just as he incorporated their opinions on Roman matters into his works,[20] so he will certainly have discussed with them Roman authors and points of Latinity.

The occasions on which Plutarch could consult his western friends may not have been frequent, and he would not have importuned them on minor matters. It does not follow, however, that he had no other help in Delphi or Chaeronea. For a man of his class and time, reading and writing were very different processes from their modern counterparts. It is clear, for instance, that much of the elder Pliny's literary work was done through the agency of freedmen and slaves.[21] Such agents would be particularly useful when they knew a language unfamiliar to their master, and such bilingual scribes and assistants are well attested.[22] Plutarch was easily rich enough to afford such helpers, even if he could not borrow them from a learned friend like Mestrius. Authors of his time were expected to use them, and acknowledgement was not the rule.[23] Plutarch may have inspected Latin texts for himself, but there is no sign that he did so extensively.

Moreover, the literary code of his time allowed wide liberties. No shame was attached to adapting large portions from the work of an earlier author, again without the necessity of acknowledgement. Plutarch himself does this in the *Coriolanus*, where his

---

[19] e.g. *Cic.* 4. 6–7, *Cato min.* 68. 2, *Brut.* 4. 8, 17. 5, *Flam.* 5. 7. Mestrius: see especially *quaest. conviv.* 684 F-685 A, 734 C–D. Cf. also *de frat. am.* 479 E, an exchange turning on the word μόρια between Plutarch and a Roman.

[20] *Rom.* 15. 3–4, *Numa* 8. 20, *Otho* 9. 3, 14. 2, *quaest. Rom.* 271 C.

[21] Pliny, *Epp.* 3. 5. 10–17.

[22] Pliny, *NH* 25. 7 (a freedman of Pompey translating the medical notebooks of Mithridates VI), *ILS* 7753.

[23] *Cic. ad Att.* 6. 2. 3, *ad fam.* 16. 21. 8; Quintilian, 10. 1. 128; A. Gell. 13. 9. 1, 15. 6. 2. Cf. H. Peter, *Wahrheit und Kunst* (1911), 442: 'fremde Mitarbeit wurde damals allgemein als selbstverständlich angesehn, trat aber neben dem Verfasser, den der Titel nannte, in das Dunkel zurück.'

main source, Dionysius of Halicarnassus, is only mentioned incidentally in the final comparison: no source at all is named in the *Sertorius*, though it clearly draws heavily on Sallust.[24] These borrowings might include, as well as matters of fact, judgements of value. Thus Plutarch shows no trace of having read the Roman poets subsequent to Cicero whom he describes as 'gifted' or the work of the orator that he calls 'very beautiful'.[25] Quotations found in the exemplar might be carried over into the adaptation, sometimes with the name of the immediate source attached to the list of authorities.[26] An author might rely extensively on his memory, citing the rough tenor of his original rather than the exact words, and sometimes introducing considerable errors.[27] In Plutarch such freedom is all the more to be expected because of his literary purposes. His aim was to depict character and provide examples for imitation, not to write history or compete with the standard authors.[28] Though he abhors deliberate falsehood, he is not bothered by casual inaccuracy.

All these considerations, the availability of helpers, the prevailing conventions, affect the question of Plutarch's Latin sources. It is usually conceded that he may not have used some of the authors and works that he mentions only incidentally: for example, though he observes that the oration delivered by Fabius Maximus at his son's funeral is extant, he borrows his judgement of its style from others.[29] But there is equally little reason to think that he personally inspected all the authors that he cites extensively. The elder Cato was no stylist for a man who had difficulty following a Latin sentence, yet when writing his

[24] *Alc.* 41. 4, cf. D. A. Russell, *JRS* 53 (1963), 21–8. *Sertorius*: H. Peter, *Die Quellen Plutarchs in den Biographieen der Römer* (1865), 61–5, B. Maurenbrecher, *C. Sallusti Crispi Historiarum Reliquiae* 1 (1891), 27–31. P. A. Stadter has shown that Polyaenus draws similarly on Plutarch's *mulierum virtutes*: *Plutarch's Historical Methods* (1965), 13–29. 'Durchaus verkehrt und unhistorisch ist es, von der Nichtangabe der Quellen eine absichtliche Irreführung der Leser abzuleiten', E. Stemplinger, *Das Plagiat in der griechischen Literatur* (1912), 185.

[25] *Cic.* 2. 5, *Luc.* 42. 4.

[26] Cf. J. R. Hamilton, *Plutarch, Alexander: A Commentary* (1969), 124–5, discussing *Alex.* 46. 1; Stemplinger, op. cit. 182.

[27] Cf. Russell, art. cit. 22; an error of Polyaenus in transcribing Plutarch, Stadter, op. cit. 24.

[28] *Cimon* 2. 2–5, *Per.* 1–2. 4, *Nic.* 1. 5, *Aem.* 1. 1–5, *Alex.* 1, *Demetr.* 1, *Pomp.* 8. 7. Cf. pp. 103–6 below.

[29] *Fab. Max.* 1. 8–9.

Life Plutarch quotes him frequently. To infer that Plutarch himself had used Cato is to ignore the circumstances of his time. In order to write a *Life* for which a Latin source was indispensable, he may have had a translation or extracts made by an assistant: the occasional inaccuracy of his translations may be due to this helper, since the person need not have been perfectly bilingual or scrupulously careful.[30] Shorter quotations may have been supplied by interested friends. Sometimes Greek versions of Latin works will have been already available. Sallust's *Histories* were translated near the time when Plutarch wrote the *Sertorius*, which is evidently based on them.[31] It is hard to believe that Augustus, whose *Res Gestae* were set up in cities of the East both in Latin and in Greek, did not also secure a wide audience for other of his works by having them translated. Plutarch's knowledge of the emperor's *Autobiography* may derive from such a version.[32]

Even if Plutarch did not make extensive use of Latin sources, he had no lack of material for those of the *Lives* that touch Roman history. The old view that he found his information already digested in earlier biographies has been generally abandoned: Plutarch had a deep interest in history and antiquities, and read extensively in Greek histories.[33] Such works, some of them written by Romans, will have supplied most of his information about Roman history. Thus the basic material for the *Coriolanus* appears to have been drawn entirely from Dionysius of Halicarnassus.[34] Sometimes the Greek sources will have been supplemented or replaced by Latin ones, for which

[30] On this see Rose, *The Roman Questions of Plutarch* (1924), 16–18; add *Cic.* 7. 8 = Pliny, *NH* 34. 48 (*domi habere*, 'to have at hand', rendered as ἐπὶ τῆς οἰκίας ἔχειν).

[31] *Suda*, Z 73 Adler.

[32] *Cic.* 45. 6, 52. 1, *Brut.* 27. 3, 41. 7, *Ant.* 68. 2 = H. Malcovati, *Imperatoris Caesaris Augusti Operum Fragmenta*⁴ (1967), *Opera Historica* frs. 8–10, 12, 17. This remains true, even if Nicolaus of Damascus' Βίος Καίσαρος was based on the *Autobiography* and appeared shortly after it (cf. Jacoby, *FGrHist* II C, p. 264): cf. the multiplication of histories commemorating Pompey's exploits. See now the papyrus fragment from a Greek version of Augustus' funeral oration for Agrippa, L. Koenen, *Zeitschrift für Papyrologie und Epigraphik* 5 (1970), 217–83. There is, however, no evidence for a Greek translation of Pollio's *Histories*: R. Häussler, *Rheinisches Museum* 109 (1966), 339–55.

[33] See now P. A. Stadter, *Plutarch's Historical Methods* (1965), 125–40; J. R. Hamilton, *Plutarch, Alexander: A Commentary* (1969), xliii–xlvi.

[34] D. A. Russell, *JRS* 53 (1963), 28. For a conspectus of the Greek sources of the Roman *Lives*, see Theander, *Plutarch und die Geschichte* (1951), 67–8.

Plutarch used translations or the advice of others. To this basic material he added freely from his own store of knowledge gathered by autopsy, conversation, or incidental reading. Not improbably he preferred to work from memory and by dictation: that will have facilitated the insertion of extraneous material and welded the whole evenly together.[35]

Though Plutarch depended on others for information, the stamp that he gave to that information is his own. When his sources are extant, he can be shown to have adapted them to his own purpose, clothing them in his style and vocabulary and imposing his own interpretation on the material before him.[36] The views that he expresses on Roman history, therefore, can be taken to be his: they may not be original or profound, but they are a part of his attitude to Rome.

[35] Memory: *Per.* 24. 12, *Crass.* 35. 3. Dictation: there is no explicit evidence, but this appears to have been common practice when a work was written at speed, as Plutarch's evidently were: Cic. *ad Att.* 13. 25. 3, Quintilian, 10. 3. 19–22. Plutarch's use of γράφω and its cognates, e.g. *Demosth.* 3. 1, of course does not show that he wrote in his own hand: cf. Rom. 16: 22, I Cor. 16: 21, Col. 4: 18, I Pet. 5: 12, etc. So also *scribo* in Latin: e.g. Cic. *ad Att.* 14. 6. 2, 12. 3, 21. 4.

[36] Style: e.g. on Plutarch's prose rhythm, A. W. de Groot, *A Handbook of antique Prose-Rhythm* (1918), 40–58. Vocabulary: e.g. Hubert Martin, Jr. *GRBS* 3 (1960), 65–73, *AJP* 82 (1961), 164–75. Interpretation: e.g. D. A. Russell, *JRS* 53 (1963), 26–8, and below, pp. 89–102.

X

THE *PARALLEL LIVES*:
VIEWS OF ROMAN HISTORY

WHEN Plutarch turned to writing biography, he adopted a genre for which convention had long since drawn up flexible rules. Polybius had distinguished biography from history as a field closer to formal laudation, in which the writer was bound to magnify the actions of his subject: and even the historian sometimes had a duty to be partial.[1] Plutarch, who came to biography as a philosopher and not as a historian, was not likely to adopt more stringent standards than Polybius. In his essay on Herodotus, he expounds a doctrine of historiography that preferred lenience to severity, patriotism to impartiality, optimism to pessimism.[2] The *Lives* show the application of these principles. Faced with a fault in his hero, the biographer should treat it as an artist treated a blemish in his sitter's face, drawing as little attention to it as truth allowed.[3] Truth itself was as much the business of the moralist as of the historian to discern: Plutarch more than once decides matters of fact by reference to character.[4] He is much more ready to detect and criticize malice than favouritism in his authorities, though in the conventional way he deplores both as an obstruction in the search for truth.[5] This assimilation of factual to moral criteria was encouraged by the language, in which the same word served for both 'a lie' and 'an error', 'preferable' and 'more creditable', 'probable' and 'equitable'.[6]

An author for whom truth and goodwill are so closely akin can be expected to allow his opinions and interests to shape his narrative, and in fact the *Lives* reveal many of their author's views, for example on the virtues of the female character.[7] The

---

[1] Polybius, 10. 21. 8; 16. 14. 6.   [2] *De Herod. malign.* 854 E-856 D.

[3] *Cimon* 2. 3-5.

[4] e.g. *Solon* 27. 1, *Cato min.* 52. 6-8, *Ant.* 6. 1-2, *Pomp.* 49. 13-14.

[5] *Per.* 13. 16.   [6] Viz. ψεῦδος, βελτίων, εἰκός.

[7] P. A. Stadter, *Plutarch's Historical Methods* (1965), 1-12.

Lives also reveal a coherent set of beliefs about Roman history, and these in turn help to reveal Plutarch's view of Rome in his own time. For brevity and clarity, three topics will be considered: the reign of Romulus, the beginning of Roman intervention in Greece, and the decline of the Roman republic.

The foundation of Rome had been a subject of interest to the Greeks long before the beginning of Roman historiography. Many influences came to shape the tradition: borrowings from Greek legend, the desire to reconcile conflicting chronologies and to give a rational explanation of myths. The legend also served as propaganda. Greek writers hostile to Rome seized on incidents from the legend of its foundation to belittle its claims or to find early models for its later crimes. Other Greeks laboured to replace this picture with one more agreeable: the Romans were in fact of the same race as the Greeks, their customs were no less enlightened, their heroes models of bravery and moderation. Under the emperor Augustus, when the victory of Actium had ended the need for propaganda against the East, a crop of writers sprang up to promote the message of reconciliation and concord.[8]

In depicting Romulus, therefore, Plutarch was faced with abundant but conflicting evidence. The *Life* shows the use of several sources, almost all now lost, of whom the principal appear to be Fabius Pictor, Varro, and the learned king, Juba of Mauretania.[9] Despite the admittedly fabulous material, Plutarch's aim is no different from that of the other *Lives*: to record the memorable facts about his subject,[10] to trace his life from birth through education and deeds to his death, with emphasis on those incidents that best revealed his character.[11] The result is a typically Plutarchean hero, a warrior and a statesman finally made oppressive by pride.[12]

Just as the *Romulus* is typical in its aim, so it is in the optimistic treatment of its subject. Among the various versions of the birth and upbringing of Romulus and Remus, Plutarch considers the

---

[8] E. Gabba, *Rivista storica italiana* 71 (1959), 361–8; G. W. Bowersock, *Augustus and the Greek World* (1965), 108–11, 122–39.

[9] H. Peter, *Die Quellen Plutarchs in den Biographieen der Römer* (1865), :46–62.

[10] *Rom.* 30. 1, ἄξια μνήμης. For this phrase cf. *Cato mai.* 28. 1, *Fab. Max.* 1. 1, *Alc.* 40. 1, *Cic.* 50. 1, e.g.

[11] Thus *Rom.* 6. 3, 7. 2, 14. 1–2, 26. 1, 31. 1, 32. 2.

[12] Thus cf. *Rom.* 26. 1 with *Caes.* 60. 1.

most probable to be that of Fabius Pictor, who in turn drew on the obscure Diocles of Peparethos.[13] This apparently made the twins the children of Mars: miraculously saved from the cruelty of their great-uncle, they were suckled by the wolf, and grew up to avenge their grandfather Numitor and to set their mother free from captivity. Plutarch knew that this version was rejected by some as a fiction, but he saw no reason not to follow it: chance could do extraordinary things, and Rome would not have attained her great power without divine aid at the beginning.[14] In so justifying his belief, Plutarch echoes a favourite conviction of Augustan historiography.[15]

No part of the lore of Rome's foundation had caused more embarrassment than the murder of Remus. The familiar tradition, already related by Ennius, made Romulus kill his brother with his own hand, and in time lent material to those who wished to trace Roman ruthlessness back to the city's origin.[16] New versions were duly produced. Remus had died by an unknown hand in a riot, or a certain Celer, set to guard the new walls of Rome and angered by his mockery, had struck him down. Romulus assuaged his grief by giving his brother posthumous honours, and the two were reconciled in death. This was the version favoured by Greek friends of Rome and broadcast by Roman poets of the Augustan age.[17] Faced with this divergence, Plutarch again follows the favourable version, though not without consideration for the other. While he mentions the tradition that made Romulus the murderer, he puts last, and lays most stress upon, the agency of Celer.[18] In his tolerance of the less creditable version, Plutarch differs sharply from Dionysius of Halicarnassus. The Augustan writer preferred to think that Remus had died in a riot, though for the

---

[13] *Rom.* 3. 1–8. 9 = Fabius Pictor, fr. 5a Peter, *FGrHist* 809 F 4a, Diocles, *FGrHist* 820 F 2. For Plutarch's method of citing the immediate and secondary source together, cf. *Cato min.* 25. 2, 37. 1.

[14] *Rom.* 8. 9.

[15] Cf. Livy, 1. 4. 1, 'sed debebatur...fatis tantae origo urbis maximique secundum deorum opes imperii principium'; 1. 4. 4, 'forte quadam divinitus', with the comments of R. M. Ogilvie, *A Commentary on Livy Books 1–5* (1965), 48–9, and below, p. 99.

[16] Ennius, *Ann.* 99–100 Vahlen; 'volgatior fama', Livy, 1. 7. 2. Ruthlessness: Justin, *Epit.* 28. 2. 10, cf. H. Fuchs, *Der geistige Widerstand gegen Rom* (1938), 45, n. 46.

[17] Diod. Sic. 8. 6. 3; Livy, 1. 7. 2; Virgil, *Aen.* 1. 292; Ovid, *Fasti* 4. 809–56; Dion. Hal. *Ant. Rom.* 1. 87. Cf. R. Schilling, *REL* 38 (1960), 182–99; Ogilvie, op. cit. 54.

[18] *Rom.* 10. 2–3, cf. 34. 1.

sake of completeness he was ready to relate the story of Celer. Dionysius' concern for the truth, however, could not bring him to mention Romulus as his brother's murderer.[19]

A similar attitude is shown by Plutarch's handling of another vexed question, the character of Rome's early settlers. The familiar version made the nucleus of the future population shepherds who had collected around Romulus and Remus at Alba. The brothers then went with their followers to found a new city near the spot where they had been suckled by the wolf. After the death of Remus, Romulus increased the population by establishing an asylum to which all could resort, many of them slaves and fugitives. Then, seeing his followers without wives and despised by the neighbouring communities, he devised the stratagem of seizing the womenfolk of the Sabines during a festival at Rome. The ensuing war between the two peoples was ended by the intervention of the Sabine women, so that they joined together under a dual kingship.[20]

This myth also lent itself readily to Rome's detractors. The city, they claimed, began as nothing more than a refuge for barbarians, mere runaways and outlaws.[21] The land on which it was founded had been stolen from its rightful owners: unable to find wives because of their low origin, the first settlers had taken them in open violence.[22] Plutarch's procedure is again to give a hearing to the harsher version, but to prefer the kinder. The decision to found a new city he ascribes to the desire of the two brothers to make their own settlement in the place where they had been reared, since that was the most honourable explanation: perhaps it was also true that the slaves and runaways who had gathered around them made their departure from Alba unavoidable.[23] Plutarch's formulation shows him to be aware of less flattering explanations, and these can be recovered in part from Dionysius: Numitor, the king of Alba, was afraid that the youths' followers might conspire against him, and so gave his grandsons the site for the new city.[24] Similarly,

---

[19] Dion. Hal. *Ant. Rom.* 1. 87.

[20] Cf. Fabius Pictor, fr. 7 Peter = *FGrHist* 809 F 5 (Sabine women); Cato, *Orig.* fr. 20 Jordan, Peter (asylum); Ennius, *Ann.* 101–8 Vahlen (Sabine women); Cic. *de rep.* 2. 12–13.

[21] Dion. Hal. *Ant. Rom.* 1. 4. 2, 1. 89. 1; Justin, *Epit.* 38. 6. 7–7. 1. Cf. Fuchs, op. cit. 15–17.   [22] Sallust, *Hist.* 4. 69. 17 M.; Justin, *Epit.* 28. 2. 9.

[23] *Rom.* 9. 1–2.   [24] *Ant. Rom.* 1. 85. 1–2.

Plutarch makes a Delphic oracle responsible for Romulus' willingness to admit all comers to the asylum.[25]

The supposed inferiority of the first settlers had also been used to explain the name of 'fathers' given to the first senators and of 'patricians' to their descendants. Dionysius ascribes to certain malicious authors the view that the 'patricians' were so called because only they could point out their fathers, whereas the rest of the population consisted of runaways whose fathers were slaves: he himself supposed that the first senators were called 'fathers' as wealthy men who already had children, and were therefore older and more distinguished than the other citizens, while their children were named 'patricians' after them.[26] Plutarch considers and rejects several reasons for the names, one of which is the malicious one scorned by Dionysius. The most probable view, in his opinion, is that Romulus wished the senators to look after the people with fatherly care, and so called them 'fathers'.[27]

Plutarch's treatment of the legend of the Sabine women is of the same kind. Unnamed authors reported that Romulus, persuaded by some oracle that it was Rome's fate to grow great by war, deliberately provoked hostilities with the Sabines. In evidence, it was alleged that the thirty *curiae* were named after the captured women, and thirty was too small a number for Romulus' aim merely to have been that of finding wives for his subjects.[28] To Plutarch this view seemed improbable: Romulus' real wish was at once to find wives for the Romans and to achieve confederation with the Sabines.[29] So far from numbering thirty, the women had in fact been above five or six hundred; later, by an indicative lapse, Plutarch makes them nearly eight hundred.[30] Moreover, they were not married women, except for one who was captured by mistake: all the rest were virgins, which proved the purity of Romulus' intentions.[31] Nor was it true that the *curiae* were called after the captured women, since many of them were called after places.[32]

Again, Plutarch is influenced by apologetic versions of Roman history propagated under Augustus. For Dionysius Romulus'

[25] *Rom.* 9. 3.

[26] Dion. Hal. *Ant. Rom.* 2. 8.

[27] *Rom.* 13. 3–5.

[28] *Rom.* 14. 1, 20. 3.

[29] *Rom.* 14. 2.

[30] *Rom.* 14. 7, 35. 2.

[31] *Rom.* 14. 7.

[32] *Rom.* 20. 3.

only motive is to achieve confederation with the Sabines, though the historian mentions as less plausible the explanation that the Romans needed wives or that Romulus wished to provoke war.[33] Dionysius describes all the captured women without exception as virgins, and makes them nearly seven hundred in number, with no mention of conflicting reports.[34] While he is prepared to concede that the *curiae* were named after the thirty women who reconciled Romans and Sabines,[35] he makes no mention of the account criticized by Plutarch, that they were named after the women originally captured by Romulus. Livy, though less anxious than Dionysius to purify the tradition, ascribes to Romulus only the motive of seeking wives for his subjects, and considers it indubitable that the captives numbered more than thirty.[36] Again, the two Greeks stand in contrast. Plutarch, while he rejects the traditions unfavourable to Romulus, does not follow Dionysius in suppressing them.

Plutarch's bias in Romulus' favour is visible in many other parts of the *Life*. Thus he rejects the tradition that Tarpeia, who betrayed the Capitol to the Sabines, had been appointed to guard it by Romulus: that made him out to be a fool, and in fact Tarpeia was the daughter of the guard.[37] Again, Plutarch agrees with the Augustan historians.[38] The story of the death of Tatius is told so as to absolve Romulus of all blame: he failed to avenge his co-regent's death, not because he was glad of it, but to avoid causing faction among his subjects.[39] Among the various versions of Romulus' death, Plutarch acknowledges the one that made the senators his murderers, but gives much greater emphasis to that of his miraculous disappearance and the vision of Julius Proculus.[40] Here Plutarch is closer to Latin writers of the Augustan period than to Dionysius, who preferred to make Romulus the victim of the senate or the newly enrolled citizens.[41] The Greek was perhaps too heavily influenced by recent events to admit this miracle with all the others.[42]

[33] Dion. Hal. *Ant. Rom.* 2. 31. 1.　　[34] Ibid. 2. 30–1.
[35] Ibid. 2. 47. 3.　　[36] Livy, 1. 9. 1, 13. 7.
[37] *Rom.* 17. 2.
[38] Livy, 1. 11. 6, Dion. Hal. *Ant. Rom.* 2. 38. 2. Ovid, however, makes Tarpeia the *custos, Fasti* 1. 261.　　[39] *Rom.* 23. 1–5.
[40] *Rom.* 27–8.
[41] Livy, 1. 16; Ovid, *Fasti* 2. 475–512; Dion. Hal. *Ant. Rom.* 2. 56.
[42] R. Syme, *The Roman Revolution* (1939), 306, n. 2, 313–14.

Plutarch's depiction of Romulus is visibly intended to flatter its subject, and strongly resembles versions propagated under Augustus, when Rome became concerned to placate Greek opinion and to reconcile it to the new order.[43] It does not, however, follow that Plutarch wrote like Dionysius for the express purpose of winning goodwill for Rome.[44] It has already been seen that his conception of biography predisposed him to favour friendly over unfriendly traditions. This tendency was reinforced in the *Romulus* by the fabulous nature of the subject. Believing that a narrator should choose the more creditable of two versions when in doubt,[45] Plutarch was all the more likely to indulge his subject when the truth was admittedly beyond recall. Moreover, though he is biased in Romulus' favour, he does not have the extreme bias of Dionysius. The Augustan writer could not be induced to mention the story that Romulus killed Remus, or that he had been urged by an oracle to make war on the Sabines.[46] Plutarch, while he does not accept such traditions, is not embarrassed by them. Here again he obeys his own rules of biography. If a painter suppressed every blemish in his subject, the portrait would not be lifelike.[47] The question whether the *Parallel Lives* are written with the ulterior motive of winning goodwill for Rome requires separate consideration:[48] but an analysis of the *Romulus* does not help to answer it affirmatively.

The account of the liberation of Greece which is the core of the *Flamininus* is the product of a similar view of biography. Here again the author is concerned to portray character through deeds, though his propensity to reduce it to one basic drive, in this *Life* ambition,[49] is here more easily realized. Again, Plutarch inclines to present his subject favourably, and the same general notions of Roman history are present. Yet the *Flamininus* has an important difference from the *Romulus*. In the other *Life*, though

---

[43] E. Gabba, *Rivista storica italiana* 71 (1959), 365; G. W. Bowersock, *Augustus and the Greek World* (1965), 123–4.

[44] Observe e.g. *Ant. Rom.* 1. 4–5, 1. 89. 1. Cf. E. Schwartz, *RE* 5 (1903), 958–60 = *Griechische Geschichtschreiber* (1957), 355–7; Gabba, art. cit. 368.

[45] *De Herod. malign.* 855 F, ὁ δ' ἱστορίαν γράφων ἃ μὲν οἶδεν ἀληθῆ λέγειν δίκαιός ἐστι, τῶν δ' ἀδήλων τὰ βελτίονα δοκεῖν ἀληθῶς λέγεσθαι μᾶλλον ἢ τὰ χείρονα. On the fabulosity of the *Theseus and Romulus*, *Thes.* 1, *Rom.* 12. 6.

[46] Contrast *Ant. Rom.* 2. 32. 1 with *Rom.* 14. 1.

[47] *Cimon* 2. 3–4.

[48] Below, pp. 103 ff.

[49] φιλοτιμία: *Philop.* 15. 1, *Flam.* 5. 7, 7. 2, 9. 5, 13. 2–3, 20. 1, 22. 4.

the sources used by Plutarch can be partly reconstructed from the extant ones, they can only be observed indirectly. Much of the *Flamininus*, however, is adapted from Polybius, and in particular from the eighteenth book of which a large part survives for comparison.[50] In certain places Plutarch can be seen adding material from elsewhere, but these insertions are sharply demarcated: there is none of the interweaving of traditions visible in the *Romulus*. He treats his source with freedom, but that is a characteristic of his adaptations, and no reason to suspect an intermediary.[51] Plutarch had read Polybius for himself.[52]

In Greece, Flamininus' ambition is manifested as the desire to be hailed as the saviour and liberator of the Greeks. Hence one of his first actions in his province is to offer peace to his antagonist, Philip V of Macedon, on condition that the Macedonian will let the Greeks be independent and will remove his garrisons. When Philip refuses, it becomes clear to all, even to those who had favoured his cause, that the Romans have come, not to fight the Greeks, but to fight the Macedonians on behalf of the Greeks. As a result of this impasse, both Philip and Flamininus send ambassadors to the Roman senate.[53] Plutarch has in fact drastically compressed the narration of Polybius. In the lost seventeenth book, Polybius narrated the conference between Flamininus and Philip on the banks of the Aous, in which Flamininus had indeed made the King's abandonment of his Greek possessions an indispensable condition of peace,[54] and this is clearly the occasion meant by Plutarch. He has omitted, however, the later conference held between the combatants and their respective allies at Locrian Nicaea in November 198.[55] From Polybius' detailed and suggestive account it emerges that, while the allies wanted Flamininus to force upon Philip the conditions

---

[50] Established by H. Nissen, *Kritische Untersuchungen über die Quellen der vierten und fünften Dekade des Livius* (1863), 290–2; cf. H. Peter, *Die Quellen Plutarchs in den Biographieen der Römer* (1865), 80–1, R. E. Smith, *CQ* 38 (1944), 89–95.

[51] Cf. D. A. Russell, *JRS* 53 (1963), 28, on Plutarch's use of Dionysius in the *Coriolanus*.

[52] Cf. C. Theander, *Plutarch und die Geschichte* (1951), 52–3; P. A. Stadter, *Plutarch's Historical Methods* (1965), 108–10, 129.

[53] *Flam.* 5. 8, 7. 1.

[54] Livy, 32. 10. 2–8, especially 3.

[55] Polybius, 18. 1–10. 2. On the date see F. W. Walbank, *A Historical Commentary on Polybius* 2 (1967), 548–9.

offered at the Aous or else to defeat him once for all, the Roman was ready to comply with the king's suggestion that the matter be referred to the senate.[56] Only then were the embassies sent. Plutarch, besides omitting to explain how they came to be in Rome, gives an entirely different impression from Polybius of Flamininus' motives and disposition.

After the senate had rejected Philip's terms, the issue was decided by the battle of Cynoscephalae in June 197. Plutarch's account again compresses Polybius' and introduces significant changes.[57] Before the battle, Plutarch represents the Romans as eager to defeat the Macedonians, whose name recalled the exploits of Alexander, while the Macedonians, thinking Rome greater than Persia, hoped to prove Philip more glorious than Alexander. Similarly, Flamininus haranguing his troops before the battle reminds them that they are about to fight the best of adversaries, the Macedonians, before the noblest of spectators, the Greeks.[58] In the corresponding passage of Polybius, there is no mention of Alexander or Persia: that is imported by Plutarch, who habitually liked to regard great events in history as inspired by earlier examples, notably that of Alexander.[59] In Polybius, so far from glorifying the Macedonians, Flamininus recalls their previous defeats at Roman hands: here it is Plutarch's patriotism that has led him to recast the original.[60]

Plutarch ends his account of the battle with the statement that the Aetolians were to blame for letting Philip escape, since they had started to plunder his camp while the Romans continued the pursuit.[61] In this he has not merely absorbed the prejudice that made Polybius belittle the Aetolian contribution to the victory: Polybius makes clear that the Romans were no less greedy for booty than the Aetolians, and implies that they were to blame for Philip's escape.[62]

---

[56] Polybius, 18. 9–10. 2. On this suggestion, apparently initiated by Flamininus himself, see Walbank, op. cit. 559–60.

[57] Polybius, 18. 18–33; *Flam.* 7. 4–8. 9.   [58] *Flam.* 7. 5–6.

[59] Cf. *Caes.* 11. 5–6, *Pyrrh.* 19. 2, *Pomp.* 2. 2–4.

[60] Polybius, 18. 23. On Greece as τὸ κάλλιστον θέατρον cf. p. 52, n. 21 above. For Plutarch's rewriting of a speech in his source, cf. also *Cor.* 35. 2–9, 36. 2–3 with Dion. Hal. *Ant. Rom.* 8. 48–53; D. A. Russell, *JRS* 53 (1963), 26. There is therefore no reason to assume another source, though Plutarch has added from elsewhere the bad omen that attended the oration of Philip, *Flam.* 7. 7.

[61] *Flam.* 8. 9. αἰτίαν ἔλαβον may, however, mean only 'were blamed'.

[62] Polybius, 18. 27. 1–6.

At the Isthmia of 196, Flamininus staged the famous declaration of Greek independence. This part of Plutarch's account, where his patriotic sympathies and his own memories were engaged, clearly betrays his intervention. In Polybius, the ten commissioners sent by the senate arrive in Greece with a resolution ordering Philip to free the cities of Greece in which he has garrisons, including the 'three fetters' of Acrocorinth, Demetrias, and Chalcis, and to hand these last over to the Romans. When the Aetolians spread the report that Rome plans to retain these cities for itself, Flamininus is forced to urge the commissioners to make the liberation of Greece unconditional; they then agree to free the lower city of Corinth immediately, but retain the three fetters for a short while longer. Polybius then narrates Flamininus' declaration at the games, emphasizing the general doubt that the Romans would honour their promises. After describing the general elation that greeted the declaration, he adds his own brief comment: it was amazing both that the Romans should have undergone so much trouble and expense to secure the freedom of Greece and that chance should have put no obstacle in the way of fortune.[63]

In Plutarch's account, the commissioners merely advise Flamininus to retain the three fetters: details irrelevant to the biographer's purpose, like the decree of the senate and the arrangements for the other occupied cities, are shorn away. The Aetolians then spread agitation among the Greeks with specious accusations: the Romans are merely replacing the old yoke of Greece with a smoother, but heavier, one, Flamininus has set the foot free and bound the neck. Thus the Aetolians kindle Flamininus' innate ambition, and he persuades the commissioners to surrender the three cities.[64] The accusations that Plutarch gives to the Aetolians are his own composition,[65] a substitute for the technicalities in Polybius; and the biographer has put the return of the three fetters before the declaration at Corinth in order to heighten the dramatic effect.

The description of the declaration itself follows Polybius

---

[63] Polybius, 18. 44–6.

[64] *Flam.* 10. 1–3. The language used of the Aetolian agitation, λαμπροὶ λαμπρῶς τὰς πόλεις ἀνερρήγνυσαν, is of course sarcastic: for this use of λαμπρός, like καλός, cf. Demosth. 21. 174, Lucian, *de merc. cond.* 30.

[65] The metaphor of the yoke is borrowed from a remark of Philip, cf. *de Herod. malign.* 855 A; for that of the foot and the neck cf. *praec. ger. reip.* 814 E.

closely, though Plutarch characteristically does not mention the general mistrust of Roman intentions, and adds from elsewhere one striking detail, that of the birds stunned by the shout of joy.[66] Then he returns to Polybius, and describes in similar language the attentions paid to Flamininus after the games. What follows, however, appears to be his own concoction. Taking his cue from Polybius' comment on the event, Plutarch represents the Greeks at their celebrations meditating on their country's history. The famous heroes of Greece had won battles, but brought no good to their fatherland: with a few exceptions, all the great victories of the Greeks had been won at one another's expense. Now foreigners, with only slight traces of a common ancestry with the Greeks, who might not have been expected even to give them advice, had undergone the greatest dangers and toils to free them from cruel despots and tyrants.[67] Again, Plutarch's hand is visible. The comparison between wars fought by Greeks against Greeks and by Romans on their behalf recalls not only the principle on which the *Parallel Lives* are constructed, but also other of Plutarch's works, like the declamation on the fortune and the virtue of the Romans. Plutarch's own views can be recognized in the comment on internecine war between the Greeks and in the belief that the Romans and the Greeks were of kindred race.[68]

The *Flamininus* cannot be considered entirely without reference to the accompanying biography, the *Philopoemen*: this is the only pair in which the subjects are taken from the same period. Here Plutarch undertook to depict a man who was remembered as the last of the Greeks, and had his own claim to be their liberator.[69] The fact that Philopoemen's love of liberty had set him at odds with the Romans does not embarrass his biographer. For Plutarch, the growing power of Rome over Greece was the divine will, the destined revolution of Fortune's wheel: even so, Philopoemen is commended for his stubbornness and

---

[66] *Flam.* 10. 8–10, cf. Val. Max. 4. 8. 5.

[67] *Flam.* 11. 3–7. It is apparently by coincidence that Livy has also invented a meditation for the Greeks at this point, though his emphasis is different: 33. 33. 4–8.

[68] Internecine war: cf. *de Pyth. orac.* 401 C–D. Kinship: e.g. *Rom.* 15. 4, *Cam.* 22. 3. On this notion cf. J. Palm, *Rom, Römertum und Imperium in der griechischen Literatur der Kaiserzeit* (1959), 13–14, 31, G. W. Bowersock, *Augustus and the Greek World* (1965), 131.

[69] *Philop.* 1. 7, 11. 3, 15. 5.

independence.[70] The view that Rome's greatness resulted in-evitably from the collaboration of the gods and fortune appears to be Plutarch's own conviction,[71] and he therefore sees no injustice in the subjection of his country. Yet, because his notion of freedom is sufficiently elastic,[72] he can regard both Philo-poemen and Flamininus as the liberators of Greece. Like the *Romulus*, the *Lives of Philopoemen and Flamininus* show Plutarch strongly, but not blindly, prejudiced in Rome's favour. Polybius' account is altered to make Flamininus act from sincere phil-hellenism, but the biographer does not conceal what he considers faults in his subject's character.[73] While Plutarch magnifies Flamininus' liberation of Greece, he also praises Philopoemen for resisting the approach of Roman power. Again, he obeys his own biographical rules. Faults should be neither emphasized nor entirely concealed; each *Life* should focus attention on the subject, even if that entailed discrepancies of fact or emphasis between one *Life* and another.[74] The tendencies revealed in these two *Lives*, like those in the *Romulus*, can be explained in terms of the author's stated aims, the depiction of character and the improvement of the reader: they do not require, though they do not exclude, a diplomatic explanation.

About half of Plutarch's Roman *Lives* are drawn from the last century of the republic, from the Gracchi to Antony. These reveal a view about that period of Roman history that is con-sistent with itself and with Plutarch's larger view of Rome. His historical notions are neither original nor profound, but they are another useful index of his attitude to the Rome of his own time.

Plutarch shares a general conviction in the decline of Roman morals under the republic. Already in the time of the elder Cato the state no longer preserved its purity, but had been exposed to many bad examples; as censor, Cato found it difficult to end extravagance, since the majority had already been seduced by it.[75] The last decades of the republic were even more a time

[70] *Philop.* 17. 2–5, *Flam.* 24. 4.   [71] Cf. above, pp. 69, 90, and below, p. 100.
[72] Cf. below, p. 120.
[73] *Flam.* 13. 1–3, 19. 7, 20. 1–2.
[74] On this 'biographical distortion' in the *Flamininus*, R. E. Smith, *CQ* 38 (1944), 94; cf. p. 80 above.
[75] *Cato mai.* 4. 2–3, 18. 2. Cf. Polybius, 6. 57, 31. 25; Posidonius, *FGrHist* 87 F 59, 112; Livy, 39. 6. 7.

of corruption and decline, when the Romans had lost their ancient uprightness.[76]

Internal decay was inevitably reflected in Rome's dealings with her subjects. Plutarch does not spare details of Roman brutality and greed: the plundering of Epirus by Aemilius Paullus, the attempt to abolish the memory of Philopoemen after the sack of Corinth, Sulla's plundering of Athens and the Greek sanctuaries, the misfortunes of Plutarch's own city during the same war.[77] So surprised were the Asians by Cato's modesty that when his servants tried to find him lodgings, they were often scorned for not using threats or insults. Cato warned his hosts that not every visitor would be like himself: if the Romans were not placated, they would use the occasion to obtain their desires by force.[78] Similarly, Cicero was in Cilicia when greed was at its height: governors resorted to plunder as if mere theft were a disgrace, and corruption was so general that those who practised it with moderation were admired.[79]

The most potent evidence of Rome's decline was the outbreak of civil war. The ancient generals of Rome won obedience from their troops by their own virtue: those of Sulla's day turned their arms against each other and therefore had to compete for the favour of the legions.[80] At Pharsalus, men of sense reflected on the pass to which greed and contention had brought the empire. Instead of living at peace or fighting still-unconquered nations, Pompey and Caesar were now to fight each other with no regard for their country or their reputation.[81] The only hope now was monarchy. There was no other way for Rome to escape faction and misgovernment.[82]

Thus the way was prepared for the final outcome: a monarch sent by divine favour to put an end to civil war. For this end the old collaboration of heaven and fortune was revived. Some thought that the destined physician for Rome's ills was Pompey, but the will of the gods gave the outcome to Caesar and his fortune.[83] Or rather, since Caesar's ambition earned its due reward,[84] heaven had another candidate. The aged Cicero once

---

[76] *Phoc.* 3. 3, *Sulla* 1. 5.
[77] *Aem.* 29; *Philop.* 21. 10–12; *Sulla* 12–14; *Cimon* 1–2, 1.
[78] *Cato min.* 12. 3–6.   [79] *Cic.* 52. 3.
[80] *Sulla* 12. 11–12.   [81] *Pomp.* 70.
[82] *Brut.* 55. 2, *Caes.* 28. 6, 57. 1, *Pomp.* 5. 4–5, 75. 5.
[83] *Caes.* 28. 6, *Pomp.* 75. 5.   [84] *Caes.* 60. 1.

had a dream in which a young boy of senatorial family was selected by Jupiter himself to become Rome's leader and bring civil war to an end. The next day the orator saw the young Gaius Octavius for the first time, and recognized him as the appointed saviour.[85] Thus the fortune of Caesar was transferred to his heir, and nothing could thwart the youth's inevitable supremacy.[86] Even the noble Brutus had to yield. It was merely by chance that he had entered battle for the second time at Philippi, before he could hear of the young Caesar's defeat at sea. Affairs no longer allowed a plurality of leaders, but required a monarchy; and so god decided to remove the only obstacle in the way of the one man who could rule, and deprived Brutus of his good fortune.[87]

In making the advent of monarchy the inevitable and desirable outcome of civil strife, Plutarch shows himself, as in his account of Romulus, under the influence of Augustan propaganda.[88] As usual, however, his sympathies are too wide for him merely to follow a party line: even if the course of history was predetermined, men were still free agents and their actions subject to praise and blame. Just as Plutarch can praise both Flamininus for freeing Greece and Philopoemen for resisting him in the cause of freedom, so he is generous in praise of those who opposed Caesar and his heir. Plutarch's portrait of Pompey is one of the most favourable in the *Lives*, and is coupled with that of Agesilaus, whom Xenophon had placed in the canon of Greek heroes. Pompey's cause in the civil war is that of freedom: so also is that of Caesar's assassins.[89] Similarly, Plutarch's picture of the young Caesar is far more shaded than that of a court historian like Nicolaus of Damascus, in the same way that his view of Romulus differed from that of Dionysius. For Plutarch

---

[85] *Cic.* 44. 3–6. From Augustus' autobiography, fr. 4 Malcovati.

[86] *Cic.* 44. 7, *Ant.* 33. 2–3, 56. 6, 67. 3.

[87] *Brut.* 47. 7.

[88] For the τύχη of Augustus, cf. his *Commentarii*, fr. 4, 12 Malcovati, Nicolaus of Damascus, *FGrHist* 90 F 130, sections 38, 55, 83, 113. Augustus as the bringer of peace: e.g. Ehrenberg and Jones, *Documents illustrating the reigns of Augustus and Tiberius*², no. 98(a) lines 4–16, 98(b) lines 32–41 = R. K. Sherk, *Roman Documents from the Greek East* (1969), no. 65 A and D, on which see now U. Laffi, *Studi classici e orientali* 16 (1967), 49–53, 56–7. The same sources will be responsible for other miraculous details in Plutarch: *Cic.* 49. 6, *Caes.* 66. 1, 66. 13 (cf. Nicolaus, F 130, section 83), 69. 2–4.

[89] *Cato min.* 53. 3, *Brut.* 10. 4, 14. 1, *Ant.* 89. 3.

the young Caesar is no less the enemy of freedom than his father.[90] The meeting at Bononia that sealed the second triumvirate moves the biographer to an indignant outburst: nothing could have been more barbarous or savage than an exchange in which each partner allowed his friends to be murdered.[91] The youth's conduct at Philippi was undistinguished, and the account of it given in his autobiography, so Plutarch implies, was mendacious.[92] Later he was as dishonourable in his treatment of Antony as of his other allies.[93] But it is characteristic of Plutarch's methods that, while he condemns the young Caesar in the *Lives* of Brutus and Antony, in the *Cicero* he dwells on his attempt to save the orator from the other triumvirs.[94] When it suits his biographical purpose to heighten the contrast between the hero of a *Life* and his antagonists, Plutarch is ready to condemn the future Augustus. When a different moral lesson could be drawn, that of the righteous avenging of a great orator, he follows imperial propaganda.[95]

Plutarch treats Roman history of the late republic with the same tendencies and preconceptions as that of earlier Rome. While there is a general bias in Rome's favour, there is also room for criticism and condemnation. Plutarch is not imprisoned in the confines of any historical scheme, because he has none. Yet his views are the reflection of his circumstances and times. Other educated Greeks, prosperous and influential by Rome's good-will, must have recognized the author of the *Parallel Lives* as one of themselves. Plutarch's attitude to Rome, at once engaged and casual, appears to emerge as an anomaly. It becomes necessary to ask why he wrote the *Parallel Lives*.

[90] *Cic.* 46. 1, *Brut.* 39. 8, 54. 5, *Ant.* 89. 2.
[91] *Ant.* 19. 4, cf. *Cic.* 46. 2–6, *Brut.* 46. 2–3.
[92] *Ant.* 22. 1–2, *Brut.* 41. 7 = Aug. *Opera Historica*, fr. 12 Malcovati.
[93] *Ant.* 53. 1, 58. 7.
[94] *Cic.* 46. 3–5.
[95] Cf. *Cic.* 49. 5–6; Vell. Pat. 2. 66; R. Syme, *The Roman Revolution* (1939), 318.

XI

THE *PARALLEL LIVES*: PURPOSE

THE *Parallel Lives* are written by a man interested in Roman history and sympathetic to Rome. So much is clear. It is tempting to go further, and to see in them Plutarch's conscious intent to infect the reader with his own enthusiasm. The view is still expressed that he wrote to prove to the Romans that the Greeks were not contemptible *Graeculi* but had produced great men of action, and correspondingly to prove to the Greeks that the Romans were no barbarians.[1] Such a view, if correct, would have an evident bearing on Plutarch's attitude to Rome and on the cultural conditions of his time. It must be examined.

Such a diplomatic purpose would not be inconsistent with another, undisputed aim of the *Parallel Lives*, that of deriving moral benefit from the study of character. The contemplation of virtuous deeds automatically inspired imitation: moreover, when the observer understood the motives behind them, he would acquire his own inclination to virtue.[2] Hence Plutarch insists frequently on a double purpose: he wishes to demonstrate the character of his subjects, and to bring himself and his readers to imitate them.[3] It is this same purpose that causes him to choose great men for his theme. Not only were they of exalted character, but the transactions in which they were involved, by putting them under moral stress, revealed their natures with

---

[1] Clearly formulated by K. Ziegler, *RE* 21 (1951), 897; since then, observe E. Gabba, *Rivista storica italiana* 71 (1959), 369, H. Homeyer, *Klio* 41 (1963), 157. Against, A. Dihle, *Abh. Akad. Wiss. Gött.* Phil.-Hist. Kl. 37 (1956), 103, J. Palm, *Rom, Römertum und Imperium in der griechischen Literatur der Kaiserzeit* (1959), 39–42.

[2] *Per.* 2. 4, τὸ γὰρ καλὸν ἐφ᾽ αὑτὸ πρακτικῶς κινεῖ καὶ πρακτικὴν εὐθὺς ὁρμὴν ἐντίθησιν, ἠθοποιοῦν οὐ τῇ μιμήσει τὸν θεατήν, ἀλλὰ τῇ ἱστορίᾳ τοῦ ἔργου τὴν προαίρεσιν παρεχόμενον. Since Plutarch clearly does not mean to deny that imitation affects character (cf. *Per.* 1. 4), μόνον has perhaps disappeared before τὸν θεατήν. The language is Peripatetic: cf. Dihle, op. cit. 57–87.

[3] *Cimon* 2. 3–5, *Per.* 1–2. 4, *Nic.* 1. 5, *Demosth.* 11. 7, *Aem.* 1, *Alex.* 1, *Demetr.* 1. 1–6, *Pomp.* 8. 7. Cf. (most recently) J. R. Hamilton, *Plutarch, Alexander: A Commentary* (1969), xxxvii–xxxix.

particular clarity.[4] Moreover, the observation of famous men at critical junctures naturally gave more pleasure than that of lesser men at trivial ones: and to give pleasure was a subsidiary part of Plutarch's purpose, since amusement made instruction easier to absorb.[5]

While Plutarch might have pursued simultaneously both a moral and a diplomatic purpose, however, it is curious that he should so frequently refer to the one and never to the other. It is true that the *Lives of Epaminondas and Scipio*, which were probably the first in the series,[6] may have set out Plutarch's programme more fully than any of the extant ones, but there is no reason to think that he proposed an aim there that he was not to mention again. Nor is it likely that he suppresses mention of his diplomatic mission in order to carry it out more effectively. Two writers of an earlier age can be compared. Cornelius Nepos justifies his praise of Greek generals by reminding his readers in his preface that Greek and Roman values were not always the same: and where the context requires it the warning is recalled.[7] Dionysius of Halicarnassus in fact writes with a purpose similar to that ascribed to Plutarch, to show the Greeks that the Romans were not savages but well disposed to Greek culture and in fact of Greek origin themselves. So far from concealing his conviction, he reiterates it as often as possible in order to impress it on his readers.[8]

If the *Parallel Lives* had been consciously planned with a conciliatory purpose, they might also have been expected to show more signs of organization.[9] In fact, Plutarch appears to have added one pair after another haphazardly.[10] The same lack of plan is evident even within the pairs themselves. Plutarch would sometimes fix on one subject and then cast about for a

---

[4] *Nic.* 1. 5, τὸν τρόπον καὶ τὴν διάθεσιν τοῦ ἀνδρὸς ὑπὸ πολλῶν καὶ μεγάλων παθῶν ἀνακαλυπτομένην. *Demetr.* 1. 5, τῶν γεγονότων ἐν ἐξουσίαις καὶ πράγμασι μεγάλοις ἐπιφανῶν. *Pomp.* 8. 7, τῶν μεγίστων καὶ μάλιστα δηλούντων τὸ ἦθος ἔργων καὶ παθημάτων.

[5] On this principle *de poet. aud.* 14 F, ἐθίζειν ὥσπερ ὄψῳ χρώμενος μετρίως τῷ τέρποντι τὸ χρήσιμον ἀπ' αὐτοῦ καὶ τὸ σωτήριον διώκειν; *mul. virt.* 243 A; *de Herod. malign.* 854 F–855 A. Cf. *Rom.* 12. 6; *Per.* 1. 3, 24. 12; *Aem.* 1. 3.

[6] Cf. Ziegler, *RE* 21 (1951), 897; C. P. Jones, *JRS* 56 (1966), 67.

[7] Corn. Nep. *de vir. ill. praefatio*, 5. 1. 2, 15. 2. 3.

[8] *Ant. Rom.* 1. 4, 1. 89, 2. 12. 3, 13. 4, 17. 3–4, 18. 2, 30. 5, 4. 24. 8, 7. 70.

[9] So, rightly, Palm, op. cit. 42.

[10] e.g. *Thes.* 1. 4, *Demetr.* 1. 5.

suitable partner.[11] Even the biography of Rome's founder was approached in this way. Having gone so far back in history as to write the *Lives of Lycurgus and Numa*, Plutarch decided to proceed to the borders of myth and include Romulus.[12] Again, Dionysius forms an instructive contrast. He deliberately began his *Roman Antiquities* with the city's early history rather than its era of glory in order to dispel false impressions about its first settlers.[13] Plutarch's methods do not suit an author concerned to reconcile Greeks and Romans: they are understandable, however, if the *Lives* were intended to illustrate the working of moral laws, since the validity of such laws could be confirmed even by the random accumulation of instances.

Plutarch's moral purpose is also sufficient to explain other features of the *Lives* behind which a diplomatic purpose has been seen. The choice of men of action rather than of culture, statesmen rather than artists, has been held to show that he wished to impress Rome with the political achievements of the Greeks.[14] In fact, Plutarch's interest in character required that his subjects be men great of soul: indeed artists, by spending their skills on products of no moral value, incurred a just suspicion of baseness themselves.[15] In an early declamation Plutarch set out to show that Athens's glory lay in its statesmen and generals, not its poets and painters.[16] The choice of heroes in the *Parallel Lives* is guided by the same conviction.

The same moral purpose accounts for another feature of the *Lives* which has been held to be conciliatory, the arrangement of Greeks and Romans in parallel. The primary purpose of this is artistic. It is one of the devices that Plutarch employs to keep his reader's attention, like the frequently inserted speeches and digressions. The use of comparisons to enhance or belittle was one of the oldest devices of rhetoric, and hence it was employed by the first classic biographers, Isocrates and Xenophon, both of whom compare their subjects favourably with kings of Persia.[17] As Greeks and Romans came to know each others' history, there grew up a natural tendency to compare their respective heroes.

[11] *Thes.* 1. 4–5, *Cimon* 3. 1.   [12] *Thes.* 1. 4.   [13] *Ant. Rom.* 1. 4.
[14] Thus F. Focke, *Hermes* 58 (1923), 363: criticized by Palm, op. cit. 41.
[15] μεγαλόψυχοι: cf. *Per.* 36. 8, *Coriol.* 1. 3, *Demetr.* 1. 7. Artists: *Per.* 2. 1.
[16] *De glor. Ath.* 345 C–351 B.
[17] Comparisons: Aristotle, *Rhet.* 1368 a 19–26, Quintil. 2. 4. 21. In biography: Isocr. *Evag.* 37–8, Xen. *Ages.* 9. 1–5. Cf. Focke, art. cit. 335–9.

Some at least of Plutarch's pairs had already been linked before him.[18] In time these comparisons formed the basis of whole compilations. One of these was Cornelius Nepos' work on illustrious men, in which Greeks and Romans together were compared by headings: kings, generals, poets, historians. While Nepos hopes that his Roman readers will make allowance for Greek values, there is no sign in the extant part of the work that he intended to create understanding between the two peoples: his aim was delectation and not demonstration. In this he anticipates Plutarch, who knew of his biographies and may have been influenced by them.[19] The same practice of setting Greeks and Romans side by side for the amusement of the reader was followed by the antiquarian Varro. His *Hebdomades* appear to have grouped prominent men of the two nations by sevens, with every one illustrated by pictures to which an epigram was appended.[20]

Plutarch's comparison of Greeks and Romans is therefore primarily artistic, but it also served his moral purpose. To study virtue in action, it was useful to observe two examples in different contexts: the observer could then distinguish what was essential to each virtue from what was accidental.[21] A Greek and a Roman paired together made a particularly rewarding subject, since the difference of their backgrounds ensured a clear view of the virtue which they had in common.

It is above all Plutarch's treatment of Greek and Roman history that makes it impossible to see a diplomatic purpose in the *Lives*. To take his Greek audience first, it has already been observed with how little embarrassment he treats what had once been sensitive subjects in Roman history. In his treatment of Romulus, he grants a hearing to versions which Dionysius, deliberately aiming to win Greek opinion, suppressed; Plutarch's picture of the future Augustus is determined by his moral views,

---

[18] e.g. Polybius, 10. 2. 8–13 (Scipio and Lycurgus); Cic. *Brutus* 42–3 (Themistocles and Coriolanus). Pairs also used by Plutarch: Vell. Pat. 2. 41. 1–2 (Caesar and Alexander), *Demosth.* 3. 2 (Caecilius of Caleacte's comparison of Demosthenes and Cicero). Cf. Focke, art. cit. 349–51.

[19] On Nepos' scheme, cf. Wissowa, *RE* 4 (1900), 1412–13. Plutarch's knowledge of him: *Luc.* 43. 2, *Marc.* 30. 5, 31. 8, *Gracchi* 21. 3.

[20] Dahlmann, *RE* Suppl. 6 (1935), 1227–9.

[21] *Mul. virt.* 243 B–D, on which see P. A. Stadter, *Plutarch's Historical Methods* (1965), 9–11. On the moral function of Plutarch's συγκρίσεις, H. Erbse, *Hermes* 84 (1956), 398–424.

not by a desire to flatter the first emperor.[22] Though he often comments on Roman interest in Greek culture, he is at no pains to conceal the countervailing tradition of contempt, and in fact devotes a *Life* to the most eloquent of its representatives, the elder Cato. Here Plutarch portrays his subject without reserve, retailing his witticisms on garrulous and insincere Greeks, his mockery of philhellenic Romans, and his tirades against Greek culture and Greek doctors.[23] Nor is Plutarch unwilling to express his disapproval of the darker sides of Roman culture: militarism, luxury, and greed.[24]

If Plutarch is unconcerned to conceal Roman vices, he is equally unsparing of his fellow Greeks. In the Rome of his day, their love of faction was 'the Greek failing', a subject for jokes.[25] Yet Plutarch, no doubt influenced by his own experience, fills his biographies with rivalry between Greeks, Themistocles and Aristides, Pericles and Cimon, Nicias and Alcibiades. The wickedness and contentiousness of prominent Greeks, so he averred, was responsible for their country's ruin.[26] Plutarch shows himself equally insensitive to Roman notions of Greek veracity. A story told by Theophanes of Mytilene about Rutilius Rufus is dismissed as the slander of an honest man by a rogue; similarly, Plutarch tells with obvious repugnance how the rhetorician Theodotus of Chios advised Ptolemy XII to welcome the fugitive Pompey and then to murder him.[27] Theodotus is not the only wicked teacher in the *Lives*; there are also Theodorus, who betrayed Antony's son Antyllus, Rhodon, who caused the death of his pupil Caesarion, and Gorgias, whom Cicero rightly blamed for leading his son Marcus into immorality.[28]

The freedom with which Plutarch expresses his opinions in the *Lives*, untrammelled by requirements of tact, disproves the theory of a diplomatic purpose. He did not write to bridge a gap between Greeks and Romans, because in his society there was none. To ascribe to him the motives of a Dionysius or a Nicolaus is to ignore a hundred years of imperial history. He himself was the friend of powerful Romans. Members of his society passed

[22] Above, pp. 89–94, 100–2.   [23] *Cato mai.* 12. 6–7, 22–3.
[24] *Publ.* 15. 3–6, *Luc.* 39. 2, *Numa* 26. 13.
[25] Dio Prus. *Or.* 38. 38, cf. Tac. *Ann.* 4. 55. 1.
[26] *Flam.* 11. 6.   [27] *Pomp.* 37. 4, *Brut.* 33. 3–6.
[28] *Ant.* 81. 1 (Theodorus), 81. 4 (Rhodon), *Cic.* 24. 8–9 (Gorgias).

easily into the ranks of the equestrian and even the senatorial orders at Rome. The most notable of all these favoured Greeks is perhaps the man to whom the *Parallel Lives* are dedicated, Sosius Senecio. A commander of Trajan's armies and twice *consul ordinarius*, Sosius may be from a province of Asia Minor.[29]

To deny that Plutarch sensed a gap between Greeks and Romans, and tried to bridge it, is not to say that the old tensions had vanished from every part of society. On the Roman side, the appellation 'Greek' could still be used in insult. That was the language of boors however, as Plutarch observed: a needy Roman client might resort to it when outmanœuvred by Oriental rivals.[30] For that adventitious nationalism Plutarch and his Roman friends will have had the same contempt. Among Greeks also, hostility to Rome was far from dead. A bold politician might hope to win the support of the populace by denunciation, open or oblique, of the ruling power, and rebellions against Rome could still occur even in Greece itself.[31] But these sentiments are the social counterpart of Roman attacks on *Graeculi*. Their source is among the city mobs, the poor and discontented who had Rome to blame for their subjection.[32] In his *Political Precepts* Plutarch curtly dismisses the politicians who play on such sentiments.[33] His Greek friends will have had the same opinion of their compatriots who hated Rome as his Roman friends for the impecunious clients who abused their Greek rivals.[34]

It does not follow, therefore, because the *Parallel Lives* have no diplomatic purpose that national antipathies had disappeared. But equally there is no reason to assume Plutarch

[29] Above, p. 55.

[30] *Cic.* 5. 2. Cf. Juvenal, 3. 61, 78, Lucian, *de merc. cond.* 17 (on which see G. W. Bowersock, *Augustus and the Greek World* [1965], 146, n. 2).

[31] Denunciation: *praec. ger. reip.* 814 C, on which see below, p. 113. A rebellion in Greece is attested under Pius: Lucian, *Peregr.* 19, *HA* Pius 5. 5, *AE* 1929. 21.

[32] Note Plutarch's comment on τὸ δυσκολαῖνον καὶ μεμψιμοιροῦν of the populace, *praec. ger. reip.* 818 E. Cf. the false Nero of 69 to whom paupers and slaves flocked on Cythnos *rerum novarum cupidine et odio praesentium*, Tac. *Hist.* 2. 8. 2; cf. p. 18 above.

[33] *Praec. ger. reip.* 814 C.

[34] Two supposed representatives of national antipathy are purposely omitted here. Tacitus' aversion for Greek vanity and loquacity (e.g. *Dial.* 15. 3, *Ann.* 2. 53. 3, 55. 1–2, 88. 3) is a literary convention: it does not show that 'a general resentment angered the Roman as he contemplated the tide of Hellenism resurgent all around' (R. Syme, *Tacitus* [1958], 513). The well-born Apollonius of Tyana has been labelled a 'Römerfeind' because he deplored Greek affectation of Roman manners (L. Hahn, *Rom und Romanismus im griechisch-römischen Osten* [1906], 140, 157, 201), but the matter is not so simple, cf. pp. 126–8 below.

unaware of contemporary currents.[35] It will be seen that certain of his essays, notably the *Political Precepts*, are written with a clear political intention. What he is concerned with in those is, not to heal a breach between Greeks and Romans, but to urge concord on the Greeks themselves. Hostility to Rome is far less important a subject than hostility between rival politicians.[36]

The *Parallel Lives* do not reveal a cleavage between Greeks and Romans, but rather their unity. They express an age in which Greeks became Roman consuls and commanded Roman armies, when emperors and future emperors could hold the archonship at Athens.[37] Indeed, if Plutarch's contemporaries felt that national vanities had entered into the writing of the *Parallel Lives*, it may have been in the prominence accorded by the author to Athens, where he had been a student and was an honorary citizen. Not every citizen of Smyrna or Ephesus will have agreed that Athens was the most venerable of all cities or that her buildings had had no rivals until the Rome of the Caesars.[38] When a scholar of Smyrna produced a *Catalogue of Romans and Smyrnaeans*,[39] he showed himself an inhabitant of the same Graeco-Roman world as Plutarch and an heir to the same cultural attitudes. Rome was no longer merely the partner of the Greeks, but their new paragon.[40]

[35] Thus A. Dihle, while rightly denying a political purpose to the *Lives*, does so on the premiss that most educated men under the principate took no part in public affairs: *Abh. Akad. Wiss. Gött.* Phil.-Hist. Kl. 37 (1956), 103.

[36] See below, pp. 112–4.

[37] Viz. Domitian (*IG* 2/3². 1996, lines 1–2 = McCrum and Woodhead, *Documents of the Flavian Emperors* no. 121) and Hadrian (*ILS* 308 = Smallwood, *Documents of Nerva, Trajan and Hadrian* no. 109).

[38] *Dio* 58. 1–2; *Fab. Max.* 30. 7. Note also *Thes.* 1. 5, *Themist.* 15. 4, *Arist.* 27. 7, *Cimon* 10. 7, *Per.* 12. 1, 13. 5.

[39] Hermogenes of Smyrna, *FGrHist* 579 T 1 = *CIG* 3311, Kaibel, *Epigrammata Graeca* no. 305.

[40] Note [Dio], *Or.* 37. 25, τῶν Ἑλλήνων τοὺς ἀρίστους ἔστιν ἰδεῖν ἐκεῖσε πρὸς τὰ τῶν Ῥωμαίων πράγματα ἀποκλίνοντας.

XII

THE POLITICAL TREATISES

PLUTARCH'S political treatises, above all the *Political Precepts*, have a special place among his works. Besides expounding his answers to problems of his time, the reign of Trajan,[1] they are primary documents for an understanding of the relationship between Greece and Rome.

The general outline of that relationship is clear and well known. From the first establishment of their power in the East, the Romans had used the traditional unit of Greek political life, the city, as an instrument of domination. To ensure loyalty and stability, they needed agents whose interests were close to their own. It was inevitable that they should turn to the upper classes of the cities, the landowners and merchants who themselves stood to gain from settled conditions. In time, Roman influence brought about constitutional changes that perpetuated the power of the wealthy and excluded lesser citizens from the guidance of affairs. Democracies in name, the subject cities became in fact local aristocracies.[2]

It has already been seen that Plutarch himself was born into this upper class and that his Greek friends were of the same type as himself.[3] It is primarily for these, and not for the consuls and proconsuls of his acquaintance, that the political treatises are intended. The *Political Precepts* are addressed to a wealthy aristocrat of Sardis called Menemachus,[4] and the complementary work on old men in politics to an Athenian called Euphanes, a holder of high office in his city.[5] The *Political Precepts*

---

[1] For the date of the *praec. ger. reip.* and the *an seni sit ger. resp.* C. P. Jones, *JRS* 56 (1966), 72–3.

[2] Cf. p. 43, n. 25 above, and references there.   [3] Above, p. 10.

[4] *Praec. ger. reip.* 798 A–B, cf. Stein, *RE* 15 (1931), 837–8, no. 5. Note the Menemachus on a coin of Sardis, perhaps of Attalid date: Mionnet, *Description des médailles antiques*, Suppl. 7, 414, no. 443, cf. B. V. Head, *BMC* Lydia, p. xcviii.

[5] *An seni sit ger. resp.* 783 B, cf. Ziegler, *RE* 21 (1951), 674. On Euphanes' ἐπιστασία of the Areopagus, see D. J. Geagan, *The Athenian Constitution after Sulla*, *Hesperia* Suppl. Vol. 12 (1967), 54, 58–9. Probably connected with the Flavius Euphanes attested as archon in 124/5, *Inscr. Délos* 2536, lines 17–18 (on the date, P. Graindor,

found an assiduous reader in another of Plutarch's friends, Cornelius Pulcher, at once a noble of Epidaurus and an influential Roman knight.[6]

Since Plutarch's treatises are intended for the use of his own class, that class is central to his political thought. Characteristically, he is less concerned with the abstract merits of different constitutions than with the guidance of conduct.[7] Hence the treatises contain no systematic discussion of political structures, though it is not difficult to trace the underlying presuppositions.

There is no question of the inherent right of the upper class to rule. Menemachus' high birth is the cause and the justification of his desire to become a public figure, since he is one of those whom the divine purpose has set above the common run.[8] These are the 'first men', the 'politicians' of the city:[9] placed in their charge, like a suspicious and refractory animal that needs to be guarded for its own good, is the people.[10]

Plutarch's comparison is instructive. While the populace could not participate in government directly, it retained the brute power of weight and force. Though Plutarch scarcely mentions the traditional assembly,[11] it is clear that the people could make its demands felt by various means, acclamations for or against its politicians, clamours for a show or a distribution.[12] Hence there was still need for the arts of persuasion and for courage in the face of public pressure.[13]

The belief that politics was the natural calling of the privileged found confirmation in their behaviour. Other works of Plutarch besides the political treatises show the intensity of civic life. One of his essays is largely devoted to the art of resisting lobbyists:

Athènes sous Hadrien [1934], 29), cf. Graindor, *Chronologie des archontes athéniens sous l'Empire, Mémoires de l'Académie royale de Belgique,* Classe des Lettres, VIII. 2 (1922), 126; also with the deceased landowner of the same name, *IG* 2/3². 2776, B II, lines 212–13.

  [6] *De cap. ex inim. util.* 86 C–D. On Pulcher, see above, pp. 45–6.

  [7] The *de tribus reip. gen.* 826 A–827 C, is of doubtful authenticity.

  [8] *Praec. ger. reip.* 798 B, 823 E–F.

  [9] οἱ πρῶτοι: *praec. ger. reip.* 815 A, *quaest. conviv.* 679 C; cf. J. H. Oliver, *The Ruling Power* (1953), 953–8, and below, p. 114. οἱ πολιτευόμενοι: *praec. ger. reip.* 813 A, and below, p. 114.

  [10] *Praec. ger. reip.* 800 C, 802 D, 814 C (φρυάττεσθαι), 821 A, 823 E–F.

  [11] *An seni sit ger. resp.* 794 C, *praec. ger. reip.* 799 E, 810 D, cf. *quaest. conviv.* 714 A.

  [12] *Praec. ger. reip.* 817 F–818 E, 819 E–820 F, 821 E–822 C.

  [13] *Praec. ger. reip.* 801 C–804 C, 813 A–C (persuasion), *an seni sit ger. resp.* 796 B–C, *praec. ger. reip.* 822 C (resistance).

another advises the ambitious politician against ruining himself by his generosity.[14] This intensity of political life underlies the problems with which Plutarch is concerned. Without it, the cities could not exist: the competition between the wealthy provided the populace with magistrates, buildings, entertainment, often cash and food.[15] But the same rivalry was fertile in disaster. Jealousy was the cities' greatest bane: private quarrels might easily flare up, sometimes leading to open faction and provoking inevitable intervention from above.[16] This inflammability was itself a consequence of the political system. The people, constantly eyeing its leaders for signs of collusion or disagreement, could be used by the unscrupulous as an instrument of public pressure. A politician who had won its favour with benefactions might set it on his enemies.[17] There was only one way for the system to survive: those in politics must realize their common interest, and not allow themselves to be divided by hatred and jealousy. Concord, the preservation of unity in the ruling class, is the essence of Plutarch's message.[18]

The main part of his political treatises is devoted to the management of the city. That is natural, since it was the city, always needing the politician's care and attention,[19] that took most of his energy. But ruling was only a part of his task: he had also to act correctly as a subject. Those he governed were also subordinate to Roman proconsuls and procurators. This was not the Greece or the Asia of the past. The magistrate must not be dazzled by his insignia into forgetting the symbols of Rome's power before him, the tribunal and the senatorial shoes. Just as actors put all their passion and skill into the contest without ignoring the prompter, so the politician must not exceed the limits of power laid down by Rome.[20]

[14] *De vit. pud.* especially 533 D, 534 C, F, 535 B–C; *de vit. aere al.* 830 E. Note the reference to money-lenders from Corinth, Athens, and Patrae (831 A), the three chief commercial centres of southern Greece: G. W. Bowersock, *Augustus and the Greek World* (1965), 92–6.

[15] A. H. M. Jones, *The Greek City* (1940), 248–50; Rostovtzeff, *SEHRE*² 142–50.

[16] *An seni sit ger. resp.* 787 C (φθόνος), cf. *praec. ger. reip.* 809 B; *praec. ger. reip.* 825 A–D (faction), cf. *de frat. am.* 487 F–488 A.

[17] *Praec. ger. reip.* 813 A (suspicion), 818 C (injuries to citizens).

[18] ὁμόνοια: *praec. ger. reip.* 824 D, cf. B. Note that this subject is the last treated in the *Political Precepts*, as if intended to be the chief lesson of the work.

[19] *An seni sit ger. resp.* 792 E.

[20] *Praec. ger. reip.* 813 E. On the interpretation of this passage, see below, Appendix II.

Again, Plutarch's metaphor is eloquent. The upper classes had to earn their licence to govern by maintaining order and harmony: they must not mistake the shadow of power for the reality. A slip, and the offender could be humbled by a mere edict of the proconsul, if not banished or executed.[21] Maintaining relations with Rome required no less prudence than control of the mob.

As was natural for a man who had many friends at Rome and mixed easily with Roman officials, Plutarch advises the politician always to have a friend among the most influential men in the capital.[22] The Romans were eager to promote the political aims of their friends, and with their goodwill a Greek could bring benefits to his less favoured compatriots. In return, the politician was to keep the people quiet and his city blameless before Rome.[23]

While the Romans wanted to control, they did not want to oppress: oppression was tiresome and unnecessary, as long as the ruling class played their part.[24] As a friend of Romans, Plutarch knew that they also had an interest in stability and order. It is therefore with complete consistency that he advises Greeks both to have friends at court and not to debase themselves before Rome. Some politicians, by referring every matter to the decision of the Romans, brought on them the reproach of oppression and made them masters more than they wished to be.[25] Here again the underlying trouble was dissension in the ruling class. Rather than yield to their rivals, political foes preferred to put all the city's affairs into foreign hands. Instead it was the politician's duty to keep internal conflicts inside and not resort to external arbitration.[26] The consequence of such folly was at best an unnecessary weakening of civic institutions, at worst war with an invincible adversary. Though rebellion against Rome is not a prospect on which Plutarch cares to dwell, it remained a real one. That is the meaning of his advice to politicians not to make the mob puffed up with talk of Marathon, Eurymedon,

---

[21] *Praec. ger. reip.* 824 E (edict), 813 E–F (banishment, execution).

[22] *Praec. ger. reip.* 814 C. For this use of ἄνω to denote Rome, cf. Arrian, *Diss. Epict.* 1. 10. 2, ἀναβάς.   [23] *Praec. ger. reip.* 814 C–E.

[24] Cf. Aristides, *Or.* 26. 64 K. φρουρῶν δὲ οὐδὲν δεῖ τὰς ἀκροπόλεις ἐχόντων, ἀλλ' οἱ ἑκασταχόθεν μέγιστοι καὶ δυνατώτατοι τὰς ἑαυτῶν πατρίδας ὑμῖν φυλάττουσιν.

[25] *Praec. ger. reip.* 814 E–F. On this passage, cf. James H. Oliver, *Hesperia* 23 (1954), 163–7, and below, p. 115.   [26] *Praec. ger. reip.* 815 A–C.

and Plataea.[27] There was no need for him to make explicit the contrast between victories won long ago over the might of Persia and the hopelessness of war with Rome.

The doctrine expounded in the political treatises is a consistent and practical one: it had to be, since they were solicited and employed by the author's contemporaries as practical handbooks. But it is not only the concreteness of his advice that shows Plutarch to be concerned with real issues. An abundance of material, literary and documentary, shows the aptness of his advice to his own time.

First, his terminology. Plutarch's political language closely resembles that of the men of his age who served their cities as secretaries, drafting the decrees and testimonials that survive on papyrus and stone. For a good reason: these officials were from the same educated class as Plutarch himself.[28] For them and for Plutarch the Roman authorities are 'the leaders',[29] their friends in the cities 'the first men',[30] 'the politicians'.[31] Public gifts are 'munificences',[32] their recompense 'honours' and 'testimonials'.[33] Plutarch's canon of political virtues is that of his time, 'mildness',[34] 'purity',[35] 'abstinence',[36] 'decorum',[37] 'gravity',[38] 'reason-

---

[27] *Praec. ger. reip.* 814 C. For the equation of Rome with Persia, cf. on ἄνω, p. 113, n. 22 above, and also the literary use of σάτραπαι to denote Roman officials, e.g. Philostr. *VS* 524, cf. E. L. Bowie, *Past & Present* 46 (1970), 33, n. 95.

[28] L. Robert, *REA* 62 (1960), 325–6 = *Op. min. sel.* 2. 841–2.

[29] οἱ ἡγούμενοι: *praec. ger. reip.* 814 C, cf. Robert, art. cit. 326–9 = *Op. min. sel.* 2. 842–5.

[30] οἱ πρῶτοι: *praec. ger. reip.* 815 A, and above, p. 111, n. 9. Cf. Robert, *Hellenica* 13 (1965), 212–13, and also the δεκάπρωτοι and εἰκοσάπρωτοι responsible for collecting taxes: D. Magie, *Roman Rule in Asia Minor* (1950), 1. 648, 2. 1516–17, Rostovtzeff, *SEHRE*² 390–1, 706–7, n. 47.

[31] οἱ πολιτευόμενοι: *praec. ger. reip.* 813 A, cf. *an seni sit ger. resp.* 790 D. On the development of the term from this meaning (cf. *Syll.*³ 850, line 15, of A. D. 145) to that of *curialis* in the late empire, cf. Robert, *L'Antiquité classique* 35 (1966), 382.

[32] φιλοτιμίαι: *praec. ger. reip.* 822 C. Cf. Robert, *Les Gladiateurs dans l'Orient grec* (1940), 276–80.

[33] τιμαί, μαρτυρίαι: *praec. ger. reip.* 821 F, ψευδώνυμοι τιμαὶ καὶ ψευδομάρτυρες. Cf. Robert, *Hellenica* 3 (1946), 22–3, 13 (1965), 207.

[34] πραότης: *praec. ger. reip.* 800 B, 808 D, 809 E, 810 E, 815 A, 819 B, 824 D. Cf. Robert, *Hellenica* 13 (1965), 223.

[35] καθαριότης: *praec. ger. reip.* 800 C, E. Cf. A. Wilhelm, *JÖAI* 17 (1914), 36, 120; Robert, *Hellenica* 4 (1948), 38–41.

[36] σωφροσύνη: *praec. ger. reip.* 800 F, 807 A, 823 A. Cf. Robert, *Hellenica* 13 (1965), 222.

[37] κοσμιότης: *praec. ger. reip.* 800 F, 817 B. Cf. Robert, op. cit. 222–3.

[38] σεμνότης: *praec. ger. reip.* 801 D, 813 C, 823 E. Cf. Robert, op. cit. 222, *Revue de philologie* 41 (1967), 12, n. 4.

ableness',[39] 'trustworthiness'.[40] Just as for Plutarch the exercise of these virtues incites others to imitation, so inscriptions regularly honour benefactors for the example they set to others.[41] Similarly, when Plutarch lists as the greatest benefits that a city can enjoy 'peace, freedom, abundance, populousness, concord', his words are echoed by inscriptions that celebrate the terms of local magistrates as times of 'peace, lawfulness, abundance, concord'.[42]

Since Plutarch's political terminology is that of his time, it is not surprising that the institutions that he presupposes can also be illustrated by contemporary evidence. The embassies to proconsuls and emperors that recur in his treatises appear also in scores of texts; several such ambassadors pride themselves, like Plutarch's ideal politician, for having used their influence with the Romans to benefit their cities.[43] Plutarch mentions as a characteristic object of such a mission a treaty of concord with another city: such treaties are frequently attested in the high empire, one of them between Plutarch's two cities of Chaeronea and Delphi.[44] The intervention of Roman governors in local affairs is no less familiar: thus at Corinth a proconsul approves the sale of public land to a benefactor of the city.[45] Within the

[39] ἐπιείκεια: praec. ger. reip. 821 D. Cf. Robert, Hellenica 13 (1965), 223.

[40] πίστις: praec. ger. reip. 805 B, 812 C, 818 B, 821 B–C, 822 F. Cf. Robert, Revue de philologie 1 (1927), 105 = Op. min. sel. 2. 1060. Note how many of the above terms or their cognates recur in the decree of the Lycian κοινόν for the benefactor Opramoas, TAM 2. 905 (IGR 3. 739), col. III, lines 54 ff.: lines 61 (πρῶτος), 64 (πολιτευόμενος), 70, 82, 87 (φιλοτιμίαι), 76–7, 83–4, 92–3, 97 (τιμαί), 78, 84, 94 (μαρτυρίαι), 81 (σωφροσύνη), 81 (κοσμιότης), 80, 86 (σεμνότης), 74 (ἐπιείκεια).

[41] An seni sit ger. resp. 790 C–791 C, praec. ger. reip. 806 B–F. Cf. e.g. IG 5. 1. 1432, lines 25–6, with the observations of Robert, Annuaire de l'École des Hautes Études, IVᵉ sect. 1968–1969 (1969), 165.

[42] εἰρήνη, ἐλευθερία, εὐετηρία, εὐανδρία, ὁμόνοια, praec. ger. reip. 824 C; εἰρήνη, εὐνομία, εὐετηρία, ὁμόνοια, IG 12. 5. 906. Cf. A. Wilhelm, Ἐπιτύμβιον Swoboda (1927), 340, Robert, Études anatoliennes (1937), 257–8.

[43] Embassies: de exil. 602 C, an seni sit ger. resp. 793 D, praec. ger. reip. 804 E, 805 A, 808 B, 812 E, 815 D, 816 C–D, 819 A. Friendships: praec. ger. reip. 814 C–E. Cf. e.g. 814 C, ἐκ φιλίας ἡγεμονικῆς ... μεγάλα τὰς πατρίδας ὠφελήσαντες with Th. Wiegand, Milet 1, 2: Das Rathaus no. 7 b, lines 12–13, ταῖς τῶν ἡγουμένων φιλίαις τε καὶ ξενίαις καταχρώμενος εἰς τὰ τῆς πατρίδος συμφέροντα. Robert, REA 62 (1960), 326–9 = Op. min. sel. 2. 842–5; G. W. Bowersock, Augustus and the Greek World (1965), 10–11, 86–7, Greek Sophists in the Roman Empire (1969), 43–6.

[44] ὁμόνοια: praec. ger. reip. 808 C. Cf. D. Kienast, Jahrbuch für Numismatik und Geldgeschichte 14 (1964), 51–64. Chaeronea and Delphi: Syll.³ 816.

[45] Corinth, 8. 3, no. 306, on which see Robert, Hellenica 1 (1940), 47–8 and now REG 79 (1966), 754–5; from the Opramoas dossier again, cf. TAM 2. 905 (IGR 3.

9

cities, documents reveal the prevalence of many of the practices that Plutarch deplores. Thus the gladiatorial shows that he so often mentions with disapproval are illustrated by hundreds of inscriptions;[46] similarly, when he advises the politician to refuse gifts of statues and pictures, and to be content with a more modest reward, he appears to be setting a standard not usually reached by his contemporaries.[47]

Another item reveals Plutarch in opposition to a trend of his time. Urging Menemachus to use his Roman friends for the benefit of Sardis, he remarks disparagingly on those Greeks who desert their cities and instead use their influence to become administrators of imperial property and managers of provincial finance.[48] Elsewhere he observes that many of the most respectable and influential live abroad, escaping the trouble, the distractions, and the bother which their native cities cause.[49] In a third passage, he is more explicit: men from Chios, Galatia, and Bithynia are not content with influence among their own citizens, but yearn to climb ever higher in office at Rome, until they are appointed *consules ordinarii*.[50] Plutarch was observing a momentous transformation in his own society. The same Greeks whom the Romans had supported in their cities now found their local responsibilities tedious and insufficient. Some became knights and senators at Rome. Others, cultivated men, took up residence in cities where their arts would be more highly appreciated than in their own. Still others merely abstained from public office. The first of these notable absentees is an exact contemporary of Plutarch, Dio of Prusa. Soon Plutarch's friend Favorinus of Arelate was to be compelled by Hadrian to serve his native province.[51]

739), col. II line 81, III line 97, IV lines 28, 103. Cf. Magie, *Roman Rule in Asia Minor* (1950), 2. 1391–2, n. 61, 1504, n. 29; above, p. 113, n. 25.

[46] *Praec. ger. reip.* 802 D, 822 C, 823 E, *de soll. anim.* 959 C-960 A, *de esu carn.* 997 C. Cf. Robert, *Les Gladiateurs dans l'Orient grec* (1940), *Hellenica* 3 (1946), 112–50, 5 (1948), 77–99, 7 (1949), 126–51, 8 (1950), 39–72.

[47] *Praec. ger. reip.* 820 C–D. However, Plutarch's recommendation that the politician should decline (παραιτεῖσθαι) extravagant honours reflects a common feeling, cf. Opramoas again, *TAM* 2. 905 (*IGR* 3. 739), col. VIII, line 100.

[48] *Praec. ger. reip.* 814 D. For an example of this practice, cf. Fronto's letter to Pius on behalf of Appian, p. 162 van den Hout.

[49] *De exil.* 605 B–C.

[50] *De tranqu. animi* 470 C.

[51] Dio: *Or.* 49. Favorinus: Philostr. *VS* 490. See now G. W. Bowersock, *Greek Sophists in the Roman Empire* (1969), 30–42.

The fact that the emperors had to intervene to check this tendency again shows Plutarch's attunement to Roman wishes. There is nothing anti-Roman in his advising Greeks not to hunt for positions in the Roman administration. He saw rightly that there was no shortage of such careerists: the shortage that was soon to become a crisis was of Greeks who were willing to stay and serve their cities, as he himself had.

A final indication that Plutarch is concerned with real problems is provided by the addressee of the *Political Precepts*. Faction, which receives such emphasis in the treatise, appears to have been endemic in Menemachus' city, Sardis. At some time before Plutarch wrote, Sardis had been plunged into armed conflict with Rome by the enmity of two of its citizens, Pardalas and Tyrrhenus, of whom Pardalas was subsequently executed.[52] It is possible that the same troubles are referred to in letters attributed to the wizard Apollonius of Tyana, which show that the dissension involved every segment of the population and was exacerbated by strife between exotically named Orders.[53] That strife was recurrent in Sardis is indicated by Plutarch's treatise on exile, addressed to a rich man who had been banished from there. Though unnamed, he may well be the same Menemachus, a victim of the very ambition that Plutarch's *Political Precepts* had warned him against.[54]

Plutarch is not delineating an ideal republic or legislating for an imaginary city: he writes for his contemporaries, even if they found his standards uncomfortable or antique. His advice may be brought into conjunction with that given by other Greeks of his period. None of these comes closer to him than Dio of Prusa. A large number of Dio's surviving speeches are addressed, at the same time as Plutarch's treatises, to cities of the Greek East.[55] Like Plutarch, Dio's primary concern is with the

[52] *Praec. ger. reip.* 813 F, 825 C–D. Several personages of that name are known at Sardis, *OGIS* 470, *ILS* 1988, *Sardis* 7. 1, nos. 22, 91, 122, 127. The *idiologus* attested in 123 (*PIR²* I/J 448) lived too late to be Plutarch's Pardalas.

[53] *Epp. Apoll.* 38–41, 56, 75–6. Brought into conjunction with Plutarch by Wilamowitz, *Hermes* 62 (1927), 296 = *Kleine Schriften* 4 (1962), 451, cf. also *Hermes* 60 (1925), 310–11 = *Kl. Schr.* 4 (1962), 398. Note also Rev. 3: 1–6.

[54] *De exil.* 600 A, 601 B, 604 B. So G. Siefert, *Commentationes philologicae Ienenses* 6. 1 (1896), 74, n. 1. Note also the banished poet Julius Polyaenus, who may be from Sardis, *Anth. Pal.* 9. 7 = A. S. F. Gow and D. L. Page, *The Greek Anthology: the Garland of Philip* (1968), lines 3947–52. Cf. however Gow and Page, op. cit. 2. 465.

[55] Dio Prus. *Or.* 31–51. The majority of these appear to be later than Dio's return

establishment of concord, though in a wider application: peace not only between rival politicians but between rival cities. Both draw on a common stock of arguments and illustrations. These were no longer the days of ancient Greece:[56] power belonged to others, before whom the eastern cities were as children.[57] Greeks who struggled for mastery over one another were scrambling for trifles and bringing disgrace upon themselves.[58] It was better to acquiesce in the peace that Roman power had established through the world.[59]

Plutarch and Dio both understood what Rome wanted. Just as Plutarch urges the Greeks not to make the Romans masters more than they wish to be, so Dio advises his hearers that the Romans prefer free men rather than slaves for subjects.[60] The cities should not ask higher approval for their every decision, acting like patients afraid to move without their doctors' advice.[61] Plutarch exhorts politicians to keep Rome out of local disputes and instead to yield to one another: Dio urges the people of Prusa not to take their complaints to the proconsul but to settle them without interference, and tells quarrelling cities to arbitrate their own disagreements and to make as many concessions as possible.[62] Another famous speaker of the period, Polemo, is praised by his biographer for the same policy: he benefited the Smyrnaeans by preventing their lawsuits from being taken outside the city.[63] Like Plutarch, Dio and Polemo were the friends of emperors and consulars.[64] All three knew that Rome's interest coincided with that of their own class.

The similarity between Dio and Plutarch is more, however, than the similarity of two educated Greeks drawing on a common

from exile under Nerva: H. von Arnim, *Leben und Werke des Dio von Prusa* (1898), 314 ff., 435 ff. The possible exceptions are *Or.* 31 (A. D. Momigliano, *JRS* 41 [1951], 149–53) and *Or.* 47; *Or.* 37 is spurious. Cf. Rostovtzeff, *SEHRE*² 586–7, n. 18, G. W. Bowersock, *Greek Sophists in the Roman Empire* (1969), 110–12.

[56] *Praec. ger. reip.* 813 E; Dio, *Or.* 31. 161–2, 43. 4.

[57] *Praec. ger. reip.* 814 A; Dio, *Or.* 32. 51. Cf. Aristides, *Or.* 23. 62 K.

[58] *Praec. ger. reip.* 814 A, 824 E; Dio, *Or.* 34. 46, 38. 38.

[59] *An seni sit ger. resp.* 784 F, *praec. ger. reip.* 805 A, 824 C; Dio, *Or.* 31. 162. Cf. Aristides, *Or.* 23. 54, 63 K.

[60] *Praec. ger. reip.* 814 F; Dio, *Or.* 31. 111.

[61] Plutarch ibid.; Dio, *Or.* 31. 112, cf. 48. 13.

[62] *Praec. ger. reip.* 815 A–C; Dio, *Or.* 34. 44, 48. 2, 10.

[63] Philostr. *VS* 532.

[64] Dio: *PIR*² D 93. Polemo: *PIR*² A 862. See now G. W. Bowersock, *Greek Sophists in the Roman Empire* (1969), 44–5, 111.

source of platitudes. Both are responding to the particular exigencies of their time. In the contemporary opinion of the biographer Suetonius, the reign of Domitian had been a time of unusual honesty and justice in the government of the provinces, and was followed by a sharp decline.[65] The abundant evidence for provincial maladministration and unrest under Trajan is partly an accident of survival: it was also a period of literary abundance. But while circumstances like those attested under Trajan had prevailed for centuries of Roman rule, not all was as it had been. Senators sitting in judgement on their peers felt freer than they had under Domitian to overlook the misdemeanours of accused proconsuls; and the burdens imposed by a new era of foreign warfare will have exacerbated discord in the tributary cities.[66] It is therefore no coincidence that two Greeks honoured by Trajan preached concord to the eastern cities in such similar terms. Nor is it surprising that the younger Pliny, sent by Trajan to establish tranquillity in Bithynia,[67] should have found practices so similar to those that vexed Plutarch: extravagant distributions, jealousy between politicians, wasteful embassies and buildings, citizens who ruined themselves by their munificence or tried to escape public burdens altogether.[68]

No emperor or proconsul could disapprove the lessons that Plutarch was concerned to inculcate: friendly relations with Rome, avoidance of discord, gentle but firm control of the populace. But questions remain. Is there an undertone of resignation in Plutarch's advice? As an admirer of the Greek past, does he reveal a muted yearning for his country's ancient freedoms? Is it his aim to preserve the remnant of that freedom against the encroachment of Roman power?[69]

---

[65] Suet. *Dom.* 8. 2. On the provinces under Domitian, H. W. Pleket, *Mnemosyne* 14 (1961), 296–315; P. A. Brunt, *Historia* 10 (1961), 221.

[66] Cf. Brunt, art. cit. 217–20; Rostovtzeff, *SEHRE²* 355–9.

[67] Pliny, *Epp.* 10. 117.

[68] Pliny, *Epp.* 10. 116–17 (distributions), 81 (jealousy), 43–4 (embassies), 17 B–18, 37–40 (buildings), 110. 2 (munificence), 58. 1, 113 (escape): on the text and the significance of 10. 113, cf. G. W. Bowersock, *Augustus and the Greek World* (1965), 148, n. 3, C. P. Jones, *Phoenix* 22 (1968), 137–8; against, F. A. Lepper, *Gnomon* 42 (1970), 570–1.

[69] Thus J. Bleicken sees 'schmerzliche Resignation' in Plutarch's advice: 'die politischen Begriffe Plutarchs gehören der Vergangenheit an; sein Ideal, dem er nachtrauert, ist die alte Freiheit der Stadt', *Nachr. Akad. Wiss. Gött. Phil.-Hist. Kl.*

The answer to these questions can begin with Plutarch's view of freedom. As a student of the past, he has an evident admiration for Flamininus as the liberator of Greece, and considers Nero's liberation of the Greeks his one redeeming act.[70] Since Vespasian had annulled Nero's grant, it might appear to follow that Plutarch regarded the freedom of Greece as dead. In fact, he observes in the *Political Precepts* that the cities enjoy as much freedom as 'those in power' allow, and more would perhaps not be good: when he talks of the 'liberty' permitted to the city magistrates, he clearly refers to this same limited freedom.[71] Plutarch's notion of freedom resists precise definition; in the world he knew, the term denoted everything from the condition of not being a slave to the various grades of privilege accorded by Rome to subject cities.[72] So far from regretting the absence of freedom, Plutarch welcomes the restrictions imposed on the mob by Rome: as a member of a class whose position depended on external support, he had no reason to welcome the removal of Roman control.[73]

Another sign of muted resignation might be seen in the examples that he uses to illustrate his political lessons, since they are drawn with a few exceptions from times long past, above all from the history of Greece before Alexander.[74] That is no reason, however, to infer that Plutarch's spiritual home was in classical Greece. These examples are used because Plutarch shared the general belief in the practical utility of history. If he thought

1966, 7, 231–2, cf. 236, 241–2; cf. also D. Nörr, *Imperium und Polis in der hohen Prinzipatszeit* (1966), 86, on which see now G. W. Bowersock, *JRS* 58 (1968), 261–2. Bleicken is clearly in error, however, when he attributes to Plutarch the statement that the *pax Romana* 'den Staatsmann in Griechenland unnötig mache', op. cit. 231, cf. 242, n. 37, referring to *praec. ger. reip.* 824 C: what Plutarch says is that the cities do not need politicians to ensure peace, because war has vanished (the same idea in Aristides, *Or.* 23. 54 K.).

[70] *Flam.* 10–11; *de sera num. vind.* 567 F–568 A.

[71] *Praec. ger. reip.* 824 C. On the very similar passage in [Julian], *Epp.* 35 (198, Bidez-Cumont) 408 A and this use of οἱ κρατοῦντες, see Br. Keil, *Nachr. kön. Ges. Wiss. Gött. Phil.-Hist. Kl.* 1913, 1, 12. ἐξουσία: *praec. ger. reip.* 813 E, 815 A.

[72] Cf. also Dio Prus. *Or.* 44. 11–12. On similar ambiguities in Tacitus' view of *libertas*, see Ch. Wirszubski, *Libertas as a Political Idea at Rome* (1950), 160–7.

[73] On the anti-Roman tendencies of the Greek lower classes, cf. Magie, *Roman Rule in Asia Minor* (1950), 1. 600; Rostovtzeff, *SEHRE*² 117, 126, 586–7, n. 18.

[74] Cf. Bleicken, quoted above, p. 119, n. 69. E. L. Bowie, *Past & Present* 46 (1970), 3–41, appears to class Plutarch among Greeks for whom 'the contemporary balance of politics was profoundly unsatisfactory' and who tried to 'forget the period after Alexander' (pp. 7, 18).

that the distant past was more productive of great men than
more recent times, that was another conviction that he shared
with many others.[75]

It might yet be maintained that, whatever Plutarch's attitude
to freedom or the past, the policy towards Rome that he recommended was politely negative. Rome, on this view, was gradually
stifling the vitality of the cities by an encroaching paternalism,
and Plutarch was concerned that the Greeks should not provoke
their masters into taking away the last vestiges of freedom.[76]

Certainly Plutarch urges the Greeks not to throw away their
remaining liberties. But he himself lays the blame, not on
Roman paternalism, but on the quarrelling Greeks who resorted
to outside arbitration in order not to yield among themselves.[77]
If Rome now intervened more in the affairs of the cities, that may
have been the consequence less of pressure from without than of
collapse from within. Moreover, what appears at first glance a
novelty of the age, officials sent to inspect the accounts of free or
tributary cities, does not mark a radical change in policy. When
the evidence permits a glimpse into conditions under the
republic and early empire, it often reveals the same involvement
of Roman authority in local affairs, even in those of free cities.[78]
Although the title of *corrector* given to these officials may have been
new, like other innovations it merely formalized an older practice.

The interests of Rome and of the Greek upper classes were
convergent, if only the Greeks would use their freedom discreetly.
Plutarch had no cause to look regretfully to the past, or to
protect Greek institutions against a foreign power. His object
is to see the vitality of the cities preserved not in spite of, but in
accordance with, the wishes of Rome.[79]

[75] On historical *exempla*, F. Millar, *JRS* 59 (1969), 13. On the belief in *effeta natura*,
A. N. Sherwin-White, *A Commentary on Pliny's Letters* (1966), 381, discussing *Epp.* 6.
21. 1.

[76] Thus Nörr, op. cit. 78–9, 113, considers Plutarch's patriotism intensified by the
pressure of Rome. Cf. T. Renoirte, *Les 'Conseils Politiques' de Plutarque* (1951), 44;
Bowie, art. cit. 38.

[77] *Praec. ger. reip.* 815 A. On this passage, James H. Oliver, *The Ruling Power* (1953),
953–8.

[78] Thus *IG* 5. 1. 1432, of the second or first century B.C. (cf. Broughton, *Magistrates of the Roman Republic* 1. 566, n. 9), shows a Roman praetor inspecting the finances
of Messene; cf. Cic. *ad Att.* 6. 2. 5. For Augustus' interference in cities of senatorial
provinces, including free ones, G. W. Bowersock, *HSCP* 68 (1964), 208–9, *Augustus
and the Greek World* (1965), 88. Note also F. Millar, *JRS* 58 (1968), 223.

[79] Thus, rightly, J. Palm, *Rom, Römertum und Imperium in der griechischen Literatur
der Kaiserzeit* (1959), 36–8.

XIII

ROME

PLUTARCH's writings confirm what his career and circumstances suggested. Born into a wealthy family, courted by consuls and emperors, he is in a long tradition of Greek writers friendly to Rome. It remains to be seen if larger consequences can be drawn. Is Plutarch representative of his contemporaries? If so, his attitude will be a valuable index of sentiments that were not often set down in writing, or if set down have not survived. Or was he as exceptional in his view of Rome as in the degree of his culture and learning?

To answer these questions it is necessary to recall that Plutarch's admiration for Rome is not uncritical or blind. Just as his picture of Roman history had dark shades, so also he has evident reservations about Roman culture. The luxury that he deplored in the late republic still offended him in contemporary Rome: indeed it had greatly increased.[1] The distaste with which he describes the temple of Capitoline Jupiter rebuilt by Domitian is not solely due to his dislike of the emperor, but to the opulence and vulgarity of the building.[2] Plutarch feels only contempt for the Romans who scoured the slave market for monsters and grotesques, or desecrated Plato's dialogues by having them performed over dinner by slaves.[3]

To deplore aspects of Roman culture, however, is not necessarily to be anti-Roman. It is instructive that when Plutarch condemns the staging of Plato's dialogues, he does so in one of his own in which the practice is approved by a Stoic sophist.[4] Though the sophist anticipates that it will soon be banned because of the general depravity, a more civilized Stoic of the company disagrees: he had in fact attacked the custom in Rome and so helped to bring it into disfavour.[5] When Plutarch and his friends deplored Roman vulgarity, they did not do so as

---

[1] *Luc.* 39. 2.   [2] *Publ.* 15. 3–6.
[3] *De curios.* 520 C; *quaest. conviv.* 711 B–D.   [4] *Quaest. conviv.* 711 C, cf. 710 B.
[5] *Quaest. conviv.* 711 C–D.

outsiders, but as men who had sympathy and influence in governing circles.

The bond of taste between cultivated Greeks and Romans is shown by another of Plutarch's dialogues in which again a Roman custom is deplored, that of allowing guests to bring their friends to dinner as uninvited 'shadows'. Here the speaker is in fact the Italian Caesernius, a relation by marriage of Plutarch's old friend Mestrius Florus.[6] Caesernius, like Florus, is probably from the region of the Po, an area noted for its conservatism and frugality.[7] To be a philhellene was no longer to be an admirer of corrupted tastes, but the opposite. Cultured Romans and their Greek friends now joined to decry the corruption of the age.

The need to distinguish enmity to Rome from criticism of Roman customs can be illustrated by a further example. Plutarch frequently expresses his horror of gladiatorial shows: they awakened murderous instincts in the mob and drove out the spirit of pity.[8] In this he is of a mind with other philosophic Greeks of his day, among them Dio and Apollonius of Tyana.[9] It has been inferred, of Apollonius at least, that he attacked such spectacles as a champion of undiluted hellenism and an enemy of Roman culture.[10] Yet an abhorrence of gladiatorial and other displays was part of educated taste both in Rome and in Greece.[11] To abhor them was not to abhor Roman culture, but the bloodthirstiness of the masses to whom they particularly appealed.

A more delicate problem is raised by Plutarch's attitude towards the deification of human beings. More than once he disparages the Hellenistic monarchs who assumed the titles of gods and deified their predecessors by law. While the souls of the virtuous could ascend to heaven, that stage came only after

[6] *Quaest. conviv.* 707 C–708 A.

[7] Origin of Florus and Caesernius: above, p. 48. Conservatism: Martial, 11. 16, Pliny, *Epp.* 1. 14. 6, on Patavium: cf. Pliny, ibid. 4, on Transpadane Gaul generally. Note *quaest. conviv.* 702 D on the antiquarianism of Florus.

[8] *Praec. ger. reip.* 822 C, *de soll. anim.* 959 E. Cf. also *praec. ger. reip.* 802 D, 823 E, *de esu carn.* 997 C, 998 B.

[9] Dio, *Or.* 31. 121; Philostr. *Vita Apoll.* 4. 22.

[10] L. Hahn, *Rom und Romanismus im griechisch-römischen Osten* (1906), 186; H. Fuchs, *Der geistige Widerstand gegen Rom* (1938), 49, n. 60.

[11] Cic. *ad fam.* 7. 1. 3, *Tusc. disp.* 2. 41; Sen. *Epp.* 7. 2–5, 90. 45, 95. 33. L. Robert, *Les Gladiateurs dans l'Orient grec* (1940), Chapter III.

long purification, and a mere law was not enough.[12] From these
sentiments it has been deduced that Plutarch was opposed to the
cult of Roman emperors in all its forms, whether spontaneous
or compelled.[13] Again, caution and reflection are required.
Enlightened Roman emperors did not claim to be gods on earth,
though they usually did not mind if their subjects so regarded
them. In Plutarch's day it was accounted part of Domitian's
arrogance that he had assumed the titles of Lord and God.[14]
Again, Plutarch's view is one that any educated Greek or Roman
could have held, such as the Greek who became a senator and
historian of Rome, Cassius Dio.[15]

When Plutarch surveys Roman culture, including those
aspects of it which he dislikes, he does so less from a Greek than
a Greco-Roman point of view. This same attitude can be seen
in his presuppositions about the Roman empire itself. Although
he regards himself as a Greek, and the time was yet to come when
a Greek could refer to all the inhabitants of the empire in the
first person,[16] it does not follow that he sees Rome from outside.
In the *Lives* he is consistently hostile to enemies of Rome, including the Hellenistic kings who claimed to champion Greece
against Rome.[17] He does not observe, except in quotations or
allusions, the old distinction between Greeks and barbarians.
The word 'barbarian' denotes for him any nation beyond the
frontiers of the empire, in the east or in the west.[18] In place of the
old distinction, he now employs a threefold one, barbarians,

---

[12] *Rom.* 28. 8–10, *Arist.* 6. 2–5.

[13] K. Scott, *TAPA* 60 (1929), 117–35; R. Flacelière, *REG* 61 (1948), 97. Note the
observation of A. D. Nock, *Cambridge Ancient History* 10 (1934), 489, n. 2: 'it is to be
noted that Plutarch makes outspoken criticisms of the self-deification of Hellenistic
kings without any feeling that what he says might be taken as reflecting on Roman
practice.'

[14] Suet. *Dom.* 13. 2, cf. Pliny, *Pan.* 11, 52.

[15] Cass. Dio, 52. 35. 5. On Dio's attitude to Rome, in several ways reminiscent of
Plutarch's, F. Millar, *A Study of Cassius Dio* (1964), 174–92.

[16] On this development, J. Palm, *Rom, Römertum und Imperium in der griechischen
Literatur der Kaiserzeit* (1959), 7–8, 54–5; on its insignificance, G. W. Bowersock,
JRS 58 (1968), 262.

[17] Note, on the Aetolians, *Flam.* 8. 9, 9. 6–7, 10. 2, 15. 1, 15. 4; on Antiochus III,
Flam. 15. 1, *Cato mai.* 12. 3; on Perseus, *Aem.* 8. 10, 9. 1, 12. 3; on Mithridates VI,
Luc. 7. 4, 31. 8, *Sulla* 24. 7.

[18] Greek and barbarian: *Themist.* 15. 4, quoting Simonides, Page, *Lyrica Graeca
Selecta* no. 367; *Mar.* 46. 1, quoting Plato; *praec. ger. reip.* 824 C, cf. Thuc. 2. 36. 4.
Barbarians as those outside the empire: *Cato mai.* 12. 2, *Luc.* 29. 6, *Aem.* 4. 3, *Mar.*
14. 1, *Sulla* 15. 3, 4, 21. 8, *Pomp.* 70. 4.

Greeks, and Romans.[19] The transference of the term 'barbarian'
to those outside the empire is accompanied by a transference of
values. Once Greeks regarded barbarians as savages or effemin-
ates, a threat to civilization or a worthy object of conquest.[20]
So too Plutarch now regards with apprehension the Celts and
Germans who had once threatened to destroy Rome, and
regrets that the strife of the late republic had wasted the strength
that might have been turned on the Parthians and other
enemies.[21] The same attitudes, concern for the safety of the
empire and dread of its fall, can be seen in his abhorrence of
civil war. Just as Marius nearly destroyed Rome by his quarrel
with Sulla, so the folly of Nero nearly overturned the empire
by setting in train the civil wars of Plutarch's youth. Nothing
was more to be cherished than the peace that Roman power
guaranteed.[22]

Plutarch's attitude to Rome is in a sense both Greek and
Roman: Greek, in that he saw himself as a Greek by birth and
language, Roman, in that his interests and sympathies are bound
up with the empire. It is now possible to approach the questions
posed earlier. Granted that he speaks as one of an international
society, how representative is a Greek in that society of wider
Greek opinion? The class from which Plutarch comes, which he
depicts in his dialogues and looks to for his Greek readership,
is of course not a large portion of the Greek-speaking inhabitants
of the empire. But that is unimportant: it was with this class that
wealth and power resided. What matters is to determine
whether Plutarch and his friends are representative of it, or
whether they express only one side of educated Greek opinion.
In other words, is there evidence that contemporary Greeks
who were as cultured as Plutarch were unfriendly or opposed
to Rome?

[19] Note that the present *quaestiones Romanae* and *Graecae* were originally accompanied by *quaestiones barbaricae*, Lamprias Catalogue no. 139. It is instructive that the
quaestiones Romanae contain material borrowed from Aristotle's Νόμιμα Βαρβαρικά,
the companion work to his Πολιτεῖαι of Greek cities: P. A. Stadter, *Plutarch's Historical
Methods* (1965), 31. Cf. [Dio], *Or.* 37. 26–7.

[20] Cf. Isocr. *Paneg.* 66–70, 150–6, Aristotle, *Pol.* 1252 b 5–9, 1255 a 21–32.

[21] Celts and Germans: *Aem.* 12. 4, *Caes.* 26. 2, *Mar.* 11, *Sulla* 16. 8. Regret: *Luc.*
36. 5, *Pomp.* 70. 3–5.

[22] Marius: *praec. ger. reip.* 806 D. Nero: *Ant.* 87. 9, cf. *Galba* 1. Peace: *de fort. Rom.*
317 C, *de Pyth. orac.* 408 B, *de tranqu. animi* 469 E, *an seni sit ger. resp.* 784 F, *praec. ger.
reip.* 824 C.

This question can best be answered by an examination of cases. It has been argued, for example, that the whole Greek renaissance, of which Plutarch was a precursor, was in effect anti-Roman: while there was no question of overt opposition, the exaltation of Greek culture and absorption in the Greek past constituted a rejection of the Roman present.[23] Such a view is not plausible. Besides Plutarch, it places among tacit opponents of Rome many who were clearly identified with its interests. Arrian could glorify Epictetus and Alexander, and yet as governor of Cappadocia defend the province against barbarian incursions.[24] A prince of the Second Sophistic, Herodes Atticus, could also give his name to the Roman year as *consul ordinarius*.[25] Claudius Charax, who swiftly ascended the ladder of office to a consulate in the same decade as Herodes, conducted minute investigations into the antiquities of the whole empire, east and west.[26] To glorify the Greek past was not to ignore or denigrate the present. Roman emperors encouraged the cult of antiquity and listened to declamations on subjects drawn from Greek history.[27] Archaism and antiquarianism were the fashion of the educated classes in both halves of the empire. What gave them the leisure to pursue the fashion was the security and prosperity in which they shared.

Hostility to Rome has been discovered in a philosopher contemporary to Plutarch, Apollonius of Tyana.[28] The historical Apollonius is difficult to discern: the surviving collection of

[23] Thus R. MacMullen, *Enemies of the Roman Order* (1966), 189, 'Rome's internal enemies were not the urban poor but rather . . . Greeks of the upper class, defending the purity of their cultural inheritance'; ibid. 244, 'the so-called Second Sophistic [was] perfectly harmless on the surface but anti-Roman in its implications, since its intent was the reassertion of Hellenism.' Cf. in a similar sense E. L. Bowie, *Past & Present* 46 (1970), 3–41. For the contrary view, G. W. Bowersock, *Greek Sophists in the Roman Empire* (1969).

[24] *PIR²* F 219. For a new inscription of Arrian, Bowersock, *GRBS* 8 (1967), 279–80.

[25] *PIR²* C 802 (in 143).

[26] *PIR²* C 831; *FGrHist* 103. For the inscription recording his career and identifying him with the consul suffect of 147, Chr. Habicht, *Istanbuler Mitteilungen* 9–10 (1959/60), 109–25. Bowie discounts the significance of Charax in his review of Greek historians in the Second Sophistic, art. cit. 13.

[27] Note that Hadrian restored the original name of Mantinea in place of 'Antigonea', Paus. 8. 8. 12. Declamations: Philostr. *VS* 626 (Heliodorus before Caracalla).

[28] Thus L. Hahn, *Rom und Romanismus im griechisch-römischen Osten* (1906), 140, cf. 157, 201, makes Apollonius a 'Römerfeind': cf. H. Fuchs, *Der geistige Widerstand gegen Rom* (1938), 49, n. 60.

letters contains forgeries, and the biography by Philostratus has a large admixture of romantic fiction.[29] According to Philostratus, Apollonius came from a very ancient and wealthy family of Tyana, though he promptly made the customary renunciation of worldly goods.[30] Despite this last, his attitudes may give some guidance to educated Greek opinion in Plutarch's day.

In the event, the evidence for Apollonius' hostility to Rome does not survive scrutiny. He denounced Antioch and Ephesus for their luxurious bathing establishments, and the Athenians for their addiction to gladiators.[31] Because these fashions had spread from Rome, however, it does not follow either that they had been implanted by Rome or that Apollonius expressed hostility to the capital in denouncing them. Just as educated men of both nations opposed the popular taste for bloodshed, so Romans as well as Greeks condemned baths as a source of effeminacy and luxury.[32] Cultured Greeks had no wish to see their compatriots mocked for their proverbial vices: Plutarch shares Apollonius' distaste for Greek effeminacy, and agrees with the Romans in attributing it to public nudity.[33] Similarly, when Apollonius blames the Ionians for adopting Roman customs, he does not do so as an enemy of Rome but as a conservative and a purist: it is in the same spirit that he rebukes the Spartans for adopting Ionian customs, and fortifies a Roman governor with an example from ancient Rome.[34]

So far from being opposed to Rome, Apollonius is in fact in the tradition of Greek philosophers who advised powerful Romans and regarded the empire with benevolence. When he rebukes or

---

[29] Letters: e.g. *Epp.* 59, from the king of Babylon to the king of India. The biography: see now G. W. Bowersock's introduction to the Penguin translation (1971) 16–19. The following remarks on Apollonius' attitude to Rome will be based on the letters, since these have some chance of being genuine. Naturally the biography, written on Julia Domna's orders, represents him as a friend of Rome: cf. *Vita Apoll.* 1. 38, 4. 33, 5. 7, p. 169 lines 17–25 Kayser, 5. 10, 5. 27–38, 6. 29–34, 7. 4, 7. 8, 8. 27–8.

[30] *Vita Apoll.* 1. 4, 1. 13.

[31] *Vita Apoll.* 1. 16, 4. 22.

[32] e.g. Cato the Censor, *Cato mai.* 20. 7–8; Seneca, *Epp.* 86; the elder Pliny, *NH* 29. 23.

[33] *Quaest. Rom.* 274 D–E.

[34] *Epp.* 71, cf. 72, Philostr. *Vita Apoll.* 4. 5 (Roman names); *Epp.* 63 (Spartans); *Epp.* 58, p. 361 lines 31 ff. Kayser (governor). On the addressee of *Epp.* 58, C. Cichorius in E. Norden, *Agnostos Theos* (1913), 337–42.

corrects magistrates, he does so not in disloyalty but because it is
their duty to rule well.[35] He blames the sophist Euphrates for
taking money from the emperor, not because that is itself wrong
but because philosophy should not be sold.[36] He advises Domitian on how to govern: there is no point in conquering barbarians
(for thus Apollonius, like Plutarch, designates those outside the
empire), since they do not deserve the benefits of Roman rule.[37]
A letter in the collection purports to be from the emperor
Claudius to the council of Tyana, commending Apollonius for
his beneficial influence on Greek youth. It may be spurious, but
it reflects a true estimate of his relations with Rome.[38]

A last example of supposed opposition to Rome may be seen
in the satirist Lucian. The *Nigrinus* and the essay on salaried
posts in great houses catalogue in detail the vices of the capital:
greed, deceit, pretension, counterfeit philhellenism. Wealth and
its abuse are a constant theme here and in other works. Later in
life Lucian entered the pay of the emperor and was obliged
to defend himself against the charge of inconsistency. Hence
he has been depicted as a social critic converted to established
values, an intellectual seduced into administration.[39]

Once again, criticism of Roman values needs to be distinguished from opposition to Rome: the one need not, though it
may, imply the other. Lucian in fact illustrates the cultural
bond between the educated classes of east and west. His observations on Roman decadence coincide closely, even in phrasing,
with those of educated Romans.[40] Lucian's values are typical of
the wealthy Greek, that he was.[41] His hero, the philosopher
Demonax, is a philosopher of the familiar type: he counsels and
corrects influential Romans, denounces gladiatorial shows, and

---

[35] *Epp.* 30, 31 (urging the procurators of Asia to greater severity), 54 (urging the
censors to be concerned with morals, not buildings), 58, especially p. 361 lines 2–4,
p. 362 lines 2–5 Kayser.

[36] *Epp.* 51. Cf. Pius' jibe at mercenary philosophers, *Dig.* 27. 1. 6. 7, and Lucian,
Nigr. 25.

[37] *Epp.* 20, 21.

[38] *Epp.* 53.

[39] A. Peretti, *Luciano: Un intellettuale greco contro Roma* (1946); B. Baldwin, *CQ* 11
(1961), 199–208. Against, J. Palm, *Rom, Römertum und Imperium in der griechischen
Literatur der Kaiserzeit* (1959), 44–56; G. W. Bowersock, *Greek Sophists in the Roman
Empire* (1969), 115–16.

[40] Thus cf. *Nigr.* 21 with Pliny, *NH* 29. 19, on nomenclators; *Nigr.* 30 with
Petronius, 71, on rich men's wills.

[41] *Apol.* 12, 15.

preaches concord to eastern cities.[42] The Cynic Peregrinus earns
the satirist's scorn for criticizing the emperor, who had the good
sense to ignore him, and for urging the Greeks to rise against
Rome.[43] When Lucian mocks the pretensions of wealthy
Romans, his wit is also directed at the Greeks who fawned on
them and earned a well-deserved reputation for flattery.[44]
Justifying his entrance into the imperial service, Lucian felt no
need to retract his strictures on mercenary Greeks who battened
on vulgar patrons. He had only to point out the difference
between them and one who played his part in administering the
greatest of empires.[45]

The literature of the high empire shows, not a divergence of
attitudes to Rome, but a remarkable unanimity. Plutarch is
only one of many who sympathized with Rome, consorted with
powerful Romans, and preached a lesson to eastern cities that
converged with Roman interests. The values of these Greeks,
their conservatism, their hellenism, their dislike of discord and
disturbance, reflect the values of their western friends. That the
literary and other records of the age should show such unanimity
is, in one way, not surprising. Ideas and attitudes travelled
freely: the upper classes were still secure in their wealth and their
control of affairs.

The enemies of Rome are not to be sought at this cultured and
affluent level, but below. The persecuted sustained themselves
on denunciations of Roman decadence and visions of the
impending cataclysm. If such ideas infected educated Greeks,
they were not those who led cultural opinion and erected the
literary monuments of their age. An itinerant philosopher like
Peregrinus might call on Greece to rise against Rome: but
Peregrinus had once dabbled in a persecuted religion, and
moreover he was of the Cynic persuasion, half-way between
philosophy and the rabble.[46] It is to be expected that articulate

---

[42] *Demon.* 18, 50, 51 (Romans), 57 (gladiators), 64 (concord). With *Demon.* 64 cf.
the very similar story told of Apollonius, Philostr. *Vita Apoll.* 1. 15.

[43] *Peregr.* 18 (emperor), 19 (Greeks).

[44] *Nigr.* 22–3, *de merc. cond.* 7, 24, 40. Thus, rightly, Bowersock, op. cit. 116.
Contrast Baldwin, *CQ* 11 (1961), 207: 'the bitter diatribe *De mercede conductis*, which
depicts the Greek intellectual at the mercy of the boorish Roman philistines'.

[45] *Apol.* 12.

[46] Lucian, *Peregr.* 19 (war), 11–13, 16 (Christianity). Cynics ἐν μεταιχμίῳ τῶν τε
πολλῶν καὶ τῶν φιλοσοφούντων: Lucian, *Fugit.* 4. Cf. Titus' displeasure at the word
'Cynic', Philostr. *Vita Apoll.* 6. 31.

spokesmen of such views should be rare, and that they should be known either through their enemies or because their sect, victorious later, preserved the literature of its beginnings. Education and wealth belonged together, and wealth had no cause to welcome the disruption of order or the advent of new systems.

It is customary to celebrate the capture of Rome by Greece, the rude victor tamed by the vanquished. The imperial age saw the completion of a new conquest: Greeks now became partners in an empire to which they had been subjects. Without that step, a further progression would not have been possible, to a Greek-speaking empire having its capital in the east and destined to last more than a thousand years. On one assessment, the winning of educated opinion may be held to have been bought too dear: at the price of artistic vitality and the general freedom. Another calculation will give the verdict to a system that pre-served what it admired, and stayed alive. In a transitory world, survival is itself an achievement.

APPENDIX I

Philostratus, *Epp.* 73

THE last in the collection of letters attributed to Philostratus, the biographer of the sophists, purports to be addressed to Julia Domna. Its authenticity has recently been contested by G. W. Bowersock.[1] Since the argument turns mainly on the reference to Plutarch at the end of the letter, it may be reviewed here.

The passage in question runs as follows:[2]

πεῖθε δὴ καὶ σύ, ὦ βασίλεια, τὸν θαρσαλεώτερον τοῦ Ἑλληνικοῦ Πλούταρχον μὴ ἄχθεσθαι τοῖς σοφισταῖς, μηδὲ ἐς διαβολὰς καθίστασθαι τοῦ Γοργίου. εἰ δὲ οὐ πείθεις, σὺ μέν, οἷα σου σοφία καὶ μῆτις, οἶσθα τί χρὴ ὄνομα θέσθαι τῷ τοιῷδε, ἐγὼ δὲ εἰπεῖν ἔχων οὐκ ἔχω.

Since, it is argued, the author of the letter thought that Plutarch was a contemporary of Julia Domna and a member of her circle, he cannot be Philostratus but someone who wrote much later. Though familiar with Plutarch's attack on Gorgias,[3] he was confused in his chronology. To give his fiction verisimilitude, he may have drawn on Philostratus' account of Gorgias in the *Lives of the Sophists*, which has clear resemblances to the letter.

However, the passage in question may be held to be simply an ornate way of saying, 'Plutarch should not have attacked the sophists, and deserves opprobrium for doing so.' It is a familiar feature of ancient, and especially Greek, controversial writing to treat a dead opponent as if he were still alive. A passage from Plutarch's treatise on Epicurus' precept, 'Live unnoticed', is instructive: 'if you are advising the virtuous to go unnoticed and unknown, you are saying to Epaminondas, "Do not be general", to Lycurgus, "Do not draw up laws", to Thrasybulus, "Do not kill tyrants"'.[4] That a deceased writer should be urged to stop attacking a target is less usual, but not unparalleled: thus Jerome bids Celsus, Porphyry, and Julian to refrain from their attacks on the Christian faith.[5] I do not know of

[1] G. W. Bowersock, *Greek Sophists in the Roman Empire* (1969), 104–5.
[2] Philostr. *Epp.* 73, p. 257 lines 21–6 Kayser.
[3] Known also from Isidore of Pelusium, *Epp.* 2. 42 = fr. 186 Sandbach.
[4] *De lat. viv.* 1128 E–F. Cf. [Longinus,] *de subl.* 4. 2, Eusebius, *adversus Hieroclem* 7, p. 376 Kayser.
[5] Jerome, *de viris ill. praef.*

another instance in which a living person is urged to use persuasion with a dead one, but it is not so far different from the present instances as to be an impossibility.

These examples have a perceptibly rhetorical cast. That, with the fact that the letter shows expertise in rhetorical theory, suggests that it is by Philostratus, as it purports to be. If so, it corroborates his statement that he was a member of Julia Domna's circle.[6]

---

[6] Philostr. *Vita Apoll.* 1. 3. Of course the present argument does not affect Bowersock's main contention, that modern accounts of this circle are based almost entirely on implausible conjecture.

APPENDIX II

Praec. Ger. Reip. 813 E

εὐσταλεστέραν δεῖ τὴν χλαμύδα ποιεῖν, καὶ βλέπειν ἀπὸ τοῦ στρατηγίου πρὸς τὸ βῆμα, καὶ τῷ στεφάνῳ μὴ πολὺ φρόνημα πιστεύειν,
ὁρῶντα τοὺς καλτίους ἐπάνω τῆς κεφαλῆς.

Two phrases in this sentence have caused problems of interpretation, and a third has been regarded as corrupt. To begin with the least
difficult, the κάλτιοι are evidently not military boots, as they have
often been supposed to be, but the senatorial shoes of the proconsul.[1]
It is inconceivable that Plutarch, who frequently praises the ubiquity
of Roman peace, could represent cities of Greece or Asia under the
close guard of soldiers.[2]

That helps with another problem, the meaning of βλέπειν ἀπὸ
τοῦ στρατηγίου πρὸς τὸ βῆμα. Plutarch is advising the Greek politician
to remember the proconsul's power, not his own: the στρατήγιον
should therefore be a symbol of the Greek's office and the βῆμα of
the Roman's. For that there is no need to emend the text. στρατήγιον
refers to the quarters of the city στρατηγός, the official responsible
for the preservation of order, whose insignia included the military
cloak or χλαμύς.[3] The βῆμα is the proconsul's *tribunal*.[4]

The phrase τῷ στεφάνῳ μὴ πολὺ φρόνημα πιστεύειν is obelized in
the most recent text.[5] But for this extension of the verb πιστεύειν,
'to entrust x to y' and so 'to repose x in y', note *Cato min.* 11. 8, where
the verb has similarly troubled editors: οὕτως οὐ τῷ ξίφει μόνον,
ἀλλὰ καὶ τῷ γραφείῳ τὸ ἀνυπεύθυνον καὶ ἀνυπόδικον ἐπίστευσεν.

---

[1] Thus, rightly, James H. Oliver, *The Ruling Power* (1953), 958, n. 27; but the
word continues to be mistranslated, most recently by E. L. Bowie, *Past & Present* 46
(1970), 18, n. 49, F. A. Lepper, *Gnomon* 42 (1970), 566.

[2] Peace: above, p. 125. On the lack of troops in senatorial provinces, Th. Mommsen, *Römisches Staatsrecht* 2³ (1887), 263–5, R. K. Sherk, *AJP* 76 (1955), 400–13.

[3] Thus *an seni sit ger. resp.* 784 B, 788 B, 789 C. χλαμύς: *RE* 3 (1899), 2344–5.

[4] Matt. 27 : 19, *P. Teb.* 434. Cf. LSJ⁹ s.v.; G. W. H. Lampe, *A Patristic Greek Lexicon*,
s.v. B. 2. Thus, rightly, L. Hahn, *Rom und Romanismus im griechisch-römischen Osten*
(1906), 205, n. 6.

[5] That of C. Hubert, revised by H. Drexler, *Plutarchi Moralia* V. 1 (Teubner,
1960).

CHRONOLOGICAL TABLE

This table is designed to set out the chronology of Plutarch's life and works; only those which can be dated by external evidence are included, and even so the dates given are inevitably approximate. References to 'Chronology' are to C. P. Jones, 'Towards a Chronology of Plutarch's Works', *JRS* 56 (1966), 61–74; other references are to the pages of the present work.

DATE	REFERENCE	EVENT
Between 40 and 45	13	Plutarch born
c. 60–5 (?)	14 ff.	Rhetorical period
		De fort. Alex.
		De fort. Rom.
		De glor. Ath.
		Visit to Asia
		Anim. an corp. aff.
		Visit to Alexandria
		Mission to proconsul
c. 65	13	Conversion to philosophy
		Plutarch becomes pupil of Ammonius
67	16–17	Plutarch visits Delphi with Ammonius
	17	Liberation of Greece
After 68	Chronology, 70	*De garrul.*
70	18, n. 30	Liberty of Greece revoked by Vespasian
Between 70 and 79	21–2	Plutarch's first (?) visit to Rome
After c. 79; before 93 (?)	Chronology, 71; 72	*Lives of the Caesars*
c. 80	22	Plutarch in Athens
After 80 (?)	Chronology, 71	*De poet. aud.*
After 81	Chronology, 71	*De tuenda san.*
After 81 (?); before 107	Chronology, 71	*De sera num. vind.*
After 81 (?)	Chronology, 71	*De soll. anim.*

DATE	REFERENCE	EVENT
83 (?)[1]		Plutarch present at the Pythian games
After 83 (?)[2]		*De def. orac.*
Between *c.* 85 and *c.* 88	22, 55	Sosius Senecio *quaestor Achaeae*; meets Plutarch (?)
Between *c.* 85 and *c.* 95	Chronology, 71	*Consol. ad ux.*
Winter 88/9	22	Plutarch in Rome (?)
Between *c.* 90 and *c.* 100	Chronology, 71	*Praec. coniug.*
After *c.* 90; before 116	Chronology, 72	*Quom. adul. ab amico internosc.*
91/2	23, 52	*De frat. am.*
After 92; before 100 (?)	Chronology, 61–2	*De cohib. ira*
92 or 93	22 ff.	Plutarch in Rome
93 (perhaps 94)	24	Expulsion of philosophers from Rome
After *c.* 95	Chronology, 72	*De E Delph.* *De animae procr. in Tim.* *De Pyth. orac.*
18 September 96		Assassination of Domitian
Winter 96/7	27	Plutarch present at Athenian Dionysia
After 96 (possibly earlier)	26, 31	Plutarch becomes priest of Apollo at Delphi
After 96	Chronology, 72	*De curios.* *Amat.*
After 96; before 114	Chronology, 72	*Praec. ger. reip.*
After *praec. ger. reip.*	Chronology, 72	*De cap. ex inim. util.*
After *praec. ger. reip.* (?)	Chronology, 72; 117	*De exil.*
Between *c.* 96 and *c.* 120	Chronology, 72; 33	*Parallel Lives*
After 97 (?)	Chronology, 72	*Adv. Col.*
Between 98 and 117	29	Plutarch receives *ornamenta consularia*

[1] R. M. Ogilvie has argued for this as the dramatic date of the *de def. orac.* (*Phoenix* 21 [1967], 108–19). An earlier one is perhaps preferable.

[2] Ogilvie, art. cit., argues for a date between 95 and 115, mainly on the grounds of affinity with other works.

DATE	REFERENCE	EVENT
After 99; before 116	Chronology, 72–3; 56	*Quaest. conviv.*
After 100 (?)		*De laude ips.*
After *c.* 105		*Quaest. Rom.*
After 107		*De primo frigido*
After *c.* 107	Chronology, 73	*De tranqu. animi*
After *c.* 110		*An seni sit ger. resp.*
c. 115		*De Is. et Osir.*
c. 115		*Mul. virt.*
Before 116		*De prof. in virt.*
After 117	34	Plutarch becomes *procurator Achaeae*
c. 120	Chronology, 66; 34	Death of Plutarch

BIBLIOGRAPHY

THE following is a list of all books (including commentaries), articles, and reviews cited in the foregoing notes. The following are excluded: articles in *RE*, collections of inscriptions and the like, editions of texts, and handbooks.

ALFÖLDY, G. *Die Legionslegaten der römischen Rheinarmeen = Epigraphische Studien* 3 (Cologne, 1967).

ARNIM, H. VON. *Leben und Werke des Dio von Prusa* (Berlin, 1898).

BALDWIN, B. 'Lucian as Social Satirist', *CQ* 11 (1961), 199.

BARNES, T. D., 'Hadrian and Lucius Verus', *JRS* 57 (1967), 65.

—— 'Philostratus and Gordian', *Latomus* 27 (1968), 581.

BARROW, R. H. *Plutarch and his Times* (London, 1967).

BEHR, C. A. *Aelius Aristides and the Sacred Tales* (Amsterdam, 1968).

BIRLEY, A. R. 'The Roman Governors of Britain', *Epigraphische Studien* 4 (1967), 63.

BIZARD, L. 'Inscriptions de Béotie', *BCH* 29 (1905), 99.

BLEICKEN, J. 'Der Preis des Aelius Aristides auf das römische Weltreich', *Nachr. Akad. Wiss. Gött.* Phil-Hist. Kl. 1966, 7, 223.

BOURGUET, É. *De rebus Delphicis imperatoriae aetatis* (Montpellier, 1905).

BOWERSOCK, G. W. 'Eurycles of Sparta', *JRS* 51 (1961), 112.

—— 'Augustus on Aegina', *CQ* 14 (1964), 120.

—— 'C. Marcius Censorinus, Legatus Caesaris', *HSCP* 68 (1964), 207.

—— *Augustus and the Greek World* (Oxford, 1965).

—— 'Some Persons in Plutarch's *Moralia*', *CQ* 15 (1965), 267.

—— 'Zur Geschichte des römischen Thessaliens', *Rheinisches Museum* 108 (1965), 277.

—— 'A New Inscription of Arrian', *GRBS* 8 (1967), 279.

—— Review of D. Nörr, *Imperium und Polis in der hohen Prinzipatszeit*, *JRS* 58 (1968), 261.

—— *Greek Sophists in the Roman Empire* (Oxford, 1969).

—— 'Suetonius and Trajan', *Hommages à Marcel Renard I*, Collection Latomus 101 (1969), 119.

—— Review of R. K. Sherk, *Roman Documents from the Greek East*, *AJP* 91 (1970), 223.

—— Introduction to *Philostratus: Life of Apollonius of Tyana*, translated by C. P. Jones (Harmondsworth, Middlesex, 1971).

Bowie, E. L. 'Greeks and their Past in the Second Sophistic', *Past & Present* 46 (1970), 3.

Breitenbach, H. R. 'Der Alexanderexcurs bei Livius', *Museum Helveticum* 26 (1969), 146.

Briscoe, J. 'Rome and the Class Struggle in the Greek States 200–146 B.C.', *Past & Present* 36 (1967), 3.

Brunt, P. A. 'The Revolt of Vindex and the Fall of Nero', *Latomus* 18 (1959), 531.

—— 'Charges of Provincial Maladministration under the Early Principate', *Historia* 10 (1961), 189.

Calderini, A. *Aquileia romana: Ricerche di storia e di epigrafia* (Milan, 1930).

Cameron, A. 'Iamblichus at Athens', *Athenaeum* 45 (1967), 143.

Cameron, A. and A. M. 'Christianity and Tradition in the Historiography of the Late Empire', *CQ* 14 (1964), 316.

Cameron, A. M. 'The "Scepticism" of Procopius', *Historia* 15 (1966), 466.

Chilver, G. E. F. *Cisalpine Gaul* (Oxford, 1941).

Clairmont, Ch. W. *Die Bildnisse des Antinous: Ein Beitrag zur Porträtplastik unter Kaiser Hadrian* (Rome, 1966).

D'Arms, J. H. *Romans on the Bay of Naples: A Social and Cultural Study of the Villas and their Owners from 150 B.C. to A.D. 400* (Cambridge, Massachusetts, 1970).

Daux, G. *Chronologie delphique* (Paris, 1943).

Degrassi, A. *I Fasti consolari dell'impero romano dal 30 avanti Cristo al 613 dopo Cristo* (Rome, 1952).

Deininger, J. *Die Provinziallandtage der römischen Kaiserzeit von Augustus bis zum Ende des dritten Jahrhunderts n. Chr.* Vestigia 6 (Munich, 1965).

Desideri, S. *La 'Institutio Traiani'* (Genoa, 1958).

Dihle, A. *Studien zur griechischen Biographie*, Abh. Akad. Wiss. Gött. Phil.-Hist. Kl. 37 (1956).

Drexler, H. 'Zur Geschichte Kaiser Othos bei Tacitus und Plutarch', *Klio* 37 (1959), 153.

Einarson, B. 'Plutarch's Ancestry', *CP* 47 (1952), 99.

—— 'Plutarch's Ancestry again', *CP* 50 (1955), 253.

Erbse, H. 'Die Bedeutung der Synkrisis in den Parallelbiographien Plutarchs', *Hermes* 84 (1956), 398.

Évrard, É. 'Le Maître de Plutarque d'Athènes et les origines du néoplatonisme athénien', *L'Antiquité classique* 29 (1960), 108 and 391.

Flacelière, R. 'Sur quelques passages des *Vies* de Plutarque', *REG* 61 (1948), 67.

—— 'Rome et ses Empereurs vus par Plutarque', *L'Antiquité classique* 32 (1963), 28.

FLACELIÈRE, R. 'Plutarque, "De Fortuna Romanorum"', *Mélanges . . .
offerts à Jérôme Carcopino* (1966), 367.

FOCKE, F. 'Synkrisis', *Hermes* 58 (1923), 327.

FUCHS, H. *Der geistige Widerstand gegen Rom in der antiken Welt* (Berlin,
1938).

FUHRMANN, M. 'Das Vierkaiserjahr bei Tacitus', *Philologus* 104
(1960), 250.

GABBA, E. *Appiano e la storia delle guerre civili* (Florence, 1956).

—— 'Storici greci dell'impero romano da Augusto ai Severi', *Rivista
storica italiana* 71 (1959), 361.

GEAGAN, D. J. *The Athenian Constitution after Sulla, Hesperia* Suppl.
Vol. 12 (1967).

GERNENTZ, W. *Laudes Romae* (diss. Rostock, 1918).

GOODENOUGH, E. R. 'The Political Philosophy of Hellenistic Kingship', *Yale Classical Studies* 1 (1928), 55.

GRAINDOR, P. *Chronologie des archontes athéniens sous l'Empire, Mémoires
de l'Académie royale de Belgique*, Classe des Lettres VIII. 2 (1922).

—— *Athènes de Tibère à Trajan* (Cairo, 1931)

—— *Athènes sous Hadrien* (Cairo, 1934).

GROAG, E. 'Prosopographische Beiträge. II. Q. Pompeius Sosius
Priscus', *JÖAI* 18 (1915), Beiblatt 265.

—— *Die römischen Reichsbeamten von Achaia bis auf Diokletian* (Vienna,
1939).

—— *Die Reichsbeamten von Achaia in spätrömischer Zeit* (Budapest,
1946).

HABICHT, CHR. 'Zwei neue Inschriften aus Pergamon', *Istanbuler
Mitteilungen* 9–10 (1959/60), 109.

—— 'Epigraphische Zeugnisse zur Geschichte Thessaliens unter
der makedonischen Herrschaft', *Ancient Macedonia* (Thessaloniki,
1970), 265.

HAHN, L. *Rom und Romanismus im griechisch-römischen Osten* (Leipzig,
1906).

HAMILTON, J. R. *Plutarch, Alexander: A Commentary* (Oxford, 1969).

HANSLIK, R. 'Die Auseinandersetzung zwischen Otho und Vitellius
bis zur Schlacht von Bedriacum nach Tacitus', *Wiener Studien* 74
(1961), 113.

HATZFELD, J. *Les Trafiquants italiens dans l'Orient hellénique* (Paris,
1919).

HÄUSSLER, R. 'Keine griechische Version der Historien Pollios',
Rheinisches Museum 109 (1966), 339.

HEAD, B. V. 'On the Chronological Sequence of the Coins of
Boeotia', *Numismatic Chronicle*, 3rd ser. 1 (1881), 177.

HELMBOLD, W. C. and O'NEIL, E. N. *Plutarch's Quotations* (Baltimore,
Md., 1959).

HOLLEAUX, M. 'Décret de Chéronée relatif à la première guerre de Mithradates', *REG* 32 (1919), 320 = *Études d'épigraphie et d'histoire grecques* 1 (Paris, 1938), 143.

HOMEYER, H. 'Beobachtungen zu den hellenistischen Quellen der Plutarch-Viten', *Klio* 41 (1963), 145.

JANNORAY, J. 'Notes sur la chronologie delphique du Ier siècle après J.-C.', *REA* 47 (1945), 46, 243.

JONES, A. H. M. *The Greek City from Alexander to Justinian* (Oxford, 1940).

—— 'The Greeks under the Roman Empire', *Dumbarton Oaks Papers* 17 (1963), 1.

JONES, C. P. 'The Teacher of Plutarch', *HSCP* 71 (1966), 205.

—— 'Towards a Chronology of Plutarch's Works', *JRS* 56 (1966), 61.

—— 'Julius Naso and Julius Secundus', *HSCP* 72 (1968), 279.

—— 'A New Commentary on the Letters of Pliny', review of A. N. Sherwin-White, *The Letters of Pliny: A Historical and Social Commentary*, *Phoenix* 22 (1968), 111.

—— 'A Leading Family of Roman Thespiae', *HSCP* 74 (1970), 223.

—— 'Sura and Senecio', *JRS* 60 (1970), 98.

KAHRSTEDT, U. *Das wirtschaftliche Gesicht Griechenlands in der Kaiserzeit* (Bern, 1954).

—— 'Zwei Probleme im kaiserzeitlichen Griechenland', *Symbolae Osloenses* 28 (1950), 66.

KAPETANOPOULOS, E. 'Leonides VII of Melite and his Family', *BCH* 92 (1968), 493.

KEIL, BR. 'Ein λόγος συστατικός', *Nachrichten von der königlichen Gesellschaft der Wissenschaften zu Göttingen*, Phil.-Hist. Kl. 1913, 1.

KIENAST, D. 'Die Homonoiaverträge in der römischen Kaiserzeit', *Jahrbuch für Numismatik und Geldgeschichte* 14 (1964), 51.

KOENEN, L. 'Die "laudatio funebris" des Augustus für Agrippa auf einem neuen Papyrus', *Zeitschrift für Papyrologie und Epigraphik* 5 (1970), 217.

KOUMANOUDES, S. N. 'Πεμπτίδης', *Χαριστήριον εἰς 'Αναστάσιον Κ. 'Ορλάνδον* 2 (Athens, 1966), 1.

KRAUSS, FR. *Die rhetorischen Schriften Plutarchs und ihre Stellung im plutarchischen Schriftenkorpus* (diss. Munich, 1912).

LAFFI, U. 'Le iscrizioni relative all'introduzione nel 9 a. C. del nuovo calendario della Provincia d'Asia', *Studi classici e orientali* 16 (1967), 5.

LARSEN, J. A. O. 'Roman Greece', *An Economic Survey of Ancient Rome*, edited by Tenney Frank, 4 (Baltimore, Md., 1938), 259.

LEO, FR. *Die griechisch-römische Biographie nach ihrer literarischen Form* (Leipzig, 1901).

LEPPER, F. A. *Trajan's Parthian War* (Oxford, 1948).

LEPPER, F. A. Review of A. N. Sherwin-White, *The Letters of Pliny: A Historical and Social Commentary*, *Gnomon* 42 (1970), 560.

LEVICK, B. M. *Roman Colonies in Southern Asia Minor* (Oxford, 1967).

MACMULLEN, R. *Enemies of the Roman Order: Treason, Unrest, and Alienation in the Empire* (Cambridge, Massachusetts, 1966).

MAGIE, D. *Roman Rule in Asia Minor* (Princeton, N.J., 1950), 2 vols.

MARTIN, H. 'The Concept of *Prāotēs* in Plutarch's *Lives*', *GRBS* 3 (1960), 65.

—— 'The Concept of *Philanthropia* in Plutarch's *Lives*', *AJP* 82 (1961), 164.

MARTIN, J. M. Summary of dissertation, *John of Salisbury and the Classics*, *HSCP* 73 (1969), 319.

MILLAR, F. *A Study of Cassius Dio* (Oxford, 1964).

—— 'Epictetus and the Imperial Court', *JRS* 55 (1965), 141.

—— Review of A. N. Sherwin-White, *The Letters of Pliny: A Historical and Social Commentary*, *JRS* 58 (1968), 218.

—— 'P. Herennius Dexippus: the Greek World and the Third-Century Invasions', *JRS* 59 (1969), 12.

MOMIGLIANO, A. D. Review of *The Cambridge Ancient History, Vol. 10*, *JRS* 34 (1944), 109.

—— Review of Ch. Wirszubski, *Libertas as a Political Idea at Rome*, *JRS* 41 (1951), 146.

—— *The Development of Greek Biography* (Cambridge, Massachusetts, 1971).

MOMMSEN, TH. 'Über die Quellen der Chronik des Hieronymus', *Abhandlungen der sächsischen Gesellschaft der Wissenschaften* 2 (1850), 669 = *Gesammelte Schriften* 7 (1909), 606.

—— 'Cornelius Tacitus und Cluvius Rufus', *Hermes* 4 (1870), 295 = *Gesammelte Schriften* 7 (1909), 224.

—— *Römisches Staatsrecht*[3] (Leipzig, 1887–8), 3 vols. in 5.

NISSEN, H. *Kritische Untersuchungen über die Quellen der vierten und fünften Dekade des Livius* (Berlin, 1863).

NORDEN, E. *Agnostos Theos* (Leipzig, 1913).

NÖRR, D. *Imperium und Polis in der hohen Prinzipatszeit* (Munich, 1966).

NOTOPOULOS, J. A. 'Studies in the Chronology of Athens under the Empire', *Hesperia* 18 (1949), 1.

OGILVIE, R. M. *A Commentary on Livy Books 1–5* (Oxford, 1965).

—— 'The Date of the *de defectu oraculorum*', *Phoenix* 21 (1967), 108.

OLDFATHER, W. A. 'A Friend of Plutarch's Grandfather', *CP* 19 (1924), 177.

OLIVER, J. H. 'The American Excavations in the Athenian Agora, Twentieth Report: Greek and Latin Inscriptions', *Hesperia* 10 (1941), 237.

—— 'Two Athenian Poets', *Hesperia* Suppl. Vol. 8 (1949), 243.

OLIVER, J. H. *The Ruling Power: A Study of the Roman Empire in the Second Century after Christ through the Roman Oration of Aelius Aristides*, *Transactions of the American Philosophical Society*, n. s. 43, pt. 4 (Philadelphia, Pa., 1953).

—— 'The Roman Governor's Permission for a Decree of the Polis', *Hesperia* 23 (1954), 163.

PALM, J. *Rom, Römertum und Imperium in der griechischen Literatur der Kaiserzeit* (Lund, 1959).

PERETTI, A. *Luciano: Un intellettuale greco contro Roma* (Florence, 1946).

PETER, H. *Die Quellen Plutarchs in den Biographieen der Römer* (Halle, 1865).

—— *Wahrheit und Kunst: Geschichtschreibung und Plagiat im klassischen Altertum* (Leipzig, 1911).

PFLAUM, H.-G. *Les Carrières procuratoriennes équestres sous le Haut-Empire romain* (Paris, 1960–1), 4 vols.

PHILIPPSON, A. and KIRSTEN, E. *Die griechischen Landschaften 1, 2: Das östliche Mittelgriechenland und die Insel Euboea* (Frankfurt, 1951).

PLASSART, A. 'Décrets de Thespies', *Mélanges Charles Picard* 2 = *Revue archéologique* 31–2 (1949), 825.

—— 'L'Inscription de Delphes mentionnant le proconsul Gallion', *REG* 80 (1967), 372.

PLEKET, H. W. 'Domitian, the Senate and the Provinces', *Mnemosyne* 14 (1961), 296.

REINACH, TH. *Mithridates Eupator* (Leipzig, 1895).

RENOIRTE, T. *Les 'Conseils politiques' de Plutarque* (Louvain, 1951).

RICHARD, J.-C. 'Les Funérailles de Trajan et le triomphe sur les Parthes', *REL* 44 (1966), 351.

ROBERT, L. 'Études d'épigraphie grecque. III. Décret trouvé à Mylasa', *Revue de philologie* 1 (1927), 102 = *Opera minora selecta* 2 (1969), 1057.

—— 'Études sur les inscriptions et la topographie de la Grèce Centrale. VI. Décrets d'Akraiphia', *BCH* 59 (1935), 438 = *Opera minora selecta* 1 (1969), 279.

—— *Études anatoliennes* (Paris, 1937).

—— *Les Gladiateurs dans l'Orient grec* (Paris, 1940).

—— 'Un edifice du sanctuaire de l'Isthme dans une inscription de Corinthe', *Hellenica* 1 (1940), 43.

—— 'Épitaphes métriques de médecins à Nicée et à Tithorée', *Hellenica* 2 (1946), 103.

—— 'Ulpia Heraclea', *Hellenica* 3 (1946), 5.

—— 'Monuments de gladiateurs dans l'Orient grec', *Hellenica* 3 (1946), 112, 5 (1948), 77, 7 (1949), 126, 8 (1950), 39.

ROBERT, L. 'Épigrammes relatives à des gouverneurs', *Hellenica* 4 (1948), 35.

—— 'Inscriptions de la vallée du Haut Caïque', *Hellenica* 6 (1948), 80.

—— 'Hagia Marina en Phocide', *Hellenica* 11–12 (1960), 70.

—— 'Recherches épigraphiques. VII. Décret de la Confédération lycienne à Corinthe', *REA* 62 (1960), 324 = *Opera minora selecta* 2 (1969), 840.

—— *D'Aphrodisias à la Lycaonie*, *Hellenica* 13 (1965).

—— 'Inscriptions d'Aphrodisias. Première partie', *L'Antiquité classique* 35 (1966), 377.

—— 'Inscriptions de l'Antiquité et du Bas-Empire à Corinthe', review of J. H. Kent, *Corinth, Volume VIII, Part III: The Inscriptions 1926–1950*, *REG* 79 (1966), 733.

—— 'Sur des inscriptions d'Éphèse', *Revue de philologie* 41 (1967), 7.

—— 'Épigraphie grecque et géographie historique du monde hellénique', *Annuaire de l'École pratique des Hautes Études, IVe Section, 1968–1969* (1969), 161.

ROSE, H. J. *The Roman Questions of Plutarch* (Oxford, 1924).

ROSTOVTZEFF, M. *The Social and Economic History of the Roman Empire*, 2nd edition revised by P. M. Fraser (Oxford, 1957), 2 vols.

RUSSELL, D. A. 'Plutarch's Life of Coriolanus', *JRS* 53 (1963), 21.

—— 'On reading Plutarch's *Moralia*', *Greece & Rome* 15 (1968), 130.

SANTANGELO, M. 'Il monumento di C. Julius Antiochos Philopappos in Atene', *Annuario della Scuola archeologica di Atene* 3–5 (1941–3, publ. 1948), 153.

SCHILLING, R. 'Romulus l'élu et Rémus le réprouvé', *REL* 38 (1960), 182.

SCHOBER, F. *Phokis* (diss. Jena, 1924).

SCOTT, K. 'Plutarch and the Ruler Cult', *TAPA* 60 (1929), 117.

SHERK, R. K. 'The "Inermes Provinciae" of Asia Minor', *AJP* 76 (1955), 400.

SHERWIN-WHITE, A. N. *The Roman Citizenship* (Oxford, 1939).

—— *The Letters of Pliny: A Historical and Social Commentary* (Oxford, 1966).

SICKINGER, A. *De linguae Latinae apud Plutarchum et reliquiis et vestigiis* (diss. Heidelberg, 1883).

SIEFERT, G. *De aliquot Plutarchi scriptorum moralium compositione atque indole, Commentationes philologicae Ienenses* 6. 1 (1896).

SMITH, R. E. 'The Sources of Plutarch's Life of Titus Flamininus', *CQ* 38 (1944), 89.

SOTERIADIS, G. 'Fouilles préhistoriques en Phocide', *BCH* 25 (1912), 253.

STADTER, P. A. *Plutarch's Historical Methods: An Analysis of the Mulierum Virtutes* (Cambridge, Massachusetts, 1965).

STARR, C. G. 'Epictetus and the Tyrant', *CP* 44 (1949), 20.

STEIN, A. Review of J. Vogt, *Die alexandrinischen Münzen*, *Gnomon* 1 (1925), 340.

—— *Der römische Ritterstand* (Munich, 1927).

STEMPLINGER, E. *Das Plagiat in der griechischen Literatur* (Leipzig, 1912).

SWOBODA, H. 'Studien zur Verfassung Boiotiens', *Klio* 10 (1910), 315.

SYME, R. *The Roman Revolution* (Oxford, 1939).

—— 'Antonine Relatives: Ceionii and Vettuleni', *Athenaeum* 35 (1957), 306.

—— *Tacitus* (Oxford, 1958), 2 vols.

—— Review of A. Jagenteufel, *Die Statthalter der römischen Provinz Dalmatia von Augustus bis Diokletian*, *Gnomon* 31 (1959), 510.

—— 'The Lower Danube under Trajan', *JRS* 49 (1959), 26.

—— 'The Greeks under Roman Rule', *Proceedings of the Massachusetts Historical Society* 72 (1963), 1.

—— 'The Ummidii', *Historia* 17 (1968), 72.

—— 'People in Pliny', *JRS* 58 (1968), 135.

—— 'Legates of Cilicia under Trajan', *Historia* 18 (1969), 352.

THEANDER, C. *Plutarch und die Geschichte* (Lund, 1951).

—— 'Plutarchs Forschungen in Rom', *Eranos* 57 (1959), 99.

THOMASSON, B. E. *Die Statthalter der römischen Provinzen Nordafrikas von Augustus bis Diocletianus* (Lund, 1960), 2 vols.

TOWNEND, G. B. 'Cluvius Rufus in the *Histories* of Tacitus', *AJP* 85 (1964), 337.

VEYNE, P. 'Apulée à Cenchrées', *Revue de philologie* 39 (1965), 241.

VOLKMANN, R. *Leben, Schriften und Philosophie des Plutarch von Chaeronea* (Berlin, 1869), 2 vols.

VORNEFELD, W. *De scriptorum Latinorum locis a Plutarcho citatis* (diss. Münster, 1901).

WALBANK, F. W. *A Historical Commentary on Polybius* (Oxford, 1957–67), 2 vols.

WARDMAN, A. E. 'Plutarch and Alexander', *CQ* 5 (1955), 96.

WEST, A. B. 'Notes on Achaean Prosopography and Chronology', *CP* 23 (1928), 258.

WILAMOWITZ-MOELLENDORFF, U. VON. *Commentariolum Grammaticum* 3 (1889) = *Kleine Schriften* 4 (1962), 619.

—— 'Lesefrüchte. CXVII', *Hermes* 40 (1905), 161 = *Kleine Schriften* 4 (1962), 208.

—— 'Lesefrüchte. CXCVIII', *Hermes* 60 (1925), 307 = *Kleine Schriften* 4 (1962), 394.

WILAMOWITZ-MOELLENDORFF, U. VON. 'Plutarch als Biograph', *Reden und Vorträge* 2⁴ (1926), 247.

—— 'Lesefrüchte. CCXXVIII', *Hermes* 62 (1927), 295 = *Kleine Schriften* 4 (1962), 451.

WILHELM, A. 'Urkunden aus Messene', *JÖAI* 17 (1914), 1.

—— 'Inschrift aus Tenos', *Ἐπιτύμβιον Heinrich Swoboda dargebracht* (Reichenberg, 1927), 336.

WILKES, J. J. *Dalmatia* (London, 1969).

WIRSZUBSKI, CH. *Libertas as a Political Idea at Rome during the Late Republic and Early Principate* (Cambridge, 1950).

WIRTH, TH. 'Arrians Erinnerungen an Epiktet', *Museum Helveticum* 24 (1967), 149, 197.

ZIEGLER, K. 'Plutarchs Ahnen', *Hermes* 82 (1954), 499.

INDEX

The following Index covers text, appendixes, and footnotes. Romans are registered by *gentilicia*, unless more familiarly known otherwise (e.g. Sulla, Tacitus); Greeks possessing the *tria nomina* are registered by their Greek names, with their full nomenclature, when known, in brackets. All dates are A.D. unless otherwise indicated.

INDEX OF PASSAGES IN PLUTARCH

The following index includes only passages of which there is substantial discussion in text or footnotes. The *Moralia* are listed in order of Frankfurt pages, and not by alphabetical order of title.

LIVES

Arist. 6. 2–5: 123–4
Cato min. 11. 8: 131
Cimon 1. 1–2: 1, 6–7
Demosth. 1–2: 81–2
　　2. 2: 20
Flam. 7. 5–6: 96
　　8. 9: 96
　　10. 1–3: 97
　　11. 3–7: 98
Galba 2. 5: 73

Otho 9. 3: 75
　　18. 1: 77
Per. 2. 4: 103 n.
Publ. 15. 5: 23
Rom. 3–8: 89–90
　　9. 1–3: 91–2
　　10. 2–3: 90
　　13. 3–5: 92
　　14: 92–3
　　28. 8–10: 123–4
Sulla 15. 5: 41–2

MORALIA

De fort. Rom. 317 A: 70
　　318 A: 68
　　321 A: 67 n.
　　326 C: 69
De E Delph. 385 B: 16–17
De tranqu. animi 470 C: 116
De frat. am. 478 B: 52
Anim. an corp. aff. 501 E–F: 14–15
De curios. 522 D–E: 23
De sera num. vind. 567 F–568 A: 19, 22
De exil. 605 B–C: 116
Quaest. conviv. 632 A: 23
　　707 C ff.: 123
　　711 C–D: 122

Praec. ger. reip. 813 E: 112, 133
　　814 C: 113–14
　　814 D: 116
　　814 E–F: 113
　　814 F: 118
　　815 A: 111, 121
　　815 A–C: 118
　　816 C–D: 15
　　824 C: 115
De Herod. malign. 854 E ff.: 88
Adv. Col. 1107 E: 57
De lat. viv. 1128 E–F: 131
Lamprias Catalogue 204: 35
　　227: 35

B009329